DOMESTIC SOLDIERS

DOMESTIC SOLDIERS

Jennifer Purcell

Constable • London

Constable & Robinson Ltd
3 The Lanchesters
162 Fulham Palace Road
London W6 9ER
www.constablerobinson.com

First published in the UK by Constable,
an imprint of Constable & Robinson Ltd, 2010

A copy of the British Library Cataloguing in
Publication data is available from the British Library

ISBN: 978-1-84529-522-6

Printed and bound in the EU

1 3 5 7 9 10 8 6 4 2

PEFC

PEFC/16-33-111
CATG-PEFC-052
www.pefc.org

To my mom

CONTENTS

ACKNOWLEDGEMENTS

A work of this nature is never accomplished alone. Throughout the process of researching and writing this book, I have been blessed with encouragement and support from dear friends and family. I have met some wonderful people who have made contributions to this project in their own ways, and along the way I have managed to make some new friends. To all those who lent moral support, offered sage advice or helped to make my work easier, I am eternally grateful.

I would like to thank the staff at the Mass-Observation Archive at the University of Sussex who were not only incredibly helpful, but who also made life at the archive enjoyable. Special thanks to Fiona Courage, Karen Watson and Jessica Scantlebury, who were not only helpful during my research at the archive, but who also made it possible for me to pursue my research from abroad. I am also grateful to the staff at Mass-Observation for acting as my cultural interpreters as they so often did. Thanks to Simon, who not only helped with my work in the archive, but who also schooled me on the joys of cricket. Thanks also to Joy Eldridge, whose knowledge of the archive was invaluable at the outset of this project. I especially thank her for sharing with me her memories of growing up listening to women's programmes on the BBC with her mother. Special thanks to Dorothy Sheridan for sharing insights about the women, which proved integral to my research. I particularly want to thank her for working out solutions that helped me continue my work abroad. I would also like to thank the trustees of the Mass-Observation Archive for making available such an extraordinary and unique resource. All direct quotes from the diarists are copyright of the Mass-Observation Archive. I wish to thank too the archivists at the BBC Written Archives Centre at Caversham Park in Reading for their assistance in this project.

To Sandra Koa-Wing, thank you for your support and encouragement throughout my time at Sussex and in the early days of writing. I will always remember your laugh and the brightness with which you filled the archive. You are, and shall forever be, greatly missed.

Without the advice, support and encouragement of Claire Langhamer and Alun Howkins, I dare say this project would not have come to fruition. I am eternally indebted to Marjorie Levine-Clark, who has been a wonderful mentor, coach and advocate over the years.

I wish also to thank my friends, old and new, who lent their support and encouragement during this process. Special thanks to Jenna Bailey, who has given generously of her time and advice in combing over numerous drafts – thank you for your support and friendship. Over innumerable cups of tea and equally numerous emails, Andrea Salter and I contemplated the life of Nella Last – I could never have survived archival work (and Nella's maddening handwriting) without you! Thanks to Susan Gustin, Laura Rey and Donna Castle for your unfailing encouragement over the years. I wish also to thank Susan Ouellette for her advice and friendship, and of course, Jane Viens, without whose help absolutely nothing would ever get done!

Thanks to Jessica Cuthbert-Smith for a keen critical eye and to Jo Stansall for her help in this process. Special thanks to Leo Hollis, without whom this book would never have reached the light of day. Thank you for the helpful advice and criticism along the way, and, certainly not least of all, for infinite depths of patience.

Finally, to my family, who has been a source of love, encouragement and inspiration. To my father for instilling in me a love of history and for helping to fire my historical imagination on so many childhood trips to American Revolution and Civil War battlefields. Love and thanks to Bill and Kim for their continual support. Love and thanks also to Doug for sharing his love of history with me and for always supporting me in my endeavours. We are blessed to have you in our lives. Without the unconditional love and support of my mom, I do not think I could have made it this far. Thanks for reading my work (really, every single scrap of paper I've ever sent your way!) and for never failing to be my number one fan all these years. Finally, to Rob, for your numerous sacrifices and support, which I can't possibly begin to enumerate here, and for patiently listening to me discourse endlessly on housewives and the Second World War, as always, my love.

INTRODUCTION

It was 2 a.m. on a frosty Saturday morning in December. Helen huddled over a coal-fired stove, straining her ears to discern any trace of the Luftwaffe growling in the distance. Night after night, she complained, they 'murdered' her sleep with each wave of planes that passed over the draughty medieval residence on the Kent coast. Whether they dropped their bombs on her village or whether they passed over on their way to deliver death on another city, the anxiety was the same. Neither was the murmur of the RAF planes on their way to the Continent comforting: their engines signalled the same death and destruction for German cities that the Nazis rained upon English cities.

Tonight, she listened for 'Firebomb Fritz', but there was no sound. After weeks of raids, it was eerily silent: a 'lovely thick fog' had descended upon the south-east coast of England, thwarting air operations for either side. Helen shivered in the silence – the stove was wholly inadequate for the sharp chill of a December night. She cursed. The one night she volunteered for fire watching duty was the one night she could have managed some sleep. 'What have I done for you, England, my England?' she bitterly mused.

It was the definitive question of the war: what were you doing for the war effort? Stated another way, as seen in the wartime pages of the classic guide to middle-class housewifery, *Good Housekeeping*, women were questioned, 'Is your conscience clear?'[1] It was a simple, but stinging, call to action that underlines the nature of the 'People's War'. Before the first month of the war was done, the phrase had been coined in the upper echelons of government in recognition of the fact that everybody was important to the war effort. Soon afterwards, the title, and the idea that everyone had a part to play in the war, was picked up in popular venues: on the BBC, on the silver screen, in the newspapers and magazines. The People's War was not – by its very definition, could not be – an entirely military affair. It galvanized everyone – woman, child and man – into action to protect Britain and to fight for a new future.

If your conscience chaffed, there were ways to soothe it. The People's War was a war of small, ordinary, even mundane, feats compounded by the millions into incredible tides of action. Certainly there were the military campaigns, the triumphs and the defeats (and sometimes the triumphal defeats) of the battlefields, in the air and on the seas: Dunkirk, the Battle of Britain, Singapore, El Alamein, D-Day, the Battle of the Bulge, for example. And, of course, these defeats and victories were composed of numerous acts of the ordinary and the courageous, the cynical and the hopeful. It was no different for those at home.

Volunteering and paid work were some of the ways civilians might assuage the conscience of those who stayed behind, but there was more to it than that. Every moment and every action counted: turning over your flowerbeds to vegetables, using less hot water, scraping the margarine paper till all the grease was gone, saying 'no' to a new pair of shoes . . . shivering on a cold December morning. The war lurked behind every act on the home front. This fact of the People's War was invigorating and powerful for some, maddening for others.

Because every act was potentially heroic, anyone could be a hero. Because there was so much to do, there was also a wonderfully empowering flexibility about the People's War. Whatever one did, or wanted to do, if it was done well and if it was deemed useful to the nation in its hour of need, it was important. But if one could be a hero, one might also be a villain; and if there was so much to do, one might not be doing enough, and the guilt could be crushing. For many, this was the day-to-day reality of the war.

It is a reality that threads its way through Mass-Observation diaries, tangled and entwined in the fabric of everyday life and relationships; sometimes the thread is barely discernible, sometimes it is a chaotic zigzag or a tangled mess; at other times it glistens like a strand of silver. In 1939, a group of intellectual avant-garde researchers, who had begun documenting everyday life in Britain two years previously, offered ordinary Britons an extraordinary opportunity: to write diaries about their day-to-day lives in wartime. The inquisitive researchers at Mass-Observation (M-O) also sent out surveys (called directives) with carefully constructed questions to understand life in Britain: what did one think about Churchill's performance? How did one feel about the Germans? Did people believe BBC news reports? Did one think British morals were slipping? Furthermore, M-O made it clear that any Briton who decided to participate wrote for an audience: their voices would be heard.

Though their names would be kept anonymous to the public, it was understood – indeed, the writers expected – that the staff at M-O read their submissions and reported on their findings to the rest of Britain through newspaper and magazine articles. (They probably did not know that, at least for the first part of the war, their observations were also distilled and reported to the government in the interests of understanding public morale.) Since M-O regarded the everyday lives and opinions of individual Britons as a crucial element necessary in exploring the true nature of British society, it was very much a part of the People's War. In fact, many of its volunteers considered their writing as a patriotic act.

The diary project was a practical response to the war. With the outbreak of conflict in Europe and the potential disruptions to postal services, the group was unsure how to carry on its mission to document everyday lives. It would continue to send its directives to the cadre of volunteers it had accumulated since 1937, but in the event that this strategy failed, M-O asked its observers to keep diaries of their experiences and post them back to the organization if, and when, possible. Thankfully, the postal service continued to operate even during the hottest periods of conflict on British soil and M-O continued to collect and analyse the observers' writings throughout the war, and indeed, well into the post-war period.

The writings of the observers leave a legacy of the war that is often forgotten. They remind us that political leaders and battles were significant, but at the same time they were often only a small part of ordinary individuals' lives. The experiences that the men and women of M-O shared with us also illustrate the extraordinary power of war to transform lives. More importantly, they offer us a human connection to the past; they tell us a story of the war, but also a story of themselves.

This book recounts the war through the eyes of six ordinary women who wrote for M-O. Women were in the vanguard of the People's War; they stepped into jobs that no one would have ever dreamed permitting them to join in peacetime, let alone excel. If women are considered in the history books, it is these women workers who are most often remembered for their contributions to the war. But there are many others, who have been rendered faceless by the tide of history: ordinary women who had families to care for, who volunteered any scrap of time they could muster, who tried valiantly to contribute in their own ways while simultaneously juggling personal and domestic obligations. Though often lost in the retelling of the war, they and their struggles were – and are – significant parts of that story.

Through these six women, we can glimpse everyday life and the thoughts, fears and personal battles of ordinary women as they lived on the edge of history, not knowing from day to day, moment to moment, how the war or their lives would play out. The tale is bounded by the events – national, international, local and personal – that these women thought important at the time; it is shaped by their words and observations. They lived across England: Sheffield, Leeds, and Newcastle in the north, the shipbuilding town of

Barrow-in-Furness in Lancashire, Kent and the Bristol coast and Birmingham. All of them were middle-aged married women and most had children.[2]

Born around 1885, Irene Grant was the eldest. Before the war, she and her family had eked out a respectable existence in the working-class suburbs of Newcastle, but always teetered precariously close to poverty. For her, the People's War offered the promise to make society more equitable: she rarely missed an opportunity to remind M-O that she was a socialist.

Nella Last was four years younger than Grant and lived in Barrow-in-Furness. She prided herself on her children and her domestic ability. The war gave her a chance to show off those skills. Though he'd rarely ever done so before the war, even her husband could not fail to recognize her abilities in wartime. Nella basked in the praise garnered from those around her, building up a confidence unknown to her in peacetime.

In much the same way as Nella, Alice Bridges found her voice in the war. She was born in 1900 and lived in the suburbs of Birmingham. The war unleashed a cheeky and playful streak that blossomed into a stubborn independence.

Natalie Tanner, who was born in 1902, enjoyed a freedom unmatched by the other women. She was not as constrained by the domestic demands that the others faced. Living in the rural countryside surrounding Leeds, Natalie was often found working in her garden, walking on the hills near her home or reading. But the social life of Leeds and Bradford always beckoned, and Natalie never failed to see a play at the local theatre, or a feature on the silver screen.

Natalie, Nella, Irene and Alice were early volunteers for M-O. Their diaries date from the beginning of the war, but observers were also recruited throughout the war by word of mouth, via advertisements and through the various articles published by the organization. Both Edie Rutherford and Helen Mitchell began writing for M-O in 1941.

Like Natalie Tanner, Edie Rutherford was also born in 1902, and although her parents were both British, she was born in South Africa and was a fierce champion of the empire. The only woman without children, she lived with her husband in Sheffield. Edie's diary was somewhat different from the other women's: her tone and insightful, often amusing, commentary on both war and local events create the feeling of a friendly chat over the morning coffee and newspaper.

Helen Mitchell was born in 1894 and spent most of the war in Kent, though when the bombing and planes became too much, she often escaped to the coast near Bristol. Helen's war was a desperate struggle to find her own voice. Her diary drips with a caustic sarcasm that reminds us that the People's War was not always empowering.

The women in this book were housewives and mothers, all of whom wrote for Mass-Observation. They were ordinary women living in extraordinary times. Through them, we can view the struggles and triumphs of everyday life during the war. We follow them into their homes, watch them cook, knit, read or listen to the wireless. Through their eyes, we watch the skies anxiously for German bombers and walk through the rubble left behind. We hear them gossip, converse or fight with family members and neighbours. We see them cheer the government at one instant and doubt it the next. We hear their worries about the future and learn of their pasts, of their hopes and joys, their fears and frustrations, their friends and families. Aware of the gravity of the times, we see them searching for ways to be a part of history and to contribute to their nation in its time of need. Finally, we watch them navigate the perennial human struggle: the fight to find voices of their own, to free themselves from others' constraints, to live and define themselves on their own terms.

In many ways, they are our mothers, our grand-mothers, our great-grandmothers. Their struggles in wartime were unique as well as universal. Their insights, their triumphs and their defeats reach far beyond the global conflict of the 1940s.

This is the story of life and war through their eyes.

CHAPTER ONE

THE LAST WAR

Helen Mitchell looked at the newborn baby boy cradled in her arms and sighed. Lonely and worn-out from the birth, the only thought she could muster was 'future cannon fodder'. It was 5 November 1917, Guy Fawkes' Day, but few celebrations were planned that autumn. More than three desperately sad years into the Great War, the nation, and indeed the entire Continent, languished in a deep state of weariness. That day, *The Times* published a short article assuring the reading public that there was 'cheerfulness at the front', yet even this sentiment was shot through with a far from comforting reality.

The 'cheerfulness' of which the article spoke was of those who lay wounded and dying on the Western Front, not knowing when death would free them from their pain, but supremely confident in the 'ultimate result': British victory. The soldiers' heroism was all the more poignant in the conditions they endured, the author explained, as Tommies fought in: 'a country sodden with water where they frequently sank, not only up to the knees or the waist, but quite often up to the neck or beyond it'.[1] Though literally devoured by the mud of Flanders, they could not be thwarted in their duty.

If Helen had opened *The Times*, which she read often, on that day, she may have seen this article, and perhaps flipped through the pages until her eyes rested upon the paper's daily requiem for the dead, the 'Roll of Honour'. Day after day throughout the war, the paper published a list of casualties, highlighting the officers lost and naming the privates who had fallen; the vast black-and-white monotony of those lists still has the power to strike one with an intense feeling of loss. Living in Newcastle at the time, Helen may have anxiously searched the names of the Northumberland Fusiliers for anyone she or her husband knew. That day, *The Times* reported twenty-six Northumberland privates who had died in recent action, a small paragraph in a sea of losses comprising over three tightly printed columns of dead.

She may have been relieved that only one officer had been lost from the Gloucester Regiment, the county where she had grown up. Or she may have wept bitterly if she recognized the name. Though she could not have known it then, the battle that had produced such devastating carnage over the past three months was to end the day after her son was born, when British and Canadian forces finally took the village of Passchendaele. The Third Battle of Ypres, more commonly known as Passchendaele, sacrificed more than 310,000 British soldiers to the gods of a war many believed futile – and interminable.

When Helen Mitchell looked at her newborn son, all she saw were the lists and lists of dead and wounded. Between 1914 and 1918, hundreds of thousands of young men lost their lives, and many more were mutilated or psychologically scarred from the action they had witnessed in the trenches during the Great War. The scale of everyday death and destruction in the trenches is unimaginable: on average, nearly 7,000 British soldiers were killed or wounded on any given day; the officers called it 'wastage'.[2] In the end, over 600,000 British soldiers were killed, and more than two million were wounded or missing.

It is little wonder, suffocating under the weight of a never-ending war, as soldiers were drowned and churned into the mud of the Western Front, that in her son Helen could only fathom 'future cannon fodder'. Indeed, Mitchell's vision in 1917 seemed eerily prophetic in 1940, when her son William, now twenty-three, was conscripted into the army. When war on the Continent emerged once again in 1939 for the next generation, those who had personally endured and remembered the random, senseless death of the trenches and the grief of the Rolls of Honour could only imagine the horror that waited.

Those who lived through the First World War continued to carry the scars of the conflict well beyond 1918. Though different in age during the war – some were married, and others young teenagers – every woman in this story felt the war deeply, and each was shaped by its long-term effects. For Helen, the trauma of the Great War was inbred in her infant, ultimately poisoning the bond between mother and son. But the scars were as varied as they were deep. Returning veterans came home to an uncertain economy and often found that their patriotic service had ruined them for the post-war world.

Edie Rutherford was a young teenager living in South Africa during the war, but her future husband, Sid, was old enough to fight. He was injured on Vimy Ridge in 1917 and suffered shell shock. Afterwards, he was sent on military duty to Burma, where he endured bouts of malaria and dysentery that adversely affected his health for the rest of his life: his military service left him suffering severe shortness of breath, heart problems and psychological trauma.

Sid and Edie met in South Africa and were married soon afterwards in Australia, where they lived until moving to Sheffield in 1934. Australia did not experience the depth of economic troubles that Britain did during the 1920s, but Sid's war disabilities nonetheless made it difficult for him to keep a job for any significant length of time. Reasoning that he could never reliably provide for a family, and feeling it unwise to bring up children they could not afford, Edie and Sid decided to forgo having children. Furthermore, Rutherford explained to M-O, her husband's shell shock made it difficult to cope with the inevitable racket raised by children. As it was, Edie's diary had to be suspended when he was home because she used a typewriter, and the noise was too much for him.

Like Sid and Edie, Irene Grant's young family struggled to survive the severe economic downturns in 1921–2 and the more famous global depression of the early 1930s. The mounting casualties of the Great War that so depressed Helen Mitchell instead motivated Irene to create life. She couldn't bear to send her husband to the Western Front without having his child, so Irene and Tom conceived a baby girl just before he left for France in 1918.

After Tom returned from France, they had another child. 'But that', Irene confessed, 'was a mistake.'

Marjorie was born in 1921, right as the post-war boom collapsed. Irene would have liked four children, but the economic reality of the 1920s made that hope impossible. By 1922, unemployment had soared to a national average of 15 per cent, causing the government to extend both the length of assistance and the monetary benefit of the dole for the unemployed. In July 1922, the rates given to out-of-work men, women and juveniles were raised by 3 shillings a week and the number of weeks of benefit extended from fifteen to twenty-six. The increase was welcome, but it was hardly enough.

The tension in the hardest-hit areas such as Sheffield and Tyneside rose steadily despite this intervention. On 8 December 1922, during a debate about the rising social unrest, Tom Smith, MP, made it clear that the benefit was not enough to feed a family even in the workhouse – the most despised form of welfare available for the poor. When respectable working men lost their jobs, the MP pointed out, they lost everything. 'I have seen men come in for food or relief who went to school with me,' he related:

... good living men, men who tried to maintain a decent standard of life for themselves and their dependants. The piano has gone, the watch has gone, and they have come for relief. What is worse, they have lost a good deal of their self-respect.

These hard realities, the MP argued, led previously hard-working, stable, men to become radicalized and to take action against the government. It was a dangerous situation that ultimately culminated in the General Strike of 1926, a national strike in sympathy of coal miners whose wages were cut. Over 1.5 million workers downed tools for nine days – the longest general strike in British history.

The Grants' troubles began in earnest when Irene was forced to leave her job. Her husband Tom, one of the 'respectable' working men radicalized by his experiences, was in and out of work throughout the 1920s and 1930s, and the family could have used Irene's income as a teacher to keep afloat, but in 1922 married female teachers across the country were forced to resign. The institution of the marriage bar by many local education authorities, requiring all women to leave a career once they married, was meant to help returning veterans find work. Ironically, it nearly devastated the Grants. Throughout the inter-war period, Irene and Tom's young family barely managed to scrape by on savings left over from Irene's teaching days and whatever could be laid by when Tom was in steady work. Although she never wrote about receiving unemployment insurance, it seems likely that the Grants were probably forced to turn to the dole during lean times.

Nella Last also remembered the inter-war period as a time of scarcity in which the domestic skills that her grandmother taught her as a child were indispensable, especially the 'dodges' that made the most of the ingredients she could afford. Times were not as difficult for the Lasts as they were for the Grants, however. After the Great War, Nella's husband Will had taken over his father's joinery workshop and worked steadily throughout the inter-war period. Those who had work during the depressions of the 1920s and 1930s were generally better-off than they might have been in more prosperous times, because they could take advantage of the lower cost of living that accompanied the downturns. In fact, while the Grants and the Rutherfords struggled to keep food on the table and to pay the rent, the Lasts bought a new house with the help of inheritance money from Nella's father. Will was never an ambitious businessman, but with Nella's wise household management they were able to raise their two growing boys.

Nella and Will were married three years before the First World War, and when he enlisted in the navy, they moved to Southampton, where they spent most of the war. While Will worked in the shipyards, Nella took care of their young son Arthur and volunteered at the local hospital. Nella fondly remembered helping the injured soldiers write letters home and entertaining them. She enjoyed bringing a smile to their faces or a glint of light to their eyes with her jokes and light-hearted 'monologues'. Nella and Will's second son, Cliff, was born during Will's service on the south coast. The birth left Nella desperately ill, but a kindly doctor took care of her and secured a month's leave for Will to help her recover. Though her health was touch and go for a few weeks, looking back on it, Nella figured she was happier in Southampton than at any other time in her life.

Alice Bridges recalled the First World War and the 1920s as a particularly difficult time. Born in 1901, she was only thirteen when war broke out. Her father was out of work for most of the war and did not serve in the military. Instead, he insisted that he was the 'chosen one of God' and left work for days and weeks at a time to pray at home. This left her mother to fend for the family, and Alice soon became her mother's main support. Although her mother worked hard to feed and clothe six children on her own, there was never enough and Alice remembered 'many hungry days' during the war and afterwards. She believed that these lean years, and the endless hours she helped her mother, 'ruined' her health.

Even in the 1940s, when she wrote for M-O, Alice's health was always delicate, but for eight years in the 1920s, between the ages of twenty-two and thirty, she suffered severe illnesses. When she married in 1928, her doctor warned her against having a child, as it might put Alice in grave danger. Les and Alice waited almost five years until her health improved before they had Jacqueline. Although she wanted two children, Alice stopped at one. It was not her health that barred her this time, but rather Les' behaviour that convinced her not to have more. After the birth of their daughter, he became jealous that Alice's attention was focused elsewhere, and left her to do all the work. Once she realized Les would not lift a finger to help with Jacq, she decided one child was enough.

Natalie Tanner made the same decision after giving birth to her son in 1933. She considered having three children, but with her husband busy building a thriving engineering firm, and because she felt the first two years of the baby's life were too 'trying' without the help of a nanny, James would be her only child. Although they remembered the large-scale destruction and grief of the war, both Natalie and Hugh were too young to participate directly in the First World War.

Instead, Natalie came of age during the economic crises of the 1920s, when she threw her support behind the Labour Party. She spent most of her early twenties campaigning for Labour candidates, and even carried out a term as Poor Law Guardian herself. For a stint of two years her radical leanings led her into membership of the International Labour Party (ILP), known especially for its staunch pacifism amid the jingoism of the Great War.

After getting married in 1926, Hugh and Natalie moved to Spain for five years; they left in 1931, the year in which the Spanish Second Republic was established. The republic soon, however, became overwhelmed by the infighting that would eventually blow up into the Spanish Civil War. When war did break out there in 1936, Natalie became involved in organizing relief efforts for the Republicans who fought against General Francisco Franco's Fascists. It was this work that brought Natalie into contact with communists, for whom she gained great respect. Although she accused them of 'tactical stupidity' and usually voted Labour, she was nonetheless a staunch supporter of the idea of communism and the Soviet Union from this time onwards. In fact, at a theatre production in 1941, she was appalled by the fact that everyone stood up for 'God Save the King', but sat down when the 'Internationale' was played. Natalie remained standing, and angrily instructed the rest of the audience to pay respect to the national anthem of their new ally, the Soviet Union.

The frequent playing of 'God Save the King' during the Second World War was one of the many annoyances with which Helen Mitchell coped. 'Why must we so frequently save the King?' she muttered when the BBC seemed to play the song continually after Italy capitulated in September 1943. Helen's less than patriotic feelings sprang from a deeper well than the simple, though exasperating, repetition of the patriotic tune:

they can be traced to an unfulfilling marriage and a tragic realization that there was no escape from it. This revelation came to her in 1936, when Edward VIII abdicated the throne to marry a divorcee.

On 11 December 1936, it was announced that King Edward VIII abdicated the throne in order to marry the American divorcee, Wallis Simpson. To Mitchell, everything about this episode illustrated the fundamental problems of British society and its conservative stance towards marriage. It was a poignant reminder of her own situation. If the stigma of divorce could not evade even the king, neither could she be immune; if she chose to leave her own loveless marriage, the shame of it would stalk her, too. She was fascinated by the prospects of divorce, and eagerly corresponded with friends who succeeded in breaking away from their unhappy marriages in the 1940s, but something in the abdication kept Helen from leaving her husband. The abdication slammed the door and turned the key on her domestic prison.

Helen married Peter in 1915 and followed her new husband to Newcastle, where he spent the First World War as an engineer. He was shy and hard working, and she was running from a desolate childhood – the youngest child by nine years, Helen's mother frequently told her she was unplanned and unwanted. Helen saw little of her husband while they lived in Newcastle, and they spoke even less. She remembered that their first years together were awkward. Neither knew much about the 'facts of life', nor was she 'very thrilled about "sex"'. Upon reflection, she figured he 'knew as little about the job as I did'. They 'managed to produce a son after 2 years', but Helen was intensely lonely. Soon after giving birth, she 'got less keen on the sex business' and felt her husband had little interest in her outside the bedroom. He threw himself into his work and rarely noticed her.

After the war, they moved to the outskirts of Aberdeen, where initially, the isolation was maddening. Helen spent these years alone in mind and spirit. She knew no one, felt painfully rejected by her husband and found little comfort in motherhood. Being the youngest child, she had had no experience with infants. They made her nervous and self-conscious, and she had no idea how to care for her own child, no one to help her and very few tender feelings towards him.

By the time William was seven, Helen seems to have finally settled into life in Scotland. For several weeks in the autumn of 1926, she presented a local radio programme on 'Prominent Women of the Eighteenth Century', but it would be three more years before she truly came into her own.

In September 1929, she left Aberdeen to study drama and elocution at the Royal Academy of Music (RAM) in London. Helen never explains how she convinced her husband to let her leave, or if indeed she *did* convince him. Nonetheless, she did leave, and since her sister-in-law lived in London, it seems likely that Helen stayed with her during her studies. At the academy, Helen was introduced to a new and exciting world. She found something at which she excelled – receiving bronze and silver medals for outstanding performances on her annual examinations. Helen also discovered kindred spirits in her fellow actors, writers and producers. And for the first time in her life, she felt truly accepted.

The ensuing years in Aberdeen were the happiest of her life, and night after night the house was filled with music and laughter. She put on bridge evenings and staged plays, poetry readings and concerts, inviting amateurs and professionals alike to her home for grand social evenings. With her husband, Peter, she founded a local Shakespeare society; both Peter and William spent their spare time together building sets for the plays. This period would see the bond between father and son strengthened, as the carpentry shed offered the perfect environment for intimate talks, and a place where William eagerly soaked up his father's knowledge and technical skills.

Though Helen watched with some sadness as she was increasingly shut out of the close relationship developing between Peter and William, the 1930s were the height of her life. She had made new friends at the RAM and, with a newfound confidence, blossomed in Scotland. With her workaholic husband rarely home, her son at boarding school for most of the year in England, and an efficient servant to take care of the house, domestic life faded into the background and her social life was in the ascendant.

The abdication crisis in 1936 was the first shock to bring her back to reality. The final blow came a year later when, tired of his work, Peter uprooted Helen from the Aberdeen she had grown to love and sequestered her in an old, rambling house in a quiet village in Kent with few friends and fewer reliable servants. Helen was given no say in the relocation; the decision to move was entirely her husband's.

Moving to Kent would place Helen in the centre of the storm that would soon break over Britain. But while she could not know the struggles she would soon endure in wartime, Helen braced herself for the domestic battle of her life.

CHAPTER TWO

WAR, AGAIN

Irene Grant was on edge. All week, she was nervous and irritable, preoccupied with fears of what lay ahead. 'War is unthinkable,' she said to her husband, as if the words were a talisman to ward off impending doom, but her thoughts would not be still. The prospect of a new war recalled the last one, the supposed 'war to end all wars'. This time, it would be worse. Her neighbour, the wife of a coal miner, told Irene that 'young people' did not realize the terror that awaited them, and she confided, 'I'd rather be dead.' Images of the coming death and horror flickered across Irene's thoughts like a nightmarish newsreel, yet the anticipation of nagging day-to-day wartime realities could not be suppressed. She knew prices would rise and food would be scarce, as had happened in the last war. Irene had barely managed twenty years ago – how would she feed her family this time?

While Grant imagined the worst, Natalie Tanner piled into the car with her family. Two other families followed the Tanners into the Yorkshire countryside to take advantage of a warm August afternoon and to enjoy what Natalie called an 'ordinary middle-class picnic'. The next day, she went out to pick blackberries while her six-year-old son James tumbled and wrestled with the farm cat's new kittens. Natalie stayed within earshot of the phone, in case news might come, but, 'war or no war', the blackberries needed to be gathered in and jam had to be made. The fact that Radio Luxembourg continued to broadcast reassured Natalie that war was more distant than some feared. The radio station beamed popular programming, including jazz and American-style soap operas, from the tiny European nation to a large audience in Britain. It was the only commercial radio station available in northern England and Scotland, sponsored mainly by American manufacturers, hawking cosmetics, household goods and packaged foods. The radio station, with one of the most powerful transmitters in Europe, would have either been shut down or taken over by Germans if the situation was more grave.

Tanner took the radio's continuation to mean that Prime Minister Neville Chamberlain was wavering and would back down, as he always had in the past. The political situation would once again stabilize, she believed. But this was wishful thinking in the wake of the Nazi–Soviet non-aggression pact – making allies of Germany and Russia – signed just days before, on 23 August. In response, Britain signed a pact with Poland, promising support if Hitler were to invade.

To keep her anxious mind from worrying about war, a week after the Nazi–Soviet pact was signed, Nella Last decided to go down to her local Women's Voluntary Service (WVS) centre. The WVS was established in May 1938 as a way to mobilize women across Britain for war. Before the war, they tried to anticipate their community's – and their nation's – needs in the event of hostilities. During the war, WVS women could be found in their distinctive green uniforms amid the rubble and debris of air raids, handing out reviving cups of tea, soothing traumatized victims and caring for the wounded. They were also involved in a surprising array of projects: they ran canteens for soldiers and war workers, knitted socks and gathered books to send to servicemen, organized neighbourhood salvage drives and helped out wherever there was a need. Their motto was: 'The WVS never says no'.[1]

When Nella walked down to her local WVS centre on 31 August, she found many women there, undoubtedly also trying to occupy their thoughts. As the volunteers knitted evacuation blankets, they were told of the new sewing machines that were to be installed for making pyjamas and hospital supplies, if war should come. As they nervously chatted together, they discussed how they might plan their household duties to allow them time to volunteer at the centre if their services were needed.

Nella was amazed that no one talked about the 'big issues' as they worked, but on the way home she overheard people who were convinced that the British–Polish pact had called Hitler's bluff and that he would now back down. She was not so sure, for she was haunted by an old 'prophecy' her father had heard long ago: Prince Edward would never become king, and in 1940, a war would begin that 'would end things'. Now, as she remembered Edward VIII's abdication, she had a 'cold feeling in my tummy when I think the first came true'.

The next day, 1 September, events made the prophecy seem even more foreboding. Natalie Tanner was shocked to learn of the Nazi invasion of Poland on the 10.30 news. That day, the Nazis introduced the world to Blitzkrieg, or 'lightning war', as 1.5 million troops streamed into Poland in a swift and well-coordinated attack, involving armoured Panzer divisions and devastating air support. Europe was stunned and Poland overwhelmed. 'Something had gone wrong with appeasement,' Tanner thought. Nonetheless, she was convinced that Chamberlain would once again evade a direct conflict, as the British government had consistently failed to support Abyssinia, China, Spain and Czechoslovakia in the recent past against Italian, Japanese and German aggression.

But if the government had been negligent in its duties to defend weak states against strong, it was not entirely blind to the threat of future hostility against Britain. Rearmament and defence spending rose in earnest from 1937, and conscription was introduced in early 1939. Air Raid Precautions (ARP) was created by Act of Parliament in late 1937, and soon afterwards 250,000 body bags were ordered to prepare for the eventuality of bombings on civilian targets. Evacuation schemes were devised to move children and mothers with young children quickly out of the city centres that were expected to be the targets of this deadly onslaught.

The Spanish Civil War, which started in 1936, offered a powerful example of the realities of total warfare, heralding a new era of combat that exempted no one from the horrors of war. The awesome destruction of massive aerial bombing was demonstrated in April 1937, when German and Italian bombers supporting General Francisco Franco's Fascist troops devastated the Basque town of Guernica in three hours. Marxist scientist J.B.S. Haldane reported that nearly 2,000 people were killed there, 'many', he said, 'roasted alive' from the fires started by incendiary bombs. It was this action, and others across Spain and China (which endured similar attacks by the Japanese), that led Haldane to write a handbook in 1938, entitled *Air-Raid Precautions*, intended to help ordinary British citizens understand and survive such mass civilian bombings.[2]

By 1 September 1939, Natalie Tanner was well aware of this new reality. Having lived in Spain before the Civil War, she was an enthusiastic supporter of Republican relief projects and closely followed the events since Franco's military coup in the summer of 1936. Now, having heard so much about that conflict and air raid preparations in his own country, Natalie's young son James caught the mood of his parents and joined them to listen pensively to the wireless, anxiously awaiting the air raids that would rain bombs down on his own home. Nella Last thought of her son, Cliff, who had been conscripted, and felt 'like a person who, walking safely on the sea sands suddenly finds [her] feet sinking in quicksand'. At home in Tyneside, Irene Grant could just perceive the cold edge of 'The Sword of Damocles', as she called it, hanging precariously by a single thread from above.

It fell on 3 September. That day, Alice Bridges was remembering the Munich Crisis. Almost a year to the day, on 15 September 1938, Hitler had pressed Britain and France for the annexation of the Sudetenland, an area of Czechoslovakia with a significant number of ethnic Germans. The crisis was so grave that the sixty-nine-year-old Prime Minister, Neville Chamberlain, boarded his first aeroplane and flew to Munich to meet the German leader. Claiming that he was concerned over the treatment of the German population there, Hitler told Chamberlain that Germany was ready to fight for the area. What he failed to tell the Prime Minister, however, was that the Sudetenland was also strategically important to Germany: without it, and its fortifications and resources, Czechoslovakia could not possibly defend itself. Throughout September 1938, the crisis threatened to plunge the world into another great conflict with Germany. The world narrowly averted all-out war, however, when the British and French conceded to Hitler's demands at a peace conference at the end of the month. Britons breathed a collective sigh of relief when Chamberlain returned home with Hitler's promise that this was his last demand. The peace lasted only six months: Hitler invaded Czechoslovakia in March 1939.

To Alice Bridges, war between Britain and Germany had been 'inevitable' since the Munich Crisis, but still, as she awaited the Prime Minister's address on 3 September, she told her diary that she 'hoped against hope for peace'. Regardless of the impending threat, she decided not to evacuate her daughter from their home in Birmingham. Jacqueline was delicate like her mother and very particular about the food she ate, and Alice worried that a new family could not, or would not, take care of her daughter properly.

Others had, however, decided to part with their children in the interests of safety. Hoping to avoid the mass chaos and panic that was expected to erupt when German bombing began, the government instituted an evacuation scheme and encouraged families, especially mothers, to send their children out of the large urban areas considered primary targets. Mothers of infants, and the elderly and infirm were also expected to ship out to safer areas. Entire schools were relocated, and numerous volunteers flooded railway stations, shepherding masses of young, often frightened, children away to safety. Like Jacqueline Bridges, not all children went: less than half of London's school age children were evacuated, while a little over 40 per cent of Glaswegian children left, and in Alice's Birmingham, only 24 per cent boarded the trains leaving home. In the first days of September, more than 1.4 million people were evacuated.

When the news came through at 11.15 that Britain was at war with Germany, Irene Grant shook her head and sadly stated that neither Chamberlain nor Britain could be blamed, for they had done all they could to avoid war. At least the nervous anticipation of the last week was over. Only the day before, on 2 September, everyone seemed steeped in their own quiet waiting. Shopping in Newcastle that day, Irene noticed that the streets were eerily silent; there was none of the gaiety of 1914: 'All Seriousness', she wrote in her diary. No one, Irene noted, wanted to talk or be talked to.

Natalie Tanner missed Chamberlain's announcement, but later found out that Britain was at war when friends came round to take her to lunch in Leeds. As they were leaving, her husband Hugh called from work to tell her the news. Everyone expected the Germans to begin bombing British cities soon after the declaration of war, and Hugh pressed Natalie to stay at home, but she disregarded his advice and went to Leeds.

Within minutes of the announcement, air-raid sirens wailed across London and Britain. Irene Grant heard them from her home in Gateshead and looked out towards the sea, fearfully expecting to see the first wave of invaders. Later, when they realized the sirens were false alarms, Irene and her family drove out to the coast to calm their nerves. Mercifully, as she stared out at the serenely rolling sea cast against a brilliantly blue sky, she felt her fears slowly ebb away.

As Nella Last walked the streets of Barrow that day, she could not shake off Chamberlain's words, which echoed 'slow and solemn' through her mind. Watching men erecting defences, she looked into their eyes and realized she was not the only one who had once hoped that a 'fairy's wand' might be waved and thus avert conflict. But it was too late for fairytales.

The next day, word came that the passenger ship *Athenia* had been torpedoed by the Germans in the North Sea with a devastating loss of life. 'Horrors!' Grant exclaimed, and Alice Bridges wished fervently that the Germans would be wiped from the face of the earth for such atrocities. 'Until we do so,' she wrote, 'we shall never have any peace.' Natalie Tanner was not so vindictive. Having been born in Germany of British parents, and living the first ten years of her life there, she was fluent in the language and had several close German friends. She decided to reserve judgement and turned to Radio Frankfurt for more information. Since there was no boasting on German radio, she concluded that the sinking was a mistake. She did, however, think it odd that the recent problems with the Irish Republican Army (IRA) had been all but forgotten in the wake of war with Germany. Only a month earlier, the IRA's sporadic bombing campaign on British targets throughout 1939 had culminated with deadly force when five people were killed and sixty injured by a bomb in Coventry.

While the others reflected on the international situation, Nella Last prepared to fight the war on her own terms. Working through an unrelenting headache, she cleaned her house and went into town to have her hair cut short – an easy hairstyle would mean she would have more time to volunteer for the war effort. Knowing she needed to keep busy in order to calm her fears, she committed herself to work for the WVS as much as possible, and converted her back garden into a chicken run and vegetable garden.

When she was not volunteering or working in her garden, Nella could not keep her thoughts from turning towards her youngest son, Cliff. She watched him intently during the first weeks of the war, attempting to divine his thoughts or perhaps trying to sear the memory of his face into her mind. As he sat reading the paper one day, she noticed he was distracted, for 'He did not turn a page often.' At that moment, memories of the Great War flooded back and she saw so clearly 'the boys who set off so gaily and lightly and did not come back'; Nella fought hard to stifle a scream of horror.

Rita Grant 'growled' at her mother, Irene, and crashed about the house. War news seemed to exacerbate Rita's epilepsy, and it was all Irene could do not to take her daughter's actions personally. It also took all her strength, physical and emotional, to restrain Rita's 'ten stone of fury' during her fits. At times, Rita proved too strong for Irene and knocked her down, leaving her mother lying on the floor, weeping bitterly with hurt and frustration. After such episodes, Rita was apologetic and tried to be cheerful, but the knowledge that another seizure might strike at any time kept tension in the house high. Irene told M-O that her daughter was 'like a piece of tinder' – anything, even the 'friendliest of advice', could act as a 'match' to set her off.

During the times when Rita was episode-free, she and her younger sister, Marjorie, helped their mother with the housework, read newspapers or books, or listened to the wireless together. When their father came home from work, he and Irene had heated discussions about war. In the first weeks of war, Irene often found herself steadfastly defending the government to her husband, Tom. 'We've backed the wrong horse,' he told her on one occasion. On another, he castigated the government for failing to prepare for war properly and raged that British capitalists had made Germany the menace it was by selling Hitler the materials necessary to build his war machine. Finally, Tom was convinced that a social revolution was near: the people would revolt rather than fight another four-year war. She agreed with him on this point, but most of the time got tired of his tirades and told him to be quiet and let the government do its job.

Within a week of the declaration of war, Natalie Tanner was bored. 'Nothing happens,' she wrote in her diary and wondered what the point was in writing for M-O in the first place. Life went on as usual. On 13 September, the Tanners celebrated their thirteenth wedding anniversary with a leisurely trip to a charming country hotel in North Yorkshire. Still, although there was little excitement to report, the future was uncertain and Natalie decided she would send her son back to school as usual. In any case, it was safer there, since the boarding school was far from any major cities.

The real war for Natalie was not in Europe, but rather with acquaintances, the Bingleys, who wanted to escape the potential dangers of the city and move into one of the cottages on Tanner's farm. In addition to the fact that there was no water laid on there, and that the Tanners were already housing several evacuees, Natalie simply did not want to cope with the demanding Nancy Bingley and the couple's children: a disobedient terror of a toddler and a fussy ten-month-old. A few days later, however, Natalie gave in, and allowed her friends to move in, but soon regretted it. It did not take long before Nancy's overbearing personality harassed anyone who had the misfortune to cross her path. Soon, all the neighbours and evacuees were on an 'anti-Nancy' crusade.

If Nancy's fascist leanings and loud-mouthed demands weren't enough for the Tanners, the Bingley's toddler, Mikey, was an absolute menace. He wrecked the other kids' toys, misbehaved constantly and refused to go to bed when told. They also brought along their dog, Winnie Sims, who had mange. Aside from the Bingleys, everyone thought 'the wretched dog a nuisance as it pees all over the house and sleeps on the bed'. 'Personally,' Natalie confessed, 'I think it's the best member of the family.'

But if everyday life and its battles made the war 'fade away' for Tanner, the others couldn't quite forget the horrors that ravaged Poland, or the restrictions that were now imposed on them. All over Britain, people tried to adjust to the blackouts, evacuations, air-raid sirens and food shortages. Tommy Handley, the star of the soon-to-be incredibly popular *ITMA* (*It's That Man Again*), made his wartime debut on 19 September with a rollicking lampoon of the numerous restrictions being set out by the government. He played the part of the 'Minister of Aggravation', who took considerable joy in his new 'power to confiscate, complicate and commandeer' and 'impose as many restrictions as possible'. If anyone had a problem with his restrictions, the incomprehensible instructions that accompanied them or the new hikes in taxes he proposed, they should, Handley suggested, complain to the commissioner at 'Inland Ruin-you'.

While Handley poked fun at bureaucracy and the new constraints on British life, Nella Last worried over the safety of lorry and bus drivers in blackout conditions and about the lack of adequate bomb shelters in Barrow. She thought it abominable that the government had not done enough to care for its citizens in the event of the expected air raids. In early September, Barrow had 'no dug-outs, no air-raid shelters, no organisation', but she hoped things would soon change.

Irene Grant cursed the blackout because of the personal inconvenience of it. She simply could not fall asleep without the bedroom window open, but the blackout material made it almost impossible to do so. To surmount this problem, she removed the blackout material every night after she turned off the lights. One night, she forgot that the window was open and turned on the light, eliciting shouts from her husband. If the air-raid warden found even a sliver of light peeking from a window, the family would be handed a hefty fine. People were no longer afraid of Hitler, Irene wrote in her diary, they only had one fear: air-raid wardens!

Settling down into war life, with all its new constraints, whether done with a bit of humour, serious apprehension or patriotic resolve (or a little of each), was for many the only tangible indication that Britain was at war. Yet, the death and destruction on the Continent and fear of the unknown never seemed to lurk far away. Indeed, this dark edge of fear that crept into people's minds may have made people resistant to Handley's comedic interpretation of the official war effort in those early days. Though his programme would become one of the most popular of the 1940s, it had a rough start in 1939 and the general opinion at first was not warm towards his antics. People tried to reconcile the war and their lives, looking for an equilibrium that allowed them to feel the emotional depth of war and yet also permitted themselves to laugh, love and live as normal; but it was hard to laugh, or indeed, to act normal that September.

Some felt a twinge of guilt for allowing themselves to soak in the peacefully calm and clear September days while on the Continent, as Irene Grant reflected, 'Lives [were] mutilated and lost, misery to 1000s.' The irony was palpable; under the same cloudless skies in Europe, women and children endured starvation, terror and death at the hands of war. 'For what?' Grant wondered. When the Soviet Union crossed into a mortally wounded Poland on 17 September, Natalie Tanner, a strong supporter of communism and the Soviet Union, was unconcerned; she trusted the Soviet soldiers and believed they would bring a peaceful new order to the Poles.

Alice Bridges' 'heart turned sick' as fear of the unknown gripped her. Europe seemed to be on the edge of a precipice, waiting for the final sinew of sanity to snap and plunge the world into the ultimate battle of good and evil. As she contemplated yet 'another beautiful sunset', thoughts of Armageddon raced through her mind. 'What will it mean ... Who will win? Or shall we nearly all be in "Kingdom Come" and not care anyway?' During those first days of war, Alice battled an illness that left her so frail she was unable to venture outdoors for weeks. Although she had hoped desperately to be involved in the war effort, she could only listen to the wireless and watch the world pass the windows in her home.

Nella Last was delivered a major shock near the end of September, when she learned that her son, Cliff, had been conscripted not into the Royal Engineers, as they had hoped he would be, but rather into the Machine Gun Corps. She was devastated. Her sensitive boy, who liked fresh flowers in his room and had nursed sick animals to health as a child, would have to face another human and kill. Perhaps – she gasped to think of it – Cliff might even have to battle in close combat, plunging the hardened blade of a bayonet into the breast of another young man like himself. After the initial shock subsided, she steeled herself and resolved not to tell her husband of Cliff's fate. Her husband, Will, was 'not strong', and she feared what this shock might do to him. As it was, it had been an uphill battle 'to keep bright and cheerful so as to "keep him up" since Cliff went'. But the burden of carrying the strain of this knowledge alone and keeping cheerful quickly took its toll.

Lately, Nella had found herself stuttering, and a 'curious ridge' had developed on her fingernails. Looking in the mirror one morning, the sunlight caught a 'dusty' glint of grey hair. In all her forty-nine years, few specks of grey had ever tainted the thick 'glossy hatch' on her head. By Christmas, she thought as she peered in disbelief at the image staring back at her, she would be entirely white. Something had 'died inside' when Chamberlain made his speech on 3 September, she realized. As she looked round her empty house or was haunted by memories of her boys' childhood – a whiff of gingerbread baking in a confectioner's shop was all that was needed to remind her of times gone by – she felt as if she had built her entire life 'straw by straw', 'like a jackdaw'. Now those straws were blowing away.

Luckily, Nella thought, she had her volunteer work at the WVS to keep her busy. When her sewing machine was 'whirring', turning out hospital supplies for the centre, the rhythm enfolded her in a melody of work that had the effect of soothing music on her nerves. Indeed, she found herself so caught up in volunteering that on 30 September she was pleasantly surprised, as she reflected on her busy day, to find she had had no thoughts of Hitler all day. It was, she wrote thankfully in her diary, 'All Quiet on the Western Front'. The people of Poland must have thought differently on the Eastern Front, for Poland had been officially conquered and divided by the Germans and Soviets only two days earlier.

It would be quiet at home in Britain throughout the winter of 1939–40. Perhaps hoping that Hitler would be satiated with Poland, Britain and France failed to go on the offensive against Germany. Apart from dropping pamphlets on the German population, the Chamberlain Cabinet refused to engage in bombing missions. Britain was plunged in a morass of hopefulness, apathy and eventual annoyance at the wartime restrictions. People stopped carrying their gas masks everywhere they went, children and mothers who had evacuated to the countryside in the panic of the first weeks of war slowly filtered back to the cities in the hope of spending Christmas at home. Though some may have relaxed a bit during the 'Bore War' or 'Phoney War', as this lull is popularly known, they still coped with balancing the ordinary and the extraordinary, even if the extraordinary was no more real than a news story or simply a distant, nagging fear gently seeping into their thoughts.

CHAPTER THREE

VERY WELL, ALONE

'The lovely weather is a mockery,' Natalie Tanner sighed. Alongside the devastating events in Europe, the warm June weather with its serene, azure skies was indeed a mockery. And yet, that June, as thousands of British and French soldiers perished on the beaches of Dunkirk, and France fell to the Nazis, Natalie Tanner could often be found at the Golden Acre swimming pool near Leeds. After her swim, she went into town for lunch and a movie or theatre production, or made her way home to work in the garden.

In the spring of 1940, war clouds ominously gathered on the Continent as Hitler's Blitzkrieg sprang into action, sweeping away the false sense of security that pervaded the first quiet months of the Bore War. That spring, German forces struck out across the Western Front and the Scandinavian countries. In quick succession, Finland fell to the Soviets in March, and in April German forces overran Denmark, which capitulated without a fight. Norway refused to surrender to the Nazis, who then staged a dramatic and forceful invasion to secure their northern flank and their supply line to Swedish iron ore. In the face of fierce opposition,

British troops were forced to evacuate from Norway in early May. A little less than a month later, the Nazis received Norway's surrender from Vidkun Quisling, the leader of the Norwegian National Unification Party, whose name soon filtered into common parlance to become synonymous with 'traitor'.

On 10 May, after British forces had retreated from Norway, German troops pushed into Belgium, Luxembourg and Holland. On that day, air-raid sirens went off for the first time across cities in northern France. In Westminster, Prime Minister Neville Chamberlain's government was replaced by a coalition run by Winston Churchill. Irene Grant cheered when she heard the news; Chamberlain's handling of the war so far had convinced her that, 'The Govt lack *VIM*,' and that change was necessary if Britain were to emerge victorious. Nella Last told M-O that if she 'had to spend my whole life with a man, I'd choose Mr Chamberlain', but, 'if there was a storm and I was shipwrecked', she believed Churchill was the right man for the job. A lifelong Brummie, Alice Bridges felt Neville Chamberlain had 'besmirched the good name' his father Joseph had built in Birmingham. 'We have at last proper leadership,' she wrote in her diary. To her, Churchill was 'the first nail in Hitler's coffin'.

Five days later, the German troops poised along the river Meuse broke through French lines at Sedan in northern France and travelled 135 miles in a week to make it to the coast. The situation was grim. Refugees flooded southwards through central France from the Netherlands, Belgium and northern France, impeding troop manoeuvres. Believing Paris to be in peril, the French government gave the order for essential ministries to evacuate. Officials at the French Ministry of Foreign Affairs in Paris began throwing classified documents out of the windows and burning them on the lawn outside the Foreign Office. French Prime Minister, Paul Reynaud, soon rescinded the order to evacuate, but the gravity of the situation was not lost on Parisians who witnessed the bonfire of government papers on the banks of the Seine. Paris was in grave danger.

Once the Germans reached the coast just north of the river Somme, the British Expeditionary Force (BEF) in Belgium and northern France was cut off from the main French forces to the south. The BEF put up a good show against Rommel's Panzers near Arras on 21 May, but Belgian resistance soon began to crumble. British soldiers were sent to shore up the Belgian army, but Lord Gort, the Commander-in-Chief of the BEF, knew it was a losing battle; soon, his troops would be surrounded, and he had to get them away. Although Hitler ordered the total 'annihilation' of Allied forces, his decision to halt the German advance temporarily on 23 May gave the BEF a chance to escape.

That same day, Natalie Tanner took a young friend to lunch at an upscale hotel in Leeds. Fran angrily discussed the events on the Continent, and Natalie was surprised to learn just how 'bloodthirsty' her friend was towards the Germans. Indeed, if Fran had a chance, she told Natalie, she'd kill as many Germans as she could with her bare hands. Natalie thought the threat a bit hollow and not a little humorous when she looked at her friend's delicate fingers. Since they were enjoying a delightful meal, Tanner decided to refrain from reminding Fran that she might then have to employ those delicate hands to kill Fran's own grandfather, who was German.

The conversation then veered to examine what had let the Germans loose on the world. Much to Natalie's astonishment, Fran told her she was convinced that the world's problems could be laid squarely on the shoulders of reform movements across the globe. 'She honestly believes', Natalie told M-O,

> . . . that all our troubles are due to the fact that people want to reform the world. If only there were'nt [sic] these busy bodies who want the unemployed to get a larger allowance, and who want to tinker with the capitalist system, everything in the Garden would be lovely.

Always proud of her education, Natalie retorted to M-O that her rather unenlightened friend had read history at Oxford. 'Thank God I went to Cambridge,' she laughed to herself.

On Sunday 26 May, as events on the Continent turned bleak, King George VI called for a national day of prayer for the safety of the troops in Flanders. As thousands bowed their heads, Alice Bridges thought it was scandalous to ask 'God to put right what our Government has put wrong'. Others in Birmingham and across the country may have complied with the King, but she did not utter a prayer that day: 'I couldn't pray to [an] order,' she told M-O. Two days later, news that Belgian King Leopold had surrendered came across the wireless; Alice called it 'A BLACK DAY'. Now, she needed no official order to pray for the troops.

Around Leeds, Natalie Tanner found most people virulently indignant at the Belgian King's 'betrayal'. The local press, she said, was quite 'poisonous' about the affair and called Leopold a 'Craven King'. Privately, she thought Leopold's actions saved his people, 'If one is charitable one can argue that he did what he did in order to save the lives of his subjects'. 'After all,' she reasoned, 'it *is* debatable whether it is better to exist in a concentration camp than to be blown to bits.' On the day that Belgium surrendered, 27 May, the BEF began its heroic retreat from Dunkirk.

That day, Irene Grant's husband, Tom, came home from work blustering about British ineptitude, confident that they'd lost the war. It wouldn't be long, he said, before they begged the Germans for a peace agreement. Irene tried to ignore her husband's defeatism, but it was difficult not to worry, for the international situation heightened an already tense situation in the Grant household.

In the calm of the Bore War, Rita Grant's epilepsy had mysteriously gone silent. She seemed more light-hearted than ever, but the tension was nearly unbearable for Irene, who anxiously counted off the days and weeks that her daughter was episode-free, wondering when or if the seizures might strike again. After weeks without 'fits', Rita announced that she wanted to take a job at the local co-op. Though twenty-one years old, she had never been gainfully employed because her parents feared for her safety if she suffered an epileptic attack away from home. Despite the recent upswing in Rita's health, Irene was sceptical, and she urged her to wait a few more weeks before pursuing the job opportunity. After all, only a year earlier, a doctor had informed Irene that Rita 'would never get better, would only deteriorate'. 'Poor child!' Irene lamented upon having to tell her daughter that she could not take the job, 'Oh! don't let her have more fits!!' The night Rita asked permission to work, as the family 'sat listening to a Scottish band, knitting, embroidering and reading', the relative domestic calm was shattered: Rita suffered a 'bad major' seizure. The seizures became so severe that Irene worried desperately that if she left her daughter alone at night, she might wake up to find Rita dead.

The newly instituted rationing scheme, introduced four months earlier, in January, also weighed heavily on Irene's mind: 'How am I to feed my family?' she wondered. But each time she felt a complaint rise to her lips, Irene thought of her nephew and the other 'brave lads' caught on the beaches at Dunkirk and fought hard to swallow it. No hardship she and her family suffered could come close to what the soldiers were enduring not far from her home on Tyneside, 'We must do our best to be thankful.'

When Nella Last walked into the common room at the WVS centre in Barrow that day, she looked at the sad and drawn faces of the women. Many had sons in France, she knew, and her heart ached to think of the pain they endured. But she could bring herself to do no more than say a few light-hearted comments, and carefully avoid any mention of the present state of affairs. Any remark about the situation, she thought, would set her 'howling'. That night, she felt a 'bogey standing at my shoulder who is trying to say "everything is finished" we are done, the Germans will win.' But she waved him away and went to bed, knowing a good night's sleep would reaffirm her confidence.

When she heard the first news reports of the Dunkirk evacuation, Natalie Tanner pledged her part in the People's War, promising to grow vegetables in her garden and to knit for the forces (though, she said, 'very infrequently'). 'Digging for Victory' had already proved to be a battle in itself for Tanner. The garden near her cottage had not been used in years, and when she decided in October 1939 to produce her own vegetables, she found it an 'unholy mess'. Over the course of the winter, she worked hard to clear the area, pulling bindweed, burning rubbish and planting new crops. By May, the bindweed was still a nuisance, but crops were beginning to peek through the top of the soil.

Much to her chagrin, however, the first fruits of her labour were destroyed by what she called 'fifth columnists'. During the Spanish Civil War, 'fifth column' became a popular term for those who were willing to collaborate with the enemy to undermine the war effort from within. One of Franco's generals claimed to have won Madrid with four columns of troops and a fifth column of sympathetic townspeople. Throughout the early stages of the Blitzkrieg, fifth columnists came forth to help the Nazis in Holland, Norway and Denmark, and most Britons worried that – should an invasion come to Britain – one's neighbours might turn out to be one's enemies. For Tanner, however, as she looked at her destroyed cabbage crop, the 'fifth columnists' were no more than cattle and sheep that grazed the nearby fields.

As the Dunkirk evacuations continued, Alice Bridges listened intently to the news and wrung her hands with worry over the future. Five days after she heard the first reports, she finally pulled herself together – there were other pressing matters. Jacqueline had recently made friends with two girls whose family had fallen on hard times. Their father, Mr Cooper, was a veteran of the Great War who had had his leg 'blown off and the other one . . . terribly wounded' on Armistice Day in 1918. Recently, rheumatism had settled into his one good leg and he had begun to exhibit signs of dropsy.

Alice decided that her 'war work' would be to help 'a sufferer from our last war'. When she noticed that the children were clad in 'poor little ragged coats', Alice immediately found old 'castoffs' and refashioned them to fit them. She also spent weeks sewing dresses for the two girls and often invited their mother up to have tea. Mr Cooper's health steadily became so grave in June that he was sent to hospital. Pulling herself out of the depression that gripped her during the evacuation, Alice stewed up a pot of cream of chicken soup, raided her personal stores and took cream biscuits and three eggs to her newly 'adopted family'.

The Dunkirk evacuation would turn out to be the moment when the British snatched victory from the jaws of tragedy. 'What began as a miserable blunder . . . a catalogue of misfortunes and mis-calculations', J.B. Priestley intoned with the full gravity of the occasion in his special Wednesday evening *Postscript* broadcast, 'ended as an epic in gallantry'.[1] The evacuation at Dunkirk was the opening salvo in the People's War, and Priestley was one of the first to notice it. In that broadcast, he praised the bravery of the civilians who heeded the Royal Navy's call to action and helped out the best they could. Thousands of ships – from large naval destroyers and passenger ferries to small, private motor boats – embarked on a titanic effort to rescue troops from the beachheads and harbours around Dunkirk. Those who crossed the Channel navigated tricky shoals and floating mines only to face a scene of carnage: German artillery belching deadly fire from the French coastline and murderous planes buzzing overhead. One Luftwaffe pilot called it 'unadulterated killing'.[2] Nonetheless, small watercraft, piloted mainly by civilians, braved the shells and gunfire numerous times as they ferried soldiers from the beaches to the large ships waiting in the deeper water just offshore.

On 3 June, with the evacuations still in progress, Alice Bridges sadly noted in her diary that a friend's son was missing in the chaotic retreat. Several men had seen him wading through the water towards the transports, but none had heard from him since. 'One of the boys' who had seen him came back, Alice reported, 'all shaky with nerves'; it was the continual aerial bombing, he confessed, that had broken him down. Less than three months later, huddled in an air-raid shelter, Alice herself would soon learn the nerve required to bear the Luftwaffe's wrath.

When the Dunkirk operation began, Churchill believed around 50,000 men could be taken safely away from the beachhead; over 100,000 would be a miracle. After the week-long evacuation, over 11,000 British servicemen had perished, 14,000 were wounded and 41,000 were taken prisoner or missing, and most of Britain's weaponry and equipment remained strewn across the shores of Dunkirk. But when the last rescue ship returned to British shores, more than 330,000 British and French soldiers had been saved.

When she learned of Belgium's surrender in late May, Natalie Tanner anticipated three events: Italy would come in on the side of the Germans, France would surrender and finally, Britain would capitulate. Although the first two events did indeed occur, Natalie could never have imagined the immense impact that the evacuation at Dunkirk would have on her prediction. Defeat at Dunkirk would have inevitably sunk British morale; but instead, Britain lived to fight another day.

Soon after the epic retreat, Irene Grant was overjoyed to learn that her nephew was one of the soldiers who made it back safely. Still, she and her family feared the future: Dunkirk seemed to be a prelude to an inevitable German invasion. They knew Newcastle would be a potential target for the Nazis, yet they decided that they would not leave their home. Alice Bridges also mulled over the prospects of a German invasion. The thought of it turned her blood to ice. 'We *must* win, we *must* win,' she cried, 'I will not live under a brutal power.'

During the lovely June days of 1940, Natalie Tanner listened to events as they developed on the Continent, sleepily drifting in and out of strains of glory and battlefield bravery as she lay in bed while her husband busily dressed for work, listening again at 9 o'clock in the evening. Practically every day during the first half of June, except for 5 June – when Natalie was too depressed by the hot weather and by Churchill's now famous 'We will fight them on the beaches' speech to do anything – one could find her enjoying the weather at the local swimming pool.

She was not alone. On 10 June, Natalie arrived at the pool to find it in an utter mess from the bathers the previous day. The workers told her that at least 2,000 people had come out to swim and revel in the warm weather. She helped them clean up the bottles and trash left over from the throng of people, reflecting to herself, 'There is no doubt, the British are a litter-minded lot.' Before she could enjoy the fruits of her labour, however, a number of soldiers from the British Expeditionary Force who had escaped the onslaught at Dunkirk showed up to bathe. By the time they left, the sun had gone in and Natalie only took a quick, though refreshing, swim. Later that day, she went into nearby Bradford and talked over events with the regulars at her favourite cafe.

Across the English Channel in Paris, coal-black plumes rose from the city, obscuring the deep blue skies above. Large fires emanated from the petrol reserves that were purposely burned to keep them out of the invading army's hands, and smaller fires trickled forth from the houses and buildings that had suffered in Paris' first air raid on 3 June. In that raid, three airports were destroyed and over 200 people died. When Alice heard of the bombing, she thought of the children in Paris and worried fearfully about the fate that awaited her own child. Irene Grant called for immediate retribution. 'Get Berlin bombed,' she cried. 'Let the German people know fear. War is ruthless and must be.'

A week later, with the Germans only nineteen miles from Paris, the French government abandoned the capital and headed south. To the indignation of many French soldiers streaming into the capital from the front, the government had decided not to defend Paris. To avoid mass destruction of property and lives, the French government declared it an 'open city'. German troops walked into Paris on 14 June. 'Paris fallen,' Nella Last reported sadly. Her friends at the WVS now wondered when London would fall. The tension was nearly unbearable as Britons anxiously watched events unfold across the Channel; both Irene Grant and Nella Last confessed several times in the days after Dunkirk to feeling 'terrified' or 'frightened'.

Several days after the fall of Paris, Churchill met the French government on the run and urged them to fight, proposing a radical plan to unite the two nations officially. Although the French Prime Minister, Paul

Reynaud, was enthusiastic, he was overridden by the hero of the First World War, eighty-three-year-old Marshal Pétain, and French General Weygand. Pétain said that a Franco–British union would make France no more than a colony of Britain, and he preferred to deal with the Nazis. Weygand was confident that, once the Nazis turned their full force upon Britain, they would 'wring her neck like a chicken'.[3] It was better, they thought, to broker a peace on their own. On 22 June 1940, France signed an armistice ceasing hostilities with Germany; Britain had lost its last ally.

The news of the fall of France shook Nella Last's confidence. She now questioned everything that had carried her to this point. 'My head felt as if it was full of broken glass instead of thoughts and I felt if I could only cry . . . For the first time in my life,' she confessed, 'I was unable to "ask" for courage and strength with the certainty I would receive it.' But, as a domestic soldier, it was her duty to carry on. She sniffed sal volatile, splashed herself with water, put on a pretty flowered dress and a bit of rouge and lipstick, then went out to the garden and picked a few roses to liven up the table.

The effort revived her. She regained her composure and had tea laid by the time her husband came home. The two shared significant glances when he walked in the door and she said simply, 'Bad – very bad', then poured the tea. As she passed by him, he drew her close and leaned up against her, looking up at her with the same fear in his eyes that she had recently felt herself. But hers had gone and, feeling 'strong and sure', she bent over to kiss him. Perhaps with admiration, amazement or a mixture of both, he quietly said, 'You never lose courage or strength, my darling.' Only she knew the struggle it had been to fight off the 'bogey' this time, but she kept that to herself and smiled. Such a confession, she thought, would 'rob him of his faith'.

In the dark period between the evacuation and the French defeat, Churchill rallied the people with his unforgettable doggedness and rhetorical mastery:

> We shall fight on the beaches, we shall fight on the landing grounds, we shall fight in the fields and in the streets, we shall fight in the hills; we shall never surrender.[4]

The speech struck a chord in the British spirit and echoed down the halls of history from the moment the words were spoken, directly after the retreat at Dunkirk. When the Battle of France ended, he went to the people once again to prepare them for the mortal combat that was to come, beseeching them to:

> . . . brace ourselves to our duty, and so bear ourselves that if the British Empire and Commonwealth lasts for a thousand years, men will still say, 'This was their finest hour.'[5]

But perhaps the famous cartoonist, David Low put the situation perfectly when he drew a British soldier standing on the coast of England, turbulent seas crashing all around, chin out, defiantly shaking his fist at the Continent, 'Very well, Alone'.[6]

CHAPTER FOUR

OH GOD, WHAT A NIGHT

As Alice Bridges put the final touches on her salad, the air-raid sirens went. Quickly she dashed up the stairs of her terraced home on the outskirts of Birmingham, scooped up her seven-year-old daughter, Jacqueline, and headed for the Anderson shelter in her back garden. There was no time to get the gas masks or any personal belongings – the planes were already overhead. Once she safely settled her daughter in the shelter, the 'het-up' feeling of terror and anxiety began to evaporate. It was her greatest fear that a bomb would fall on her house before she could get Jacq to safety. Alice relaxed a bit and listened to the bombs falling near them, all the while trying to wrap her mind around the fact that by the time the planes passed overhead, the bombs had already been released. It made her feel utterly helpless. There was little to do but to run for cover and hope that the bombs were not meant for you. Alice whispered a heartfelt 'thanks to the Almighty' that they'd been spared. Only a week before, at least ten people had died and twenty had been wounded in a raid only a few minutes' walk from her house.

Somehow, in that shelter of corrugated metal with the earth and sod of her garden covering it, Alice felt invincible. 'I felt as though a magic ring had been drawn round our shelter,' she wrote in her diary. Nervous pangs pierced her heart like a 'sharp arrow' every time she felt a bomb's impact, but the arrows were not so much concern for herself and her family, Alice explained, as for the others she knew who suffered nearby.

At midnight, the All Clear went and Alice and her husband jumped at the opportunity to get the essentials they had left in the rush caused by the siren a few hours before. She put the water on for tea, grabbed the masks and coats, took them down to the shelter and went back up for the tea. Another wave of planes sounded ominously in the distance. With the searchlights above illuminating the way, she ran through the garden, a boiling pot of tea under her arm and a 'tray full of crocks and a bottle of milk' wobbling precariously with each hurried step. Nearby, one shelter suffered a direct hit and four people were killed, but Alice and the tea made it. Once she put the tray down, she had a good laugh, 'I must have looked daft . . . I breathed out, whew. It was a nice cup of tea though.'

The night before the tea dash, 23 August 1940, the waves upon waves of bombers overhead sounded to her like a 'layer pudding': 'Bless me another wave came over, then the warning, then more gun fire, more waves and so on . . . the gunfire were like the sprinkled currants.' That night she dreamed she and Jacq were machine-gunned. Later, Alice reported that few were killed that night, but one woman she knew went to hospital because she had 'smashed her face in' falling down the stairs in the rush to get to safety.

Two weeks had passed since the first siren awoke Alice from her sleep on the night of 8/9 August. Since then, she had recorded sirens about every three nights, waves of planes passing overhead, anti-aircraft fire (or 'ack-ack'), and bombs falling. The enemy aircraft that released their bombs over Birmingham that August had drawn Alice and her fellow Brummies into the Battle of Britain.

Soon after the fall of France in June 1940, Hitler and his commanders began drawing up plans for a full-scale invasion of Britain. At the same time, Hitler hoped to persuade the British government to agree to a peace settlement – the Führer insisted he 'did not wish to destroy the British Empire', but he would if his hand was forced.[1] Furthermore, Hitler wanted to knock Britain out of the war quickly and thus neutralize any threat on the Western Front that might impede his planned move east against the Soviets. Considering the rapidity with which most of Western Europe had fallen to Nazi forces, an offer of peace may have seemed attractive to some Britons. But, aside from a few British diplomats and the former King Edward VIII (now the Duke of Windsor), German attempts at peacemaking were met with a defiant cold shoulder.

According to the German invasion plan, code-named Sea Lion, German forces were to be in place by 15 September. Those forces would land at three sites on the 75-mile stretch of coastline between Brighton and Folkestone. Within the first two hours of invasion, the Nazis planned to put 80,000 soldiers ashore, 125,000 over the first three days. Parachutists would then land just inland, near Folkestone, block the Canterbury–Folkestone road and secure crossings over the Royal Military Canal, a 28-mile defensive canal stretching from Seabrook, Kent, to Cliff End, East Sussex, originally created to thwart a Napoleonic invasion. Other airborne troops were expected to hold the Downs behind Brighton. The German plan called for another ten infantry divisions (roughly 130,000 men) to be on British soil a week and a half after the initial invasion, followed by a second invasion force of Panzers and motorized divisions. Another nine divisions were to follow in the next two weeks, with eight divisions waiting in reserve.

It was an ambitious plan, and, considering the strength of the Royal Navy defending its home waters, the German Naval Command was not optimistic. Air support was crucial for the invasion to succeed. Before invasion could commence, the RAF had to be neutralized, thus leaving the Luftwaffe with a free hand to harry and distract the Royal Navy in the Channel.

The Germans bombed the Channel Islands on 28 June, killing over forty islanders. The military and about a third of the population had evacuated the islands on orders from Churchill's War Cabinet just eight days before, and, finding the islands undefended, the Nazis quickly occupied Guernsey, Jersey, Alderney and Sark in the early days of July. At the same time, in preparation for the invasion and eventual occupation of mainland Britain, the Luftwaffe began a concerted attack on shipping in the Channel. Intermittent air raids over the mainland also commenced that July and August, as German bombers flew missions over the south and Midlands to gain experience and to test their navigational systems. The air raids that Bridges experienced in August were part of this prelude to invasion. The first of these was in the early hours of 9 August, when Alice Bridges was first woken by air-raid sirens. About forty German planes had flown over the Channel from Cherbourg on missions meant primarily to harass civilians. Bombs fell on Birmingham for the first time that night, while Dover, Norwich and Birkenhead were also hit.

When the sirens went that night, Alice could hear her neighbour banging on the wall to get the Bridges' attention; Alice knocked back in acknowledgement and then extended the favour to her other neighbour, banging on the wall and awaiting a response to ensure everyone was awake. Anxious commotion followed this neighbourly exchange as Bridges endeavoured to wake her daughter, mobilize her husband, get dressed, find shoes and gather together refreshment for the shelter. Luckily, Bridges' neighbourhood was not targeted that night: it took 'an age' for everyone to assemble in the safety of the Anderson shelter. Instead, a lone bomber released his load of bombs over a suburban area in Erdington, several miles north of Bridges, before he headed home.

Alice's first encounter with the Luftwaffe resulted in a 'good night's sleep busted up'. Although nearly 200 civilians lost their lives in the intermittent air raids of July and early August, many had similar experiences to Alice's. Since sleep seemed to be the largest casualty at this time, George Orwell called them 'nuisance raids'.[2]

On 13 August, dubbed 'Eagle Day' or *Adlertag* by the German High Command, the Luftwaffe shifted its attention towards knocking out the RAF and Britain's aircraft production.[3] All three Luftwaffe squadrons were thrown at airfields and air factories, flying both daytime and night-time sorties across Britain. The night of *Adlertag*, German planes dropped numerous empty parachutes across the Midlands and in the lowlands of Scotland to unnerve the population. The New British

Broadcasting Station – a rogue radio station set up by the Germans and allegedly run by British 'patriots' in a secret English location – then announced that parachutists had landed near Birmingham, Manchester and Glasgow. The troops, purportedly dressed in civilian clothes or British uniforms, were said to be harboured by fifth columnists and were ready to neutralize anyone who got in their way with a secret 'electro-magnetic death ray'.[4] Rumours abounded, but those who bothered to check the facts would learn that no footprints were discovered near the abandoned parachutes. There were no hidden invaders waiting to massacre civilians with secret weapons.

Instead, the action was in the air. Breathtaking aerial battles occurred largely in southern England: over Kent, Hampshire, Sussex and Surrey. Residents of the south cheered and gasped as they watched Spitfires thrusting and parrying with Messerschmitts high across the summer sky like modern-day knights, while journalists and radio announcers on the ground commentated on the whole thing for the rest of the country and the world, as if it were a cricket match.

The British people were more than spectators watching or listening to the action as 'The Few' defended Britain's shores against the invader. Instead, the Battle of Britain provided opportunities for ordinary people to fight the enemy and support the war effort. On 10 July, the WVS beseeched the nation's housewives to deliver a blow to the Germans with their saucepans; any item made of aluminium, they were told, could be recycled into Spitfires, Hurricanes and other aircraft. Soon, droves of women, men and children began scouring homes and garages for the 'Saucepans for Spitfires' campaign. Kettles, saucepans, metal dishes and other kitchen implements poured in – anything thought useful, even shells of old cars, were donated. When homes were emptied, those with money to spare raided local shops for new aluminium goods that they could offer in patriotic gesture. When the drive ended after two months, the appeal had raised an estimated 1,000 tons of aluminium.

In addition to sacrificing new and used kitchen stock, one could simply invest in a new Spitfire. Recycling metal for planes could be a bit intangible, but with the 'Spitfire Fund', the Minister of Aircraft Production Lord Max Beaverbrook, itemized the cost of every Spitfire part. Five pounds bought a compass, while a few pennies bought a rivet; set down 15 shillings, and a machine-gun blast tube was yours. Cities, neighbourhoods, factories, newspapers and other groups organized collections for a grander contribution: £2,000 put a pair of wings on a fighter plane, while £5,000 bought the entire plane. (This was not, however, the true cost of building the plane: £12,000 was nearer the mark.) Those who bought a plane had the honour of naming it; some names were mundane, some patriotic, others advertising opportunities, and still others were simply unfortunate. Alice's 'City of Birmingham' graced four Spitfires, LNER sent up a 'Flying Scotsman', Marks and Spencer was proud of its 'Marksman', while any pilot must have been a bit wary of flying Portland Cement's 'Concrete'. Listening to an air battle 'called' over the air, or turning one's eyes to the skies to watch the glint and flash above, one might, as Lady Reading of the WVS put it, 'feel a tiny thrill' at the thought that perhaps one's saucepan or shilling was part of the fray.[5]

*   *   *

While aerial battles pitting fighter against fighter raged in the south, civilians across Britain began to feel the heat of the Blitz. Before 24 August, night-time raids consisted of a few aircraft roaming across wide swathes of the country, dropping bombs here and there. After the 24th, however, night bombing campaigns began to concentrate on industrial and urban areas. Industrial works, such as the 345-acre Nuffield factory (producing Spitfires) and Fort Dunlop (tyres), situated in the Castle Bromwich area close to the city centre made Birmingham an ideal mark. South of the city, Austin's plant at Longbridge, which had converted operations to manufacture both military vehicles and aircraft, added to the importance of Birmingham. Nearer Alice, in Acock's Green, Rover made engine parts, and just down the road was Serck Radiators, which manufactured all of the radiators and air coolers in the Hurricanes and Spitfires used in the Battle of Britain. British Small Arms (BSA), producing nearly half of the precision weaponry in Britain, was also very near Alice in Small Heath. Besides these major works, Birmingham produced everything from tanks to stirrup pumps (used by firewatchers to douse fires started by incendiaries) and grenades to minesweepers. Although Cadbury continued to supply the nation with chocolate and cocoa, the company also opened up Bourneville Utilities, making plane parts, rockets, respirators and munitions.

On the first night of intensified bombing for the area, 24/25 August, German bombers embarked from the Brittany coast in France and flew over Dorset, dropping bombs on Bristol and South Wales before heading into the Midlands, where bombs fell on factories in Castle Bromwich, less than five miles from Alice's home.

On 25/26 August, Birmingham experienced its worst raid to date. Woolworths and other shops in the Bull Ring were damaged, the Market Hall was destroyed and, closer to home, just five minutes' walk away, a bomb dropped in the garden of one of Jacq's schoolmates, while another lifted a house and dropped it whole in the crater left by the bomb. Overall, twenty-five people were killed or seriously injured in the raid. When the Bridges looked out of their shelter door that night, they could see the glow of fires that erupted across the city, which the German planes flocked to like 'flys [sic] to the honeypot'.

The period of 'nuisance raids' was over. After three nights of raids on Birmingham and Coventry, the Luftwaffe shifted its attention to Merseyside, which received heavy attacks on the last four nights of August. Over 1,000 people lost their lives in the raids across Britain in August alone. By the end of the month, the effects of regular air raids were noticeable, not only in the damaged landscape of Alice's Birmingham, but also in the people around her. Stomachs flipped and churned, some bought phospherine tonic to calm their nerves, and everywhere emotions were raw. Bridges' husband sulked and complained that in all the commotion, Alice had forgotten to pay attention to him. When he came down to the shelter during a raid on 30 August, he was in a huff that he couldn't find his keys. 'He was none too sweet . . . blamed me, how like a man,' she told M-O. But she kept her calm and helped him search the house, until finally she asked him to try his pockets. 'I was right, as usual. What a man.'

With nerves snapping and confidence slipping all around her, Bridges attempted to shore up morale. She taped a large sign to her window for all to see; it was similar to one her husband, Les, had noticed on the way to work. It read: 'THERE IS NO DEPRESSION IN THIS HOUSE AND WE ARE NOT INTERESTED IN THE POSSIBILITIES OF DEFEAT. THEY DO NOT EXIST.' The same day she made out her will. In admiration for her neighbours or as a mantra to bolster her own spirits, she told M-O that she was impressed with how others around her endured the Blitz: 'INDOMITABLE SPIRIT DOMINATES. THEIR CHEER-FULNESS IS WONDERFUL.'

The focus of the German bombers shifted to London soon afterwards. After a RAF raid on 26 August killed civilians in Berlin, Hitler promised to raze British cities to the ground in revenge. 'When the British Air Force drops two or three or four thousand kilograms of bombs, then', he swore as a crowd of Germans erupted in frenzied applause, 'we will in one night drop 150-, 230-, 300- or 400,000 kilograms'.[6] To those in England who wondered when the invasion would begin, Hitler assured them, 'Be calm. Be calm. He's coming! He's coming!'[7]

The London Blitz began on 7 September, just three days after Hitler promised to destroy British cities, and would continue uninterrupted for fifty-seven nights. Helen Mitchell endured the first night of the London Blitz playing cards 'in a state of fright' with her husband, son and friend in an underground coal cellar in Beckenham among other residents (whom Helen called 'bodies') of the flats where the Mitchells were living at the time. The next day, Helen's husband left for Canada, and her son went off to the army four days later, abandoning her to face the Blitz alone. Unable to carry on she left the city a week later to stay with a friend in Epsom. A landmine later obliterated the flats.

From the end of August, German ships streamed towards the Dutch coast from ports in Lubeck, Stettin and Kiel. Soon, British reconnaissance reported a build-up of ships in the invasion ports of Holland, Belgium and France. By 8 September, most of the barges, tugs and trawlers slated for Operation Sea Lion were in place. More ominously, British intelligence believed that specially trained Gestapo troops had arrived at embarkation points on the 11 August. Intelligence reports announced that, 'An expedition may be launched at any time now.' [8]

The Battle of Britain lasted until 15 September, when the RAF chased German fighters and bombers to the coast during a daylight raid on London, forcing the Germans to rely on night raids from then on. On the 17th, the RAF bombed Dunkirk and scattered the invasion fleet. Hitler now had little option but to postpone the invasion of Britain until the spring. Nonetheless, across the Channel, preparations for invasion continued to be reported by Allied intelligence well into October.

Bridges didn't write for the entire month of September, but by October, when she resumed her diary, Birmingham was once again a target despite the heavy raids on London. Sleep was becoming a treasured commodity with each passing day and, although Alice had complained in August that her sleep was cut to a *mere* seven hours, it got considerably worse.

On the night of 4 October, it wasn't the German bombers that deprived her of sleep, but her husband. He stumbled into the shelter late that night, drunk from a night out with his mates. She sent him back to the house for his dinner, but when she went in to check on him, Alice found he'd burned his meal and in a fit of anger had thrown the plate across the kitchen against the wall she'd recently painted.

> I blazed . . . I told him exactly where he got off and that I was wasting my time running a home for a man who could go out drinking, come home and make himself a damn nuisance, when at that moment there were our lads giving their lives for such as he.

Defiantly, she said that she would evacuate Jacq to safety in the countryside and find a job instead of keeping house for him. He threatened to lock her inside the house so she couldn't. She went to bed shaken, 'I cannot afford rows . . . I can face bombing better.'

In the morning, she told him he could keep some of the housekeeping money and eat his dinners out, for she wouldn't waste her time cooking for him. He balked, but then they patched things up. He admitted that he'd got drunk because he felt guilty that he was doing nothing for the war effort. She softened and defended him to M-O:

> The last war he was seventeen or sixteen when he joined up, he was in it, you see, and doing something. This war he has responsibilities, a home to pay for and upkeep, a wife and child, his job to keep or another to get, to help the war effort and yet he's in a reserved occupation.

For most of October, Alice and her family rushed down to the shelter at around 8 p.m., the time when the sirens seemed to wail as if on schedule. Some nights were relatively 'quiet', but the roar of German planes could nonetheless be heard overhead as they bypassed

Birmingham and turned their wrath on another district. Bridges and her friends held their breath and hoped that Lord Haw-Haw, the British turncoat who broadcast on German radio with seemingly uncanny accuracy (though often this was little more than rumour spread after the fact), was right. Maybe Hitler really *would* spare Birmingham for his capital since he was determined to raze London to the ground, as Haw-Haw had asserted. But the hope was fleeting. In mid-October, the Germans returned to Birmingham for several nights.

At the start of these raids, on 15 October, Bridges had a difficult time convincing her husband to take cover. He was slightly deaf and swore she was too cautious: her '2 miles away is about 10 miles', he mocked. Stubbornly, Les vowed not to move until he heard the bombs himself. Between the raids, she ran from the shelter through the garden, with ack-ack fire blazing nearby, to the house to beg him to come down, but it was no use. Finally, she absolved herself of all responsibility for him and ran back to the shelter. 'He got terribly peevish, he's a man that likes everything cut and dried and he thinks jerry shouldn't come until he's ready for him,' she huffed to M-O from the safety of her Anderson shelter.

In his own good time, Les eventually came down to the shelter with a peace offering of coffee, but not without delivering a backhanded comment that he was right. The next morning, he learned that the bombs fell only a quarter of a mile away. Alice couldn't help jesting: 'I like your 10 miles.' When the sirens went the next time, Les was in the shelter, wearing his tin hat.

On 24 October, Birmingham city centre endured a large raid that obliterated Marshall and Snellgrove's department store. Bridges listened for bombs, ready with cotton for her ears and a piece of rubber to pop in her mouth (to protect from the impact of nearby explosions) and hovered over her daughter, prepared to protect her if need be. When the bombs whizzed nearby, Alice flopped over Jacq, who was duly annoyed to be awakened. When they looked out of the shelter, the sky over town was fully alight and fires glinted across the horizon. The next night, the Carlton Cinema where she'd taken her daughter to see a George Formby movie only five days earlier was hit in a raid. That night 170 people perished throughout the city. Alice would later learn that some friends were among the nineteen casualties in the theatre. 'My interest in pictures has evaporated,' she wrote in her diary.

In November came the rain. To Bridges, the back garden and the Anderson shelter resembled the trenches of the Great War. Water poured relentlessly into the shelter from all sides. Alice and Les took turns baling out the shelter, but it was a losing battle. It wasn't long before all of the families along Bridges' street gave up and decided to brave raids in their houses, taking cover in their shelters only when absolutely necessary. At such times, they sat ankle-deep in water, watched the rain run down the walls of the shelter and waited anxiously for the All Clear, when they could dash up to their homes and escape both the bombs and the wet. In the damp, with fear and frustration mounting, Alice learned that not only ankles, but also nerves became raw. 'My young man went out this morning peevish,' she wrote, 'blaming me for the wet in the shelter, the cough on his chest, the fact that he has to wash and shave in the morning, the fact that there is a war on.' Two days of constant rain, baling, ducking for cover and foul moods finally led to a truce. They both decided they must adapt to the situation and be civil to each other, 'but if you could have conceived for one moment the hopelessness of our task', Bridges sighed after she and Les endeavoured unsuccessfully to keep their shelter dry during the raid on 5 November.

The worst still lurked in the future. On 19 November, Bridges noted the fearful devastation that Coventry had suffered on 14/15 November. The shelter was still flooded, so she and her family were forced to endure the raid in their home.

> Planes flew over in droves, right over our roof tops, hour on hour on hour . . . I sat on the bed on the floor in the corner of the big room, ready to fall on top of Jacqueline the minute I heard a bomb whizzing, wishing I had moved our heavy gramophone from overhead wondering how big a dent it would make in me.

But the night was Coventry's, not Birmingham's.

With the devastation wrought on Coventry that night, a new word was created: 'Coventration', or 'to lay waste by aerial bombardment'.[9] Around 500 tons of high-explosive bombs – five times the amount considered a 'major raid' – and 30,000 incendiary bombs obliterated the city centre. It took one woman a year to find where the Boots she had patronized for years used to stand. 'It stood in the centre of the city on a corner, and the complete street . . . is gone,' she told M-O. To her and others, though, after a year to heal, the destruction wasn't entirely bad. On the anniversary of the bombing in 1941, the same woman wrote:

> One continually gets new views through the ruins . . .
> One of the miners in this village said, 'Apart from the

loss of life, these Blitzes aren't too bad. They have cleared away lots of stuff which the Corporation would never have been able to afford.' I can endorse that. Apart from about four really interesting buildings, there is nothing at all to regret about the destruction of Coventry, as far as the actual bricks and mortar is concerned.[10]

One might find a silver lining in the destruction of uninspiring 'bricks and mortar', but there was nothing more tragic than the 568 dead that night, many of whom were rendered unidentifiable after an explosion took the roof off the mortuary and two days of rain soaked the remains. The raids injured a further 1,200 people. Nearly everyone in Coventry, which was a relatively small industrial town, knew someone who died, had gone missing or had lost their home in the raid. Soon after, a team from M-O went there to report on the ruin wrought on the city. They found 'more open signs of hysteria, terror, neurosis, than during the whole of the previous two months together in all areas'. Some were left dazed and speechless, others cried or trembled uncontrollably, and still others lashed out at rescue and support personnel. Over and over, the team of observers heard residents echo a feeling of hopelessness – 'Coventry is finished,' 'Coventry is dead.'[11]

A few days later, on the night of 19 November, it was Birmingham's turn. Sirens went at 6.50 in the evening, just as Alice was ready to serve dinner. Initially, the family took cover inside, but the bombardment became so hot and shook the house so violently that they ran down to the shelter, the gunfire shredding the air and the sky lit up as if it were day. As they settled into their Anderson shelter, the next-door neighbours, the

Brownings, came down looking for shelter. Seven of them huddled together under the corrugated steel and earth listening for hours on end to the 'clack-clack of incendiaries falling' and the shrapnel that 'fell like hail round us'.

The electric fire that Les had fitted in the shelter warmed them and soothed their nerves somewhat, but when she heard a bomb falling – and much to her annoyance, her neighbours were quick to point out and comment on each one – Alice's 'tummy turned right over'. The noise was terrifying: according to one Londoner, bombs came down 'with a tearing sound as well as a whistle; they did not fall, they rushed at enormous velocity'.[12]

Not until 2.30 in the morning did there seem to be a lull in the action, but when the Brownings decided to go back to the house, they were greeted by a massive blast. Two 'landmines' – parachute mines 8 feet long and 2 feet in diameter, which floated to the ground and caused extensive damage – landed in the street parallel to them. At the same time, a 'breadbasket' of incendiaries had fallen nearby, starting numerous fires.

The Brownings made it back to their house in safety, and, once quiet had descended, Alice mustered together her family and ventured back home too. Dinner had been left uneaten when the raid started eight hours before, and Alice's first priority beyond safety was to feed her daughter. Once inside, Alice soon discovered that the gas was cut but, luckily, electric service was not disrupted. She breathed a sigh of relief for her electric cooker – an appliance for which she often expressed gratitude in the coming days.

Ignoring the ruined dinner, she quickly heated up some sausages and the family sat down for a quick bite. In the lull, a warden came by to check on them. He told them the devastation was 'pretty awful', but at least there weren't many casualties. From the front door, where she talked with the warden, she could see hundreds of night workers streaming home from the factories and warehouses nearby. The respite was punctuated by one more violent barrage that morning, so close that it lifted Bridges off her bed and sent her flying once more towards the shelter. Later that day, after she'd recovered a little, she sat down to write in her diary. 'Oh God, what a night,' she wrote, '10¾ hours of anguish, misery, hunger and sleeplessness'.

The next two nights, Wednesday and Thursday 20 and 21 November, the Luftwaffe appeared again, but the waves did not last as long. Rain began to fall on Thursday, slowing down the raiders, but swamping the shelter once again. Water 'came in like a river', and all night they baled out the shelter, but the damp settled into Jacq's chest and brought on bronchitis.

On Friday morning, Alice pulled sixty buckets of water out of the shelter and nearly fainted from the strain. Yet she was thankful for the work, because the shelter once again became their refuge for what would become Birmingham's largest onslaught. 'The fun started' once again at dinner. Within minutes, incendiaries had started fires several houses away. Across the road and on the corner, more homes burned. While Les went out to help fight the fires, Alice and Jacq dressed and got two suitcases ready for evacuation. When Les came in, they retreated to the shelter, for Alice said she could 'stand the idea of blast but not being roasted alive'. 'The gunfire was hot and the effect of the fires . . . was terrifying because of the thought of it. All those houses were on fire, and we in the centre . . .'

Alice bundled up Jacq and soon her daughter drifted off to sleep. Meanwhile, what seemed like a thousand planes came over, delivering death and destruction. The neighbour, Mr Browning, came down during gunfire, carrying with him a cup of tea for Alice and her husband. She was thankful for the refreshment, and 'It was quite a relief having a chat to someone,' she told M-O. Soon, the raid got so hot that Les couldn't leave the shelter to get rid of the buckets of water flooding in. He could only open the door and throw the water as far out as possible, creating a huge muddy quagmire round the entrance. From inside, Alice listened apprehensively to the raid, and when a landmine exploded nearby she felt her legs and feet go cold, 'like lumps of ice'.

In the distance, she heard voices intermingled with screams and fire engines. Alice would later learn that the chaos occurred only a block away from her: incendiaries, landmines, high-explosive bombs, time bombs and a 'huge torpedo bomb' had been dropped. People were rushing out of their shelters barefoot, half-naked and dazed as ARP wardens shouted instructions to 'Throw yourselves down, get up, run, keep calm.'

It was 4 a.m. by the time Alice felt she could shut her eyes and sleep, but then a stray bomb would drop and wake her 'with a horrible tight feeling round my heart'. It was useless. The night seemed interminable; all she wanted to do was see the light of day, for then, she knew, the bombers would be gone. The All Clear finally went at 5.45, and the Bridges emerged from their shelter like ragged troglodytes. 'I felt like a person dead and devoid of feeling,' Alice scribbled in her diary.

She flicked on the radio in time to hear the BBC state, a 'raid over Midland area'. No mention of Birmingham.

No one to sympathize with their plight. It was as if the nightmare never occurred. But when she went out the next day to check on her mother, it was all too clear that hell indeed had been let loose upon her world. Shattered shop windows lay in shards about the streets, a car had been swallowed up in a huge bomb crater, dazed people walked the streets with suitcases, hoping to board buses out of town. In one section of town, Alice was so overwhelmed by the destruction that she felt she 'could have stood in the road and howled': all around her, rows of houses had been laid waste, 'nothing but dust and debris' was left. Walking through this wasteland, she may have experienced what John Strachey (a socialist intellectual who sometimes wrote for the *New Statesman* and who served as an ARP warden in Chelsea) described as the 'harsh, rank, raw smell' of a bombed street,

> [The] torn, wounded, dismembered houses . . . For several hours there was an acrid overtone from the high explosive which the bomb itself contained; a fiery constituent of the smell. Almost invariable, too, there was the mean little stink of domestic gas, seeping up from broken pipes and leads. But the whole of the smell . . . was the smell of violent death itself.[13]

On her way home, Alice met a man who was looking for water for his car radiator. He said he was off to Stourbridge and offered Alice a ride – an escape from the large-scale devastation she'd witnessed on her excursion through town and from facing another night of carnage in which her luck might not hold up. 'Well, my spirits soared,' she confided to M-O, 'I thought it was the answer to a maiden's prayer.' She ran up to the house to pack, only to learn minutes later that her hopes were dashed. Les informed her that the deal was off; the Bridges were staying in Birmingham. All Alice could do was 'shrug my shoulders and carry on'. 'What is to be, will be,' she thought. Alice exuded calm in front of her family as she waited for the night to fall, but inside, she confessed, nothing could be further from the truth. And once again, with the darkness came the sirens. But this time, she was armed with lemonade and Nut Brown Ale: 'I wasn't going to be without a pick-me-up tonight.'

The eleven-hour raid of 23/24 November was the largest of the Birmingham Blitz. Hundreds of fires were started and fire crews came from as far away as Cardiff to help fight the blazes. Through a friend, Alice heard of the disaster that occurred at the Birmingham Small Arms (BSA) factory at Small Heath that night. Bombs came down on the heavy machinery and crushed the workers below. Those who escaped the collapse ran out into the street and were machine-gunned. 'The carnage was ghastly,' she wrote, 'the fellows and girls to escape the machine gunning threw themselves over the side of the canal and committed suicide.' Over 800 people were killed and 2,000 injured across Birmingham. A further 20,000 were made homeless. Alice was one of the lucky ones. Her family was safe and her house remained standing after the raid.

Since August, when the first bombs fell on Birmingham, Alice had agonized over evacuating Jacqueline to safer destinations in the countryside and even entertained sending her to America. At the beginning of the war, official government evacuation schemes encouraged parents living in congested inner cities likely to be bombed to send their children out of the city for safety's sake (and, more importantly, from the government's point of view, to avoid mass panic when bombs fell). In the first days of September 1939, millions of children streamed out of urban areas, boarding trains destined for supposedly safe reception areas (Folkestone and Eastbourne were among the destinations), some with their mothers, but most accompanied only by brothers and sisters, classmates and teachers. Overall, 1.5 million children were resettled that first September of the war; 25,000 children and 4,500 teachers from Birmingham embarked for the Cotswolds and Wales. Alice decided at that time that Jacq was too finicky about her food, so Jacq stayed at home. As it was, since the expected bombs didn't fall that autumn or winter of the Bore War, most of the evacuees came home anyway after the initial exodus.

After the fall of France, the government created a scheme to send children overseas to Canada, America, New Zealand, South Africa and Australia. Some well-to-do families had already made arrangements to send their children abroad, but the standard £15 fare was nearly a month's salary for many workers. To ease this financial burden, passage under the plan would be free, except for some fees to cover regular needs, such as clothing and shoes. Offers poured into Eleanor Roosevelt's United States Committee for the Care of European Children to provide homes for thousands of British 'seavacuees'.[14] About 2,500 children headed to homes overseas under the official scheme before it ended in October. The overseas exodus was not without its dangers. On 20 September 1939, a large torpedo struck a ship headed for Canada carrying ninety evacuees: seventy-seven children perished.

Such tragedies weighed heavily on Alice's mind as she turned over the options available for Jacq's safety.

America was out of the question: 'Hitler and Musso couldn't withstand the pleasure of sinking our children.' No, she thought, 'If my child has to face war, then she shall face it under my care, not be sent to face a watery grave and God knows what horrors.' But with every wave of planes that passed overhead and the growing fear she could see in her child's face, the conviction to keep Jacq close weakened.

After the raid on 23/24 November, Alice was finally convinced she needed to get her daughter away from Birmingham. She went round to the school and learned that a new evacuation scheme was underway, and for the next week, she worked to find Jacq a suitable billet. It was not easy and she suffered many ups and downs – one day things looked promising and the next, her hopes were dashed. Alice feared not only for Jacq's safety, but also for her character. Alice worried that if Jacq was shipped off with one school, she might come back rough. As it was, the evacuated East Enders up the street had taught her daughter to say 'Blast'. Eventually, a respectable middle-class family in Retford, east of Sheffield, was found.

While she waited for Jacq's school to be evacuated, Bridges scoured town for clothes and other necessities to send with her daughter. Laundry had to be done too. This task was made even more onerous than normal, since water mains had been cut in the Blitz. Alice pulled up buckets of shelter water, boiled it, put soap in and then stirred a small handful of clothing or towels in the saucepan on the hot plate. Afterwards, she put the laundry in the sink, rinsed it with one cup of disinfected shelter water, and placed more clothes in the saucepan. Still, she found time to cook for neighbours and friends, who she knew went without. She sent a mince-meat suet pudding to one family and a hearty meal of creamed potatoes, cauliflower au gratin, salmon steak, one chop and mince-meat pudding to her ARP friend, Mrs Empson.

Birmingham had another raid on the night of 3 December, which sent stabs through Bridges' heart, and once again made her legs and feet feel like blocks of ice. Her daughter turned white with fear and couldn't sleep, a response that reinforced Bridges' determination to evacuate Jacq to a safer place. On 10 December, Alice and Jacq loaded themselves on an early-morning bus and made a seven-and-a-half hour journey, through Nottingham and up to Retford. Alice was delighted to meet the billeting family and Jacq was equally thrilled to learn the family had a terrier named Queenie and to see that the farm nearby had ponies. Bridges couldn't have got her daughter out of Birmingham at a more propitious time; the next night the city endured its longest raid ever.

On 11/12 December, Nazi bombers buzzed like angry hornets over the city for thirteen hours. An incendiary dropped in the Bridges' garden that night, but Les and Mr Browning made quick work of it by digging up Alice's cabbage patch and throwing the dirt over it. Several times the bombs heated up the neighbourhood, but by the end of the night, with random planes flying over, gunfire cracking away and time bombs exploding sporadically, everyone was fed up. Alice couldn't sleep and everyone was cold. 'Blast Hitler and Blast the men who have allowed our country to become impoverished to the extent of putting us in the position of this bombardment,' she fumed in her diary. By 7 a.m., everyone was 'beyond caring'. Despite the raid still going on overhead, Les went up to get ready for work and the Brownings went back home.

According to Mrs Empson, Bridges' ARP warden friend, 11/12 December's was much worse than any others, but with less loss of life. Mrs Empson had been patrolling in Acock's Green when a 'packet' of bombs came down. Six houses were demolished, and when she arrived at the scene the situation was dire. Wires were down, the water main had been hit and ice-cold water gushed into the road. Mrs Empson was left to administer first aid while her partner grabbed a constable's bike and rode to Central Control for help. As he rode off, an incendiary dropped just behind him and bounced along after him. Turning his head constantly to check on the bomb's progress, the ARP warden hadn't noticed a wire down in his path, and was thrown headlong over the handlebars. He only narrowly escaped being decapitated by another telegraph wire. When he returned with help, Mrs Empson had stories to tell that didn't end so well. Several wardens had gone into houses, never to return, and the injuries she saw were horrific. After hours aiding bomb victims and wading through the frigid water, Mrs Empson finally managed to drag herself to Central Control, where she gladly gulped the tea and toast they made for her.

The rest of the Christmas season was relatively quiet for Birmingham. Almost too quiet. On 19 and again on 23 December, Alice and her friends wondered if an invasion was afoot. It may have been quiet enough in Birmingham to entertain the possibility of a stealthy invasion, but those in Sheffield, Merseyside and Manchester were under no such illusion. Sheffield lost over 600 people in its 12/13 and 15 December raids, over 700 people perished while the docks of Merseyside burned on 20 and 21 December and Manchester burned out of control on 22 and 23 December, as many of its firefighters had been sent to help Liverpool.

Though only two miles from Sheffield's city centre, Edie Rutherford escaped the worst of Sheffield's December 1940 raids. On 12 December, the first wave of German bombers dropped thousands of incendiaries, creating a 'ring of fire' around Sheffield to act as a target for subsequent raiders.[15] The gas works north of the city was hit early in the raid and, 'with a terrifying "whoo-oo-sh", sent two hundred feet of flame . . . into the air', blasting a wall of heat that could be felt up to a mile and a half away, near Rutherford's flat on the northern edge of town.[16] Edie's flat suffered a few cracked and blown-out windows, which – out of 'patriotism' and an unwillingness to be 'difficult' – she held off applying to have fixed until 1946.

As bombs whistled relentlessly to the ground, the city's barometer jumped up and down wildly from the rush and suction of continual blasts playing havoc with the air pressure. The greatest disaster that night occurred when a bomb hit the Marples Hotel on the High Street, causing its seven floors to fall into the cellar where seventy-seven people were sheltering. Only seven survived. Most of the damage done to the city, however, was in the southern corridor that the Germans used to approach the city and in the industrial areas east of the centre. That night, in her farmhouse north of Leeds, Natalie Tanner and her family saw 'a lot of gunfire (at least a lot for us) and . . . three flares and some shells bursting' in the distance, but they were too far away to feel the impact of any of the 355 tons of bombs dropped on Sheffield that night.

Though Edie was not writing for M-O at the time, she later told M-O that she'd never forget sweeping up shards of glass the morning after, dressed in a top coat, bonnet and boots to stave off the bitter cold December morning streaming undeterred through the holes where windows once stood. Later that morning she may have picked her way into town and experienced the poignant ruins and varieties of dirt that the official account of the raid describes: 'Whole sides of sturdily-built, expensive Victorian houses fell away and crumbled,' wooden doors and plaster walls shredded by splinters of glass flung at high speed, and the long, deep channels that flying metal gouged through solid stone.

> Light flakes of ash flew everywhere near the fires. Dust from broken pavements and little gardens swirled in clouds ... explosions near craters sodden with the overflow from burst water pipes spattered mud in all directions.

A thin dirty ice formed around the smouldering ashes and charred timbers left in the wake of the bombing. In the end, all that was left was 'mud and mess and desolation'.[17]

While Sheffielders cleaned up the morning after, the Tanners inched their way through gale winds over rain-swept icy moors to James' school in Glossop. James had a role as one of the dwarfs in *Snow White and the Seven Dwarfs*. Natalie proudly reported to M-O that he remembered all his lines and brought the house down three times with his performance. On their return home, Natalie and her husband, Hugh, stopped in Leeds for dinner and a movie. When the Germans came back to Sheffield on 15 December, Natalie didn't hear the ack-ack fire from her seat at the Civic Theatre in Leeds, but those in the balcony did.

Alice Bridges spent the waning weeks of December entertaining guests at her house, picking through the wreckage caused by Birmingham's recent raid to visit friends and family, buying Christmas gifts to send to Jacq, tidying her house and securing their Anderson shelter – Les laid some concrete to stop the rain from coming in.

For Alice, the season was a bust. Christmas Eve was her thirteenth wedding anniversary, but the couple had forgone their usual party and she felt miserable and lonely. Jacq wasn't home, and Les only mirrored Alice's mood, making her even more depressed. She had asked Mrs Empson if there was anyone she might invite to Christmas dinner who was bombed-out and had nowhere to go, but it seemed everyone was settled. Christmas was 'peaceful' in more than one way: the night skies were quiet and the normally sociable Bridges had no visitors. Christmas Eve and Christmas Day were quiet for Alice, and for Britain. On Hitler's orders, there were no raids on British soil over the holiday.

The Blitz of 1940 was punctuated, however, by raids directly following the Christmas lull. On 29 December St Paul's Cathedral in London narrowly escaped the fate of its predecessor in 1666 and thereafter stood evocatively among the flames to uplift the spirit of the people, and remind them that the popular song, 'There'll Always Be an England' had some substance in its hopeful message. In the following year bombers would not visit the capital with such regularity, but the intensity and devastation of the raids ratcheted up steadily until 10 May 1941, when London experienced its worst and its last major raid of the war. Across Britain that winter and spring of 1941, other cities also suffered the wrath of the bombers.

Early in January 1941, Hitler called off the invasion and suspended Operation Sea Lion indefinitely. Still, night after night, bombers hit strategic ports; as well as London, other ports – Cardiff, Swansea, Hull, Liverpool and others – were to be destroyed according to Hitler's plan. Irene Grant's Tyneside and the huge shipbuilding facilities at Vickers in Barrow-in-Furness were also on the list.

Glasgow was targeted too, and in the course of a bombing raid on that city the Luftwaffe decided to hit Sheffield. Visibility, however, was low and the bombs were accidentally released over Leeds. This was the closest Natalie Tanner and her family got to the Blitz. They were in Bradford for the evening, taking in a play and a late-night drink when they heard the sirens. With the lethargy of those who had never experienced the bombings first-hand, they leisurely finished their drinks before they headed home. The drive passed uneventfully, but when they got home, 'We heard guns and some dull thuds. We could see the shells bursting and our door rattled a bit.' Those in Leeds were not so lucky. The bombs caused extensive damage and left fifty-seven dead.

Irene Grant and her family had just returned home after a day out visiting her mother when the first sirens went on 9 April. The Grants had thus far experienced few significant raids and the noise startled them. Rita, Irene's daughter, jumped and accidentally spilt her glass of water. Irene's husband, Tom, began to curse. Quickly, Irene and her other daughter, Marjorie, got between them to save Rita from Tom's angry blows. Soon, they began to hear the planes come over. 'So starts the most terrible night of bombs, gun-firing, [and] planes,' Irene noted in her diary. Windows shook and nearby bombs twice knocked Irene off her bed. Later, Irene learned that the fires she saw from her windows were the timber yards at Tynedock. She also reported that about five miles from her home, North and South Shields sustained heavy bombing, while Sunderland's Town Hall and many of the businesses on what Irene considered the town's 'finest street', Fawcett Street, were gutted.

That same night, on 9 April, raiders flew over Birmingham, as they did throughout the spring. This night, after so many raids and so many evenings spent shaking in fear, Alice's nerve finally shattered. All night, she trembled fearfully, and as each whistling bomb pounded the earth around her shelter, she could not help but jump in fear. When a massive bomb split the ground nearby, electric fear raced up her spine and it took every ounce of strength she had to stop her hands and legs from shaking uncontrollably.

Luckily, Jacqueline did not have to witness this raid. Only weeks before, Alice's daughter was at home after Alice had learned that the family that took Jacq in December 1940 had neglected her. Jacq came home with frostbitten feet and filthy clothes – it seemed as though they'd never been cleaned in two months. Furthermore, she complained, the billeting family repeatedly ridiculed Jacq. Sadly, it was a common story for many of the evacuees, though some endured much worse abuse at the hands of their foster families. After several weeks in Birmingham, however, Alice found Jacq another home that was a much happier environment, and her daughter thus narrowly escaped the spring raids on Birmingham.

In Barrow-in-Furness, Nella Last endured several terrifying nights of air raids over the course of that

April. When the sirens went, Nella and her husband, Will, along with their cat and ageing dog, scattered to the reinforced space under the stairs in their semi-detached home, and listened to the angry bombers growling overhead on their way to targets on Clydeside and in Northern Ireland. As they passed over the shipbuilding town, the 'devil bombers' let fly machine-gun fire and bombs on Barrow's city centre and industrial sites. Shrapnel poured down on the roof of Nella's home, which was not far from the centre of town, while 'Doors and windows shook and rattled, as if someone is trying to force their way in,' with every bomb that fell nearby.

Following each raid, Will, a joiner by trade, went into town to repair what he could and demolish what was unsalvageable. The damage Will witnessed convinced him that Nella's desire for an indoor Morrison shelter was wise, and the couple quickly sent away for theirs. With each passing raid, Nella noted more and more townspeople packing up and heading out of town. The scenes of people queuing for buses, hailing taxis or simply on foot reminded her of the chaos in France only a year earlier, when scores of scared refugees flooded the roads out of town. What would happen if Barrow had a 'big blitz', she wondered.

On 3 May, Nella hunkered down in her newly arrived Morrison shelter, waiting for 'the end' during Barrow's greatest raid. The squat indoor, coffin-like shelter with thick steel plates on top and bottom and open steel-mesh sides – large enough to accommodate two adults and two children lying down but small enough to fit into a small space – protected her from the damage done that night. The windows in her home were blasted out, doors were torn off their hinges, plaster rained down from the ceilings, walls were cracked, and the roof on the garage separated four inches from the house. Ten people were killed and 2,000 rendered homeless in Barrow's Blitz.

A week later, on the night of 10 May, the conditions over London were perfect for destruction. The moon was full – a 'bomber's moon' – and the Thames that sparkled in the light was at its ebb. Across Britain, everyone feared clear evenings and full moons. At the end of 1944, when the threat of bombers over Britain had all but evaporated, Edie Rutherford noted a beautiful moonlit evening and immediately thought of the Blitz four years earlier. 'I wonder when we will cease connecting perfect moonlight with blitzes,' she mused.

The 2,000 fires that were started in London on 10 May 1941 fanned across the city. All firemen could do was watch the conflagration grow as their hoses ran dry. Landmarks across the city succumbed in the onslaught. Bombs destroyed the Commons debating chamber and 250,000 books in the British Museum, Westminster Abbey was bombed, as was the Palace of St James, King's Cross and Temple Church, along with other notable London structures. Thousands were made homeless, almost 2,000 were seriously injured and nearly 1,500 died that night in London.

People stood the strain of these raids for as long and as best they could. Some packed up quickly after heavy raids and sought relative safety in the countryside. Others trekked nightly out of town centres and slept on moors, in caves or forests nearby to escape the bombings. In Barrow's raids, some people walked the five miles to nearby Dalton. During Plymouth's April

1941 raid, when German raiders hit the city hard for five days in one week, masses walked out of the city at night and slept in barns, in churches, in ditches or under hedges. Some bedded down on Dartmoor, wrapping their children in rugs to stave off the bitter cold nights. When daylight came, they brushed themselves off and trekked back to the city to work.

In the heaviest blitz on Birmingham, Alice Bridges had hoped to get out of the city, too, but, thwarted in her quest, she hunkered down in her Anderson shelter with a fatalistic attitude, some liquor and her diary. Although she kept a M-O diary for nearly a decade, it was during the 1940 Blitz that Bridges turned to her diary the most. From 1939 to 1949 she sometimes wrote sporadically, sending in brief diaries usually recounting a three-month time span. But with the Blitz, the difference is striking. Almost every day during the height of the Blitz, Alice wrote of her own experiences and actively sought out friends and neighbours, asked them about their stories, and told M-O about them. At significant points in her daily life, such as during the Blitz or after major tiffs with her husband, she became detailed in her writing. M-O was not only a social research group for whom she volunteered, it was a friend to whom she could turn and offload her troubles. And, during those long and sleepless nights of autumn 1940 and spring 1941, she had plenty of time to do so.

The constant barrage of the blitzes could work strangely on the mind. At times, the fear was intense – hands shook uncontrollably, stomachs churned, chests tightened and pangs struck at the heart. But the body and mind can take only so much for so long. Mundane thoughts would creep in and temporarily mitigate the fear. While Nella Last waited for 'the end', with her ceiling coming down in bits all around her, she thought of tea and wished she'd eaten the fruit salad she'd saved for another day. Friends told Alice, 'Sometimes we feel all "het-up" and quite sick and ill at the thought of what is happening and what might happen and at other times, don't care a damn.'

'Taking it' did not mean that one was impervious to the fear, but that one put on a brave face and remained outwardly calm while a titanic struggle to overcome that fear raged inside. Keeping up appearances, keeping to schedules and 'acting' normal was a crucial component in this battle. A factory roof might be blown off during a raid, office buildings reduced to rubble, but the workers came nonetheless, even if it took them hours to pick through blitzed streets or walk across miles of hills from where they sheltered for the night.

Women were under considerable pressure to keep calm in front of their families – going to sit on the stairs to cry alone or finding refuge to allow a tear to fall in the darkness of the cinema. A brave face also meant a pretty face. Forgetting one's appearance was evidence that the war had beat them.

When Alice visited her friend, Jane, who had been bombed-out during the December raids, she was concerned by Jane's appearance. Her hair was a mess, no make-up had been applied – indeed, her face was dirty – and there was a blank look in her eyes. Furthermore, the baby was fussy and the new house was a wreck. Alice sat with Jane and listened to her troubles. Bridges offered comfort by telling her that everything happened for a reason, but ultimately reminded her of her duty. She told her friend,

Don't you see that the whole happiness of this home depends on you . . . Frank [Jane's husband] is trying to make the best of it and keep bright and the baby, you can't expect him to be anything but naughty and altered if you are so altered.

Alice then bathed the baby, cleaned the kitchen floor and did some laundry for her friend. Afterwards, Bridges was pleased to see her friend had washed and powdered her face, 'We all look better for a bit of powder,' she wrote. Now Jane could provide comfort to her family and face the war once again – if only in appearance.

The Blitz lasted for nine gruelling months, from August 1940 to May 1941. Britain was given a respite from the intense bombings when Hitler's desire for lands in the east led him to turn his attention on his erstwhile ally, the Soviet Union. Invasion forces rolled into the USSR on 22 June 1941. Although bombers still visited Britain afterwards – Birmingham experienced the last of its seventy-seven raids in April 1943 – the intensity and coverage was never what it had been during late 1940 and early 1941. Over 43,000 civilians perished in the Blitz, and thousands more were injured. It would take nearly three years of war before military deaths would surpass the civilian deaths endured in nine months of the Blitz.

CHAPTER FIVE

DOMESTIC SOLDIERS

The wind and rain lashed violently against the window, and the cold and wild October morning seeped into her joints, making movement almost unbearable. Her body wanted to rest; indeed, at any other time, she would have stayed in bed all morning, hoping her husband might notice and bring her a cup of tea. It would not have been unusual, if the pain continued, for her to stay in bed the entire day or for several days. But that was before the war. This morning, 15 October 1942, Nella Last fought the pain, a determined 'I am a soldier' echoed through her mind, calling her wearied body to action. She had too much to do, too much to ever allow aching joints, a sour stomach or a splitting headache (one or more of these ailments afflicted her most mornings) to get in the way of her national service.

From the beginning of the war, Nella Last had given her Tuesday and Thursday afternoons over to the WVS, where she knitted and sewed supplies for hospitals and the armed services. In September 1941, and for the rest of the war, she sacrificed her Friday afternoons to work at Barrow's canteen, feeding soldiers, sailors and workers who passed through looking for a hot meal and a friendly face. By the summer of 1942, she added to her already full schedule of responsibilities volunteering at a local Red Cross shop that raised funds for prisoners of war. She was a central figure in the shop's inception and in its continuance in wartime, helping secure a storefront, finding and begging items from neighbours and friends to sell, cleaning and mending damaged goods to make them saleable, pricing, and running the shop on Mondays.

This schedule left only Wednesdays and the weekends, and some mornings, to manage her home – also an important wartime service. Though she found this work increasingly difficult as her volunteering expanded, filling in the cracks of her leisure and domestic time, she was nonetheless loath to take the advice of Lady Reading, the head of the WVS, who urged her volunteers to 'leave the house dirty' and let their husbands 'jolly well get on with a piece of bread' – there was war work to be done.[1] Nella's house remained respectably clean throughout the war, and before she went out to volunteer she always left a hot meal warming by the fire for her husband when he arrived home.

In between cooking and cleaning, making and mending clothes for her family, tending the garden and preparing scraps to feed her chickens, Nella's sewing machine whirred and her fingers flew across knitting for the WVS and the Red Cross shop. If she permitted herself an indulgence, it was to make 'dollies' and stuffed animals for children in hospital or to sell in the shop: rabbits with funny faces, pink 'piggies', golliwogs, little ladies and gentlemen lovingly decked out with purses and top hats – whatever her mind could conjure with her scrap bag of cloth. Rarely did her busy schedule permit an escape into the fictional world of the cinema. Instead, her leisure often consisted of no more than snatching a nap here and there or walking along Walney Island with her husband and gazing out at the Irish Sea.

As she contemplated the sea on those walks, she might have thought how her life had changed because of the war. 'Not clever, not well-educated', Nella described herself before the war broke out,

> . . . with a husband who shunned life and people and insisted I shared his views – or if I made a play and insisted on "being like other people" showed his feelings so plainly in public I quickly got back into the shell he liked so much.

In the mid-1930s, Nella suffered a severe emotional breakdown that left her almost unable to walk. After numerous treatments, her doctor explained that the cause of the breakdown was 'repression' in her marriage. 'What would happen to a kettle', he asked her husband, 'if you put a cork in the spout and tied the lid down tight and yet kept it at boiling point?' The point was lost on her husband, but Nella understood all too well.

Nella had spent most of their marriage giving in to her husband's moods and whims for the sake of domestic peace, quietly complying with his demands or trying to cheer him when he was depressed, but these efforts only papered over the trouble. Even if she was able to cheer him or draw him into conversation, Will quickly reverted to his quiet, stubborn moods, and with each compromise, she surrendered a little of herself.

When she was younger, Nella told M-O, she had been vivacious, independent and inclined to adventure, but over thirty years of marriage had changed her. Reflecting on their marriage to a young neighbour, even Will noted Nella's transformation, which he thought for the better: instead of 'gadding about dancing' (as he called it) and orchestrating romantic 'moonlit picnics', as she had done in her youth, Nella had settled down to marriage and become more like her husband. Will may have been satisfied with a more staid wife, but Nella resented the compromises she made of herself, realizing that 'peace' in the home slowly ate away at her own identity. Will was, she told M-O, a petty 'dictator' whose unanswerable trump to anything she wished to do was, 'I feed and clothe you, don't I? I've a right to say what you do.'

Increasingly, after they'd married, she stayed at home and lost touch with friends because Will did not want to go out and therefore, he made clear, neither should she. Throughout the 1920s and 1930s, Nella said, she constantly felt 'outside of things'; she had few social contacts and her husband expected to accompany her whenever she went out. If she did insist on going out, he would invariably act so rude or morose that she quickly became embarrassed and abandoned her plans. With her doctor's help, Nella realized that her 'weak mindedness and eternal giving in was killing me'. The doctor recommended a colourful hat and several solo trips to whist games, which put her on the road to recovery.

That recovery was fleeting. Bit by bit, as the 1930s came to a close, Nella found herself once again giving in, to avoid conflict in her home. By the start of the war, she had relapsed and suffered yet another breakdown.

To make matters worse, the last bright spots in her existence, her sons, were leaving home. Arthur's work as a tax accountant took him to Manchester, and Cliff was in the second call-up for the army and would be off soon. 'I felt all go – I felt so useless to help,' she confided in her diary. The war offered Nella new opportunities, and she cast around for ways to be helpful, not just on patriotic impulse – although that was certainly a factor – but also to keep her from worrying over her sons, and perhaps, like the colourful hat, in an effort to loosen the 'cork' of a repressive marriage that so often plunged her into devastating emotional throes.

Walking the streets of Barrow in the first days of the war, she stopped and stared at a 'big, brave poster': 'YOUR COURAGE. YOUR CHEERFULNESS. YOUR ENDURANCE. WILL BRING US VICTORY'. She let the words seep into memory, silently tumbling them over and over in her mind. People always told her she was cheerful, and anyone can endure, she mused. Taking a deep breath, she cast her eyes to the heavens and prayed to God to give her strength to live up to this civilian call to arms. She thought of Cliff going into the army and at that moment, as men and women rushed past her in the streets of Barrow, she 'vowed to be a soldier too'.

Little did she know how much her life would be changed by that simple vow; with it, she had enlisted in the People's War, where everyone had work to do, even if it was just to endure. But Nella went far beyond simply enduring for her country. As we have seen, she volunteered for the ARP and the WVS, and, a day after Britain declared war, she was in her garden laying out a hen house and digging up flowers to make way for cabbages, potatoes, and the other vegetables she would need to feed her family. Like a soldier, she had her hair cut into a time-saving shorter style, but by no means did this mean that she let herself go.

As a domestic soldier, it was important to uplift morale, and taking time to look ones' best was a significant part of this duty. Beautifully made-up women were so crucial to the war effort that the government never rationed cosmetics, despite the fact that make-up used valuable wartime materials such as petroleum. Indeed, women's beauty bolstered male morale, as movie star Gary Cooper informed wartime *Good Housekeeping* readers. He 'thanked God' for women's beauty in times of crisis, for, he thought, it was a tangible indicator of women's natural ability to create calm and inspire men to greatness.[2]

Nella agreed, and often had scathing opinions of women who were careless about their appearance, as she felt such attitudes undermined the war effort. She was indignant when she saw slovenly women in long trousers pushing prams along the streets of Barrow in the spring of 1942. 'Many women', she complained to M-O, 'are seizing the excuse of there being a war on to give full rein to the sloppy, lazy streak in their make-up.' Even on the days when she was overwhelmed with work, fighting a headache or backache, Nella was always careful to keep her hair tidy, her lipstick and rouge cheery and her dress feminine. She could understand and even forgive women becoming a little 'lazy' during the hottest times of the Blitz, but it had been a year since Barrow had a major raid. There was certainly no excuse to shirk one's duty, Nella thought.

Beneath this conviction about one's appearance lay the idea that a woman's foremost duty on the home front was to combat defeatism, and amongst the women at the WVS Last was known to raise a smile in a gloomy room, spreading peace and cheerfulness among her comrades at the centre. It was a skill she had honed not just throughout her marriage, but all her life.

As a child, she had tried to lighten up the unhappy and volatile home in which she grew up, and vowed never to recreate the same contentious domestic situation of her childhood when she married. Instead, she made it a point to fashion a sanctuary out of her home – a peaceful and safe haven for her husband and sons, 'where' she hoped, 'the door will close on all hurting things' after a hard day's work, play or school. If her sons ever got into an argument, she shooed them out the door and expected them to work out their differences before they came back inside. In the pursuit of creating such a refuge, however, she buried deep feelings of frustration and a nagging suspicion that she'd lost a sense of self and freedom.

In the First World War, Nella spread laughter among the injured servicemen on visits to the hospital in Southampton. And when Britain found itself in conflict again in 1939, Nella mustered her talents once more for the nation. She knew, as the government poster had stressed, that cheerfulness and endurance would help win the war. Taking the messages in the poster to heart, Nella joked around with shopkeepers on her shopping rounds and uplifted the spirits of the women in the WVS centre with a mixture of silliness and quiet, resolute confidence in the nation's cause. Indeed, Mrs Waite, the head of hospital supply, told Last that her 'saucy tongue' inspired much-needed levity at the centre and soothed her comrades' nerves when they were on edge.

* * *

Joking in the face of adversity and maintaining composure was an essential duty for the domestic soldier. For the sake of morale, it was also important to keep up the appearance that life continued as usual. This was an almost impossible task, given the scarcities of staples such as eggs and milk, and the imposition of rationing.

The availability of rations was ensured by the process of registration: each person or household registered with a retailer, and stocks were refilled according to the number of registrants at each retailer. Rationing was intended to guarantee that everyone got their 'fair share' of food at a fair price – a necessity for a country that imported most of its food and animal fodder. Ration books were issued in late-September 1939, but the official rationing scheme did not begin until 8 January 1940. At first, only sugar (12 oz), butter (4 oz), ham and bacon (4 oz) were rationed. Over the course of the war, the weekly allowances per person fluctuated according to availability, and the list of rationed foods grew to include meat, cheese, margarine, cooking fats, preserves and tea.

Edie Rutherford was an avid champion of the rationing scheme, agreeing with the social justice of 'fair shares' inherent in the programme. Those who tried to skirt the scheme were particularly loathsome to Edie, and every time she met with one, or was prodded by shopkeepers to take more than her fair share, she was furious. She knew others took advantage of the black market, or stretched the rules and received better-quality items or more than she did. But if butchers winked or shop clerks nodded, Rutherford refused to play the game.

From 1941, the distribution of milk and eggs came under the rationing scheme. One might expect about an egg a week – more for children or expectant mothers – but the reality was that – unless one kept poultry, as Nella Last did – a shell egg was a rarity. Instead, many made do with the dried eggs that were introduced in the summer of 1942. Other hard-to-find items, such as tinned food or sweets, were put on a points scheme. Points could be used at any retailer on a variety of items. One exercised a degree of choice under the scheme: an entire monthly allocation of points could be spent on a 'luxury' item such as a can of first-grade tinned salmon, or one could make the points go further by purchasing several, less exciting, foods over the course of the month. There was no guarantee of availability for any given item; the only guarantee was that people could find something on which to spend their points.

If Edie were given the authority, she would have extended rationing to even more goods than were already officially controlled. She believed that rationing would stave off wasteful behaviour, especially the wild abandon with which the residents in her block of flats squandered bread. A continual complaint of hers was that the English (she was South African) wouldn't eat day-old bread and that she regularly saw entire loaves thrown in trash bins.

Rutherford supported those who advocated adding bread to the list of rationed items, but, as bread was generally considered a staple for working-class diets, this was such an unpopular move that the government postponed making such a decision until after the war. Instead, it incrementally increased the extraction rate of wheat in flour to 85 per cent, turning the ever-popular white bread into an unattractive shade of brown and resulting in what most people considered the largely inedible 'national wheatmeal loaf'. The Minister of Labour, Ernest Bevin, pointing to the middle of one such loaf, complained at a meeting of the War Cabinet that the bread was 'indigestible', and let out a belch to make his point.[3] About 86 per cent of the population, including Rutherford, agreed with Bevin.

As it did with the national loaf, the wartime government sought to make the most out of fabric and other materials destined for the consumer market, with the so-called 'utility' products introduced in 1942. Like the National Loaf, Rutherford heartily disliked anything utility. It could be that she, like others, recoiled at the term itself. It was unattractive, it certainly had no glamour to it and, indeed, 'utility' seemed somehow to evoke all the gloom of austerity in one word. In utility, fashion took a backseat to thrift: embroidery and appliqué work were forbidden, the widths of hems and sleeves standardized, the number of buttonholes and pockets reduced (a fact that irked many men) and socks were shortened, to name some of the design limitations. In an effort to combat the gloom of style restrictions, the Board of Trade went to respected London fashion designers for smart designs that required little fabric or materials. The same principle applied to the entire line of utility goods, which included furniture, household linens and crockery. Many women, once they got over the initial revulsion of the word, with all its connotations of uniformity and ugliness, found that there was actually a reasonable range of choice and style, as well as quality.

Rutherford, however, was unmoved. To her, utility meant lack of quality, and she did her best to avoid it. Edie rarely held back opinions in her diary, a fact that M-O seemed to appreciate. When M-O sent a note thanking her for her 'piquant observations', she chuckled heartily, as did her husband. 'Well, I say just what I think,' she explained and then added, 'If everyone did, I reckon this world would progress further.'

Indeed, Rutherford was certain that the shoddiness of such products was behind the scene she witnessed in a local shop. 'Yesterday', she wrote, 'I saw something happen which I have up to now only had happen to me in a nightmare.' Edie was waiting for a woman in front of her to be served, when, 'Suddenly her pink silk knickers fell on the floor.' Shocked, the woman shot a 'wild glance' around to see who was nearby, gathered up the offending knickers, then stumbled behind the counter and into a backroom. 'I bet they were Utility pants,' Edie joked.

During the war, and until 1954 when rationing was finally lifted, the price and availability of food, furniture, clothing and other scarce commodities were as much sources of conversation (and grumbling) as the weather. Irene Grant often wondered where the rabbits she used to buy in the butcher's had disappeared to, and nearly all the women were regularly indignant about the price of less-than-appetizing produce at the greengrocer's. Grant, Bridges and Rutherford all worried over how to feed their hard-working husbands on the meagre meat rations. Like most women, their solution usually came down to sacrificing their own rations to their husbands. Five years into rationing, Irene's daughter Marjorie wondered wistfully, 'What did we used to eat in the days before the war?' Her mother responded with a mouth-watering array of pre-war foods: fresh fish, sausages, fresh tomatoes, bananas, mushrooms and fruit. Still, despite the maddening lack of variety,

Irene was thankful for rationing and points; she knew that without them, her family would have starved.

Rationing and scarcity required a great deal of ingenuity and skill on the part of the domestic soldier. Women had to navigate the uncertain food supply and come up with tasty and nutritious meals to feed their families – ideally without letting their families know how frustrating and difficult the task was – and Nella Last excelled at all of it. Her 'Gran' had taught her many cookery skills that stood her in good stead amid the austere restrictions of rationing. Nella was so successful at keeping her husband in the dark about her economies that once, at the beginning of the war, he chastised her for seeming to disregard the scarcities. 'It's time you realized there's a WAR on,' he scolded her after a particularly enjoyable lunch. She only laughed and told him not to worry, as it was well worth the happiness it gave him. His ignorance also proved her skill. Privately, she wondered what she could have done to make the meal any cheaper: two days' soup, toast with a scrape of marg and some left-over herrings on top, and apples that had been given to them cost her a mere 6d.

Nella was determined to make her home a shelter against wartime conditions and privations for her husband and her sons, when they visited. She saved 'bits and bobs', an egg white here or the rare tin of fruit there, for months in anticipation of such visits or other special occasions. Despite shortages and rationing, she made her sons feel loved and special by creating festive pre-war meals with ersatz ingredients, culinary tricks and thoughtful management – and a colourful spray of flowers to complement the experience. Her sons marvelled at her abilities and often praised her for them – little gems of recognition that lifted her spirit. Their 'cries of delight' over her domestic genius were 'enough to recompense for hours of thought and work', she told M-O.

While Nella craved the praise and recognition, she also made sure to create a certain mystique about her talents. 'It does not do to let men know about "domestic economy",' she wrote in her diary. At the same time, as more and more women entered the workforce or volunteered more of their time during the war, there was a push to get men to do more of their share around the house. A comment in *Woman's Own* magazine may have made some consider that their husband's help in the home was actually a patriotic duty during wartime. The magazine asked:

> Would your husband think he was losing caste if he helped with housework, shopping? Most still think so, especially in the industrial north, but they must change their views now wives are on war work.[4]

Yet there was also a palpable sense that letting men in on the 'secrets' of women's work might destabilize the home and women's position in it – and at the very least, create more work as a result of men's domestic incompetence.

Comedic Mrs Fusspottle, a feature also found in *Woman's Own*, famous for her wartime gaffs, such as spreading obviously ridiculous rumours about the IRA 'pinching our barrage balloons', related a humorous story about leaving her brother-in-law, Chalmers, in charge of the home for a few hours. It all started when Chalmers told her that women's work in the home wasn't difficult. In fact, he said, it was all a lot of 'female propaganda' designed to make men feel sorry for their wives, and once husbands found out that their wives in fact did very little, the 'divorce courts will be working overtime'.

No self-respecting housewife could fail to pick up the gauntlet after such provocation, and thus Mrs Fusspottle left him with a list of the things she and his wife did on a daily basis. 'You can', she told him,

> . . . sweep and dust through the house, polish the floor boards, wash up the breakfast things, clean the grates, get in the coal – remembering Total Economy – prepare the vegetables, cook the dinner, make a pudding so forth from A to Z.

But that was not all. After that, Chalmers could,

> Polish the silver in your spare time, clean round the bath . . . shake the doormats and carpets and hearth-stone the fireplaces and doorsteps, not to mention put out the Pig Wash and Waste Paper for salvage and rubbing up the door handles.

Mrs Fusspottle and her sister came home to find 'Chalmers in a sweat, all mixed up with furniture and carpets and brooms and smeared with black lead, swearing to himself, tripping over things'.[5] He'd put his broom through a pane of glass, knocked over a lamp stand and smashed the shade, spilt coal dust and ashes over the floor, broken two cups and a glass and plate while he was washing up, fallen over the pig wash bucket, and ruined dinner. So, lesson learned: perhaps it was not a very good idea to let husbands in on their wives' daily round.

On the other hand, a woman as talented as Last in domestic arts and – especially in wartime – those of scrimping and saving, was obligated to pass such wisdom to other domestic soldiers. She sent advice to Ambrose Heath, a culinary expert on the morning radio programme, *Kitchen Front*, which offered recipes and tips on rationing. Perhaps to enlighten and assist those at M-O, she also sprinkled her diaries liberally with detailed recipes. And certainly, her skills were welcomed among the women at the WVS.

The domestic know-how that helped her feed her family during the difficult inter-war period had once gone unnoticed to all but herself. In the 1920s and 1930s, Nella felt it unrespectable to let neighbours know that she employed what she referred to as 'dodges', or economies that saved the family money but did not scrimp on taste or style. In wartime, however, this changed. Under the restrictions of rationing, those 'dodges' became badges of honour.

When a colleague from the WVS appeared on her front step in late-August 1941 and asked Last to become an 'advisory cook' for mobile canteen units in Barrow, Nella was incredibly flattered. Having worked hard, day in, day out, managing a home and family with little encouragement or praise before the war, Nella slowly began to realize that the same domestic duties that had been taken for granted by her family were actually skills and talents worthy of notice. Indeed, something that she did well, something that defined her life and experience as a housewife and mother, was now flush with value. It was, as Nella might say, a 'tonic' to her spirit and a boost to her self-confidence. After Last accepted the offer, and the colleague had gone, her husband wondered aloud at the newfound vigour exuded by his wife of thirty years. 'You know, you amaze me really,' he said, 'when I think of the wretched health you had just before the war, and how long it took you to recover from that nervous break-down.' Nella wasn't surprised.

For the first time in her life, people recognized her, and with each attempt to contribute to the nation's fight she found herself more confident and more inde-pendent. Her health improved, and the woman who could not, or would not, leave the house without her husband now had an excuse – and a patriotic one at that – to strike out on her own. With each step forward, she found a voice and camaraderie never before ex-perienced. After Will commented on her energy, she thought to herself,

> He never realizes – and never could – that the years when I had to be quiet and always do everything he liked, and *never* the things he did not, were slavery years of mind and body.

The war gave her an excuse to break free from living within the boundaries of her husband's expectations, moods, whims and desires. More and more, Nella stood up to Will instead of giving in 'for the sake of peace'. His 'petulant moods' that previously had made her 'run round trying to get him in a good humour and worry and worry for days' now only elicited 'indiffer-ence' or sharp responses. As a domestic soldier, she was careful to make sure her husband's morale didn't falter, but once she ensured his relative comfort she did not have to sit at home and watch him mope. Called out on national service, she lived according to the motto, 'The WVS never says no,' and found herself involved in a number of rewarding projects, meeting a wide variety of people she would have never had the opportunity to know in the past.

Will, on the other hand, seemed content to sit by the fire, vacantly staring at the flames, ageing while she flourished. In December 1941, as the family gathered at home, the table laid with a festive embroidered tablecloth and chrysanthemums, enjoying her expertly engineered delectable Christmas fare that made the rationing scheme fade to the corners of their minds, Last was uneasy. The war weighed heavy on her mind. She thought of the 'evil' Hitler had let loose in the world, and tried to assuage her anxiety with thoughts of nearby Coniston Water: the peaceful finger-like lake cutting gracefully through the ruggedly green Furness Fells in the southern Lake District always spoke a placid incantation to Nella's spirit. But it wasn't just the war that nagged her.

She watched her husband sitting quietly in front of the fire, knowing that nothing she could do would stir him or move him to discuss anything of consequence, and had to remind herself that he was 'only fifty-three and *not* eighty-three'. She longed to be back at work, where she had made friends who chatted with her, appreciated her and responded to her efforts to cheer them when the blues descended. As the New Year approached, however, she decided not to grumble about her temporary hiatus. The holiday was almost over and she would soon go back to her wartime routine. She counted her blessings: 'I've broken loose and am free now.'

In total war, everyone was a soldier on the home front, and this fact could be empowering. On the radio, in magazines and newspapers, the British people were constantly reminded that their individual efforts added up to a massive contribution. Novelist and playwright J.B. Priestley argued in his popular Sunday evening *Postscript* radio broadcasts, which aired after the 9 o'clock evening news, that there were 'postmen soldiers, housewife and mother soldiers', and not to leave himself out, even 'broadcasting soldiers'.[6] One *Woman's Own* magazine article urged women to be careful when they filled their lamps, as one drop of paraffin wasted by each individual in England alone would add up to 37 million drops wasted (or roughly 600 gallons). A simple act such as saving kitchen scraps could, according to one Ministry of Food jingle, eventually save the empire. The most mundane activities of peacetime were infused with patriotism and value during wartime.

Women became the vanguard in the People's War. They controlled their families' consumption, fed and comforted them, and helped fill the ranks of workers and volunteers as men went off to fight. To underline the importance of women's domestic contributions, Lord Woolton, the Minister of Food, went on air in 1940 to rally women to the war effort. 'It is to you, the housewives of Britain that I want to talk tonight,' he said in a stern, authoritative voice:

We have a job to do, together you and I, an immensely important war job. No uniforms, no parades, no drills, but a job wanting a lot of thinking and a lot of knowledge, too. We are the army that guards the Kitchen Front in this war.

Without women, and their wise domestic management, many of the nation's home front policies would fail. It was up to them to 'translate national economy into domestic practice'.[7]

The success of the home front rested on women's willingness to scrimp and save on everything, from food to clothes, to fuel. As much coal as possible had to be saved for munitions, as a soldier in a Ministry of Fuel advertisement in *Good Housekeeping* informed housewives: 'Without it, our factories could not operate; not a 'plane, gun, tank or ship could be turned out, and Britain would lie open to the enemy.'[8] Practically anything lying around the house could be used for military purposes. Aluminum pots and pans, paper and even bones from the evening joint could be recycled into weapons.

Without this effort, Britain would have to divert military resources such as ships and raw materials to feed the nation. 'Save bread and you save lives,' the Ministry of Food exhorted.[9] Other advertisements stressed that lives would be lost bringing unnecessary domestic goods to Britain. 'Food wasted is another ship lost,' announced one such advertisement, which illustrated its point with a ship labelled 'food' going down into the murky waters of a wasted meal.[10] Another advertisement in *Good Housekeeping* was more blunt: 'A sailor's blood is on your head if you waste a scrap of bread.'[11] Such imagery and rhetoric was powerful for women who worried over the safety of the armed forces and merchant marine. Having lived on the coast for most of her life – her husband worked in the navy in the First World War, and Barrow was a hub for sailors, and home to the large shipbuilder, Vickers – Nella's sleep was often punctuated by nightmares of sailors drowning in rough frigid seas.

By no means did the messages of individual effort end with these entreaties. Wartime Britain was bursting with ways in which people – from soldier to pensioner, housewife to factory worker – could, or *should*, be useful to their country. Almost every aspect of a person's life had the potential to affect the war effort, from the amount of water and its temperature in their baths (as well as the amount of soap used) to their leisure time and employment, and the government (as well as consumer manufacturers) was sure to remind the people to keep vigilant. Aside from the death and destruction of war, Britons had much to worry about: they were supposed to 'Dig for victory', 'Keep your eye on your fuel target' and 'Save fuel for factories', mind the 'Squander Bug' and 'Spend less on yourself – Lend more to your country', 'Travel between 10 & 4 and don't crowd the war workers', 'Keep mum' and remember that 'Careless talk costs lives', 'Stuff the salvage sacks and starve the dustbin', 'Mend and make-do to save buying new', 'Lend a hand on the land' and 'Come into the factories'.[12] The constant barrage of messages may have elevated a personal sense of investment in the national cause and importance in the war effort, but it could also lead to feelings of guilt that one simply wasn't doing *enough*. It was difficult to keep the nagging question of the level of personal commitment to the cause at bay. An advertisement in *Good Housekeeping* encapsulated this predicament of wartime guilt perfectly when it asked: 'Is your conscience clear? There's war work waiting.'[13] One's conscience could hardly be entirely clear. There was just *so much to do*.

Nella Last generally reconciled this problem by rationalizing that she was doing as much as a woman her age (she was forty-nine when the war started) in her position could do, and she was doing it well, at that. She judged others' efforts similarly: when an elderly neighbour felt he wasn't doing enough for the war effort, she pointed out that he was doing as much as he possibly could. Indeed, she believed that with an arthritic shoulder he was going well beyond what might be expected of him in planting and maintaining a prolific garden. With a garden like that, she argued, 'Whether he wore khaki or not, he was a soldier.' Still, when confronted with the incredibly diverse problems of the war effort, she sometimes felt she could do more. Forgetting for a moment that she felt everyone could be a soldier in their own way, she once dismissed the importance of her efforts, writing, 'I wish I'd the chance – and strength – to do something worthwhile to help.'

The idea that everyone and every action was crucial to the survival of the nation was so pervasive and powerful that it seeped into the fabric of everyday life. Whether they contributed positively to the war effort or not, most were aware that they should be doing so. There was, as Helen Mitchell once told M-O, 'always some *arrière pensée* [concealed thought] behind every action'. If every action was important, every action must be scrutinized. For some, like Helen, this fact of the People's War was overwhelming.

Though she too wanted to make a difference to the war effort, Helen Mitchell could barely muster a shred of enthusiasm for the task she was given at the Red Cross depot in Minehead. Her unwilling hands slowly stitched slippers for the wounded in hospital; a feeling of futility settled deeply into the grooves of her mind as she watched the needle passing in and out of the fabric. Surely the task was useless; in all likelihood, she felt, 'They are never used, or . . . one hospital has thousands of them, and others none.'

During the war, she maintained a virulent scepticism of the 'everyday soldier' messages percolating throughout the British media, questioning not only the value of individual efforts to the war effort, but also the government's ability to capitalize on them. Although she couldn't quite buy the rhetoric of the People's War, she nevertheless felt compelled to pitch in. A few days after stitching the slippers, Mitchell wandered along one of the hills overlooking Minehead, perhaps enjoying the view out to the Bristol Channel or, looking up the coast, admiring the patchwork of light and dark greens stretching across the rolling Quantock Hills. She may have turned her attention south and gazed at the brilliant heather and wild beauty of Exmoor. Minehead was her sanctuary. Yet, as she reached the top of the hill, her peace was shattered by the sight of people gathering bracken. 'Always feel embarrassed when I meet people working,' Mitchell confessed to M-O, 'and think I ought to be doing something – would do so, if I knew what.'

Soon after this, Mitchell left Minehead to return to her home in Kent, which tenants had recently vacated. 'Bitter thought,' she wrote, 'exchanging Somerset for Kent.' She enjoyed the company and the surroundings of Minehead, but loneliness and interminable housework was all she could look forward to in Kent. For weeks after she arrived home, Mitchell set to exorcizing the ex-tenants' filth. But in wartime personal concerns had to be balanced by the continual calls of the nation, and soon Mitchell felt she must find a way to be useful. The rhetoric of the People's War and the non-stop government directives nagged her to do *something*, *anything*, but there seemed so little she *wanted to do*. She had her own talents, her own unique gifts – she loved theatre, enjoyed directing and taught elocution – but, to her, these seemed to lack the necessary gravitas in the middle of all-out war. Instead, she struggled for years, searching for work worthy of the sacrifice of war.

In 1941, she worked for a stint registering prisoners of war in London. Then, in Minehead, she did various tasks for the Red Cross: sewing or collecting items to finance relief efforts. By December 1941, a month after arriving home from Somerset, she agreed to fire-watching duty. She shivered on a few sleepless nights, watching the skies, but Helen soon learned that the mismanagement she suspected in the distribution of hospital slippers extended to include fire watching, rendering her efforts ineffectual. One night, as she prepared to go on duty, she was informed that, 'No one is expected to fire watch on Friday nights!!' She learned later that it was commonplace for people to shirk their duty: her butcher, for example, simply stayed in bed on his appointed nights. It hardly seemed worth the effort or lack of sleep, so Mitchell left.

In March 1942, only a few months after she left fire-watching duty, Helen was seized by a 'filthy temper' as she travelled to London for a lunch date with her husband. It wasn't that she was seeing her husband – usually a loathsome affair accompanied by a foul mood. This time it was the overwhelming feeling that she did little more than take up space. 'Felt I'd no right to travel, or to take someone's place in a restaurant; in fact,' she confided to M-O, 'unless I can be useful, no right to exist.' In order to justify her existence, once again Mitchell searched about for another way to be active on the home front.

She applied to the local WVS for work, and anxiously awaited their reply. She dreaded, above all, that they would stick her with evacuees – a prospect that conjured up memories of a bad experience at the beginning of the war when she took in two mothers and their babies. Two weeks after she posted the letter to the WVS, she was overjoyed to learn that her village was no longer a reception area for evacuees and, instead, she was asked to collect for the Red Cross – a task she took up with great gusto, as one who gratefully serves penance upon receiving a reprieve. Later, Helen found herself 'roped into' joining the organization and was given work at a children's canteen.

Unlike Nella Last, who found confidence and acceptance in the WVS and who looked forward to working in the town canteen, Helen could not 'imagine anything I should hate more'. To her, the WVS centre was a 'haggery' full of housewives who were uninteresting and boorish and only thought of food or cinema. To 'get straight again', and to shake off the mental exhaustion of the centre, she often felt the need to play a Bach fugue on her piano afterwards. And to prepare for her work at the canteen, she required a day of rest and quiet. She spent two weeks 'flinging food' at the children until, much to her surprise, Helen encountered a woman who 'lamented' it was her last day at the canteen. She could hardly believe her luck. Seizing the opportunity, Mitchell happily offered the woman her place and the WVS quickly receded from her life.

By June 1942, Mitchell had found volunteering at a London office a little less insufferable, but still only stayed in the job for the summer. And for all of 1942, she allowed the local constables to meet in her home after their office had been destroyed during an air raid. Even this was not without its sacrifices, since the men were 'never very accurate' in their use of the lavatory, but she nonetheless 'held her nose and said "It was for England"!'

After 1943, it seemed Helen had given up on finding active war work, though she was never free from the guilt of the People's War. She did, however, periodically collect for the Red Cross, take in boarders who had lost their homes, and tried to manage what seemed to her to be an ever-expanding slag heap of government regulations, urgings and exhortations. Helen did her best to heed these messages: she cut apples for drying according to the Ministry of Food, she was conscientious with the soap ration (even if, much to her chagrin, her servants were not), she minded salvage controls, she monitored the household use of fuel and did her best to dig for victory. But it was exhausting. She always felt 'very tired of always being accosted about this or that', and her keen eye for hypocrisy and inconsistencies made it all the more trying.

When a woman showed up at Helen's home and informed her that the eighteenth-century wrought-iron gates protecting her manicured lawn were to be taken down for salvage, she thought, 'Nice job driving round the country snooping for iron. Petrol has to be imported for the job, so why not iron instead?' And in contrast to the many advertisements equating waste of imported goods with sailors' lives lost, she wondered, 'Why are shops bursting with cigarettes if we are losing ships?' She refused to give up smoking if the government continued to allow huge quantities of cigarettes to flood the market. After the war in Europe was over, Mitchell looked back at her efforts and summed up her experience thus: 'It's all been very futile looking back, have done nothing useful as far as I can see.'

*　　*　　*

People's War messages could work positively and negatively. They could offer some a feeling of inclusion and worth, while for others it seemed there was always something more 'spectacular' one could do, and for still others the People's War could fuel a debilitating guilt. Nella Last found she had skills that had thus far been ignored, but were now appreciated at both a local and a national level, and her self-confidence increased accordingly. Even she had moments of doubt about the level of her contribution to the war effort, and this doubt spurred her to take on more work. It could be physically taxing, but she fought through their fatigue and seemed to have a genuine feeling that what she did was nonetheless useful.

Helen Mitchell, on the other hand, could never quite get comfortable in the everyday heroism of the war. There was always evidence of infuriating bungling and the sense that individual efforts, contrary to the propaganda, actually added up to nothing more than personal aggravation. One had to feel useful, but in one's own way. The messages had to align with one's identity and talents. For Mitchell, this was impossible, since she felt her talents unworthy of wartime service; yet the unrelenting calls to duty forced her into a maddening Sisyphean search for purpose in the People's War.

CHAPTER SIX

A FEW HOURS OF HAPPINESS

At first it seemed perfectly reasonable. Hugh did a great deal of work for the government and knew a number of high-ranking officials. It was entirely possible that he could be the target of some kind of conspiracy.

At the end of July 1941, Hugh and Natalie Tanner were feverishly preparing for a theatre production of *Richelieu* in Bradford. Hugh was acting in the play and Natalie was in charge of the props. Natalie spent most of the month trying to track down the perfect period candlesticks – not an easy task in wartime Britain. She searched Leeds and eventually found some that fitted the bill. But while she was out negotiating the price of the candlesticks, Hugh was at the theatre, growing increasingly 'nervy'. He fussed continually about his costume and worried over his lines. The night before the opening, he was convinced he couldn't carry on. He did, and the production seems to have been a success.

Hugh's nervousness didn't dissipate with the end of *Richelieu*, however; it only seemed to grow worse. That week, after spending a day swimming with James, Natalie came home to find Hugh feeling 'woozy'. She chalked it up to his falling asleep in the brutally hot summer sun, but Hugh had different ideas. He was convinced that the beer at the local pub had been drugged. Natalie took Hugh to see a doctor when he still felt off the next day, but her husband was positive that the doctor's assistant was a Fascist and that his prescription had also been tainted. By the end of the week, Hugh was pacing the house day and night in search of surveillance equipment.

Natalie wasn't sure what to think. She teetered between believing it was a 'persecution mania' and a plausible plot. Her husband's engineering firm delivered cutting-edge technologies needed to fight the war, and thus he had contacts at the highest levels of government. Hugh was so convincing and the circumstances – his work, his connections, the war – all made it even more so. At the very least, he believed 'they' would have him framed and arrested. It certainly didn't help matters when Hugh learned that Natalie's brother and sister-in-law had been arrested and were being held at Brixton and Holloway prisons respectively. Of course, there was cause for the government's suspicions of Natalie's relations, since the couple had been living in Italy when the war broke out and then maintained relationships with 'various doubtful people' when they later moved to Athens. Furthermore, Natalie knew that her brother had Fascist sympathies. It wasn't surprising, to her at least, that the government seized them when the two landed in Britain after their time abroad. It only added fuel to Hugh's increasing paranoia.

With this new turn of events, Hugh refused to let James out of his sight and told Natalie that 'they' were out to kidnap James. Half-believing the conspiracy theories herself, even Natalie sneaked a peek over her shoulder from time to time. But she called the doctor again when Hugh confessed one sleepless night that he believed the entire family would end up like people 'you read [about] in the newspaper, whole families, husband, wife and child being found with their throats cut'. This time she was truly frightened.

The next day, the doctor and Hugh's brother escorted him to a mental hospital in York. In an effort to find out what had happened to her husband, Natalie rang up the hospital every day for the next week, but the only answer she received was, 'Mr Tanner is still very restless.' Finally, the primary physician agreed to see her. Hugh seemed to have slipped even further away from reality. His 'restlessness', she learned, consisted of smashing windows and running around naked. Though the doctor was very 'noncommittal' about Hugh's prognosis, he did allow Natalie and James to visit him briefly. (Natalie had brought James along to soothe Hugh's fears that he'd been kidnapped.) Hugh remembered them and seemed calm, but still, Natalie reported, he was 'full of plots and counterplots'. When they went to York a week later, Hugh was once again actively 'restless' and the nurses refused to let Natalie see him.

By the end of August, Hugh was finally in a state to receive visitors and Natalie had settled into a routine of regular afternoon visits and frequent overnight stays in York. In September, Hugh was still talking of fifth columnists, but he looked better. After shock treatments in October, he was able to accompany his wife on strolls around the hospital grounds. With Hugh better, the worry that had burdened Natalie since July seemed to dissipate on those walks together, and for the first time, she was able to observe the other patients – some who were much worse than Hugh and others who were, to Natalie, shockingly young. The walks seemed to have a positive effect on Hugh as well, and soon the doctors decided that he no longer needed to be held in confinement. His upgraded status didn't last long, however. On 15 November, York had an air-raid alert that caused him to relapse. Once again, Hugh was put under close observation.

Life that autumn and winter was an emotional roller-coaster ride. Hugh's mental state seemed to shift daily, and as Christmas approached, it was obvious that he wouldn't be home to enjoy it with his family. Indeed, neither Natalie nor James made the trip to York over Christmas, but instead only managed the trip on 29 December. Natalie never explained why, but it may have been that public transport was closed for Christmas and Boxing Day. Still, Hugh's brother had a car and could have, presumably, taken the family into York for the holiday. It must have been a desperately lonely few days for Hugh. When Natalie and their son finally visited him, they found him 'very depressed and in bed', and they stayed only an hour. On the return trip home, the train was freezing and there was no buffet car. It was all 'very depressing', Natalie sighed.

After the holidays, James returned to his school near Manchester and, perhaps to share some of the emotional strain or to save time, Natalie began to stay with friends in Leeds or stay at the railway hotel. At the very least, it made the trip to York so much easier; but it also had the added benefit of restoring a little of her previous life. Staying in Leeds meant that she could spend a few hours in York and be back in Leeds or Bradford in the evening for her usual round of theatre, cinema and political talk – all without worrying over finding a way home (which would require either a taxi or a 4-mile walk from the bus).

The routine and the companionship were also much-needed diversions. The bar in the railway hotel was lively. The conversation was easy and the drink flowed with similar ease. Old friends stopped by, and new friends were made.

When a 'Major X' of the Royal Army Medical Corps (RAMC) appeared in the bar one night in January, it is not surprising that Natalie was captivated. He was worldly, intellectual, fascinating and attractive. They spent the night talking and drinking beer until 2 a.m. The next day, she went to the News Theatre, but found she couldn't focus. Afterwards, she sought him out at the hotel and once again the two fell into deep conversation. 'The attraction', she learned, 'is mutual,' but Natalie was able to break away from him in the afternoon. The snow was falling and she nearly turned back, but she had ordered a taxi several days before she met 'X' and it was waiting for her, so she returned home. The taxi made it just over a mile from her house before becoming stuck in the snow. Natalie trekked the rest of the way through the snow, the winter night silent and still. It was perfect for musing over 'X'.

The next day was a Sunday, and she spent it washing, cleaning and thinking. As she watched the snow build up outside, Natalie made up her mind that she must see Hugh – and 'X'. The major had told her that he might be deployed at any time, and with the weather looking the way it did, it was possible that she would be snowed in for a few days and might never see him again if she didn't get to Leeds soon. The next morning, despite the freezing drizzle and a foot of snow, she walked the four bone-chilling miles into the village;

but she felt wonderful. By the time Natalie arrived, she figured it was too late to go to York and sent a telegram to Hugh not to expect her. She then went to Leeds.

Natalie spent the evening and the next morning with 'X' and decided once again not to go to York. In the afternoon, she went to the cinema and saw *Ships with Wings*, an Ealing Studios film that focuses on the lives of naval officers and stars Leslie Banks and Basil Sydney. For once Tanner, who usually enlightened M-O with detailed critiques of the many movies she watched, had surprisingly little to say – she was too preoccupied with her budding affair with 'X'. 'It's all very compli-cated,' she explained. 'His own personal life is snarled as well . . . but just as I can talk to him, so he can talk to me.' For a woman who rarely disclosed her personal feelings beyond film casting or political and inter-national affairs, 'snarled as well' is an enigmatic glimpse into her own marriage. Nonetheless, Natalie confided that, if only for a fleeting moment, the two 'managed to get a few hours of happiness without hurting anyone but ourselves'.

The next day, Natalie finally made it to York and found Hugh a little better. But she was still 'dazed' by 'X'. After seeing Hugh, she settled down to answer a directive from M-O, but found she simply couldn't do it. It was all about 'feelings', she complained, stat-ing, 'I have no feelings except about X at the moment,' and apologized to M-O for not responding. But if she couldn't quite bring herself to respond to the direct-ive, she felt that M-O was a confidant and unloaded the affair in her diary. 'I have to get rid of my feelings somehow!' she wrote. Although Tanner had a number of friends, she felt awkward discussing the affair with them. 'I always feel very uncomfortable when my friends tell me of their affairs – that is when I know their husbands,' Natalie told M-O, 'it seems so frightfully disloyal somehow.'

Throughout February 1942, Natalie continued to see 'X'. On her birthday, 8 February, Natalie and 'X' celebrated until midnight, when they ordered up more drinks and toasted Hugh's birthday (his birthday was on the 9th). He was still in hospital.

The affair was still full of heat, and the relationship remained intense, but Natalie was finally feeling herself again. 'For sometime', she confessed,

I was rather like a swimmer who has dived through the breakers – X being the sea. It's a lonely . . . half drowned feeling but it's good to get through the breakers and come up and breathe. One still enjoys the sea, but one has time to enjoy the sky and the distant shore.

The two were both well aware that the affair could not last. Hugh was getting better every day and would not be in hospital forever, and soon the expected orders to the Middle East would reach 'X'. 'We are civilized human beings,' Natalie rationalized to M-O when she first met him, 'and when the time comes we'll be able to say "goodbye" without any distressing scenes.'

In the event, his departure had little of the tearful, cinematic flair that a romantic film buff like Natalie might conjure of a soldier going off to face certain death in battle. He was not sent to the Middle East, but rather received orders to replace the head of a nearby convalescent home who had taken ill. 'Not as drastic as the Persian Gulf, but almost so,' Natalie sighed. They spent the night together, walked around Leeds all morning until his train arrived, then exchanged numbers and addresses. Later that day, she met an old friend from Cambridge for dinner. He was a Roman Catholic priest whom she hadn't seen for four years, but within a few minutes of conversation, he had divined the truth. It wasn't just his dog-collar that loosened her tongue – they were close friends and, like 'X', he understood her implicitly. Over the course of the evening, she made her confession.

Natalie tried several times to ring 'X' after they said goodbye, but it was difficult. He had given her a military number and she continually ran up against officials refusing to patch a civilian through. Natalie did manage to reach him once in March, but she did not record the details of their conversation. She thought about him often, writing letters to her Cambridge friend for solace and spending a few days reading T.S. Eliot poems (both she and 'X' shared a love of Eliot), wallowing in depression. She contemplated inviting him to meet once more in town, but if she did see him again, she never told M-O. The affair was over. After eight months in York, Hugh came home and 'X' made his final appearance in the diary.

Natalie Tanner's brief but profoundly moving affair with 'X' underlines a particularly significant wartime problem. The upheavals in family life that war created – children evacuated miles away from their homes, families separated because of bomb damage, servicemen sent abroad, wives working – increased fears that the family as an institution was in mortal danger. Adultery, and worries over its increasing prevalence in wartime, was at the centre of the debate over the breakdown of marriage and family. These debates were largely focused on women's infidelity, rather than men's.

In fact, men's affairs were generally excused as a result of the extraordinary pressures of wartime and battle. It seemed entirely reasonable that a man might resort to the comfort of another woman sometime during an extended absence. Unless he reneged on his financial duties to his family or abandoned them, women's magazines encouraged wives to forgive husbands' transgressions. Indeed, agony aunts often asked wives to look at themselves *first* as the source of blame for their husbands' indiscretions. Were you always presentable and desirable when you saw your husband? Was the house clean and cheery? Were *you* cheery? Furthermore, men's affairs seemed to carry far less offence than women's did. Husbands' infidelities were waved away as simple follies that had very little meaning. Women were encouraged to believe that all was not lost; just because a husband had an affair did not mean that he had fallen out of love with his wife.

Wives, on the other hand, were judged by a different standard altogether. First, there was always the fear that when a woman was tempted into another man's bed, her heart went with her. A man had physical needs, it was reasoned, but a woman's emotional needs far outweighed her physical desires (if, indeed, society allowed her to have any physical needs!). A cheating wife, it was thought, meant that she had fallen out of love with her husband. This was certainly a more grave offence, because there was then little opportunity to salvage the marriage.

In wartime, the issue went deeper than this. The faithfulness of wives became a matter of national importance. This was especially true of servicemen's wives. Fears were widespread that women's home front affairs might distract servicemen on the battlefront from their soldierly duties. This, of course, put not only the soldier at danger, but also his comrades, and ultimately, his nation. The matter was thought to be so important in the government's eyes that servicemen's wives who were caught or suspected of adultery could lose the right to draw the allowance they were entitled to while their husbands were abroad.

Although this potential loss in income was a powerful incentive to keep mum about any affair, women's magazines stressed the emotional and psychological impacts of infidelity on the husband. To shield a husband from undue suffering, women were advised to refrain from disclosing an affair from their husbands – especially husbands abroad – unless pregnancy was a consequence of the transgression. *Good Housekeeping* urged women to self-censor anything from letters that might worry or upset husbands – be it small worries such as grouses over food shortages or larger concerns such as affairs. One woman who asked *Woman's Own* for advice about an affair was told to keep it secret, even though she had contracted venereal disease. In this case, the advice columnist assured the woman that her lack of loyalty was much graver than the disease. 'Don't make him suffer,' she advised. Ignoring the obvious consequences of venereal disease, she finished her line of reasoning with the less-than-sage advice, 'He can't know *unless* you tell him.'[1]

In the event that a serviceman *did*, however, learn about his wife's infidelity, the military greased the wheels of justice and made it easier for servicemen to seek a divorce. The army and the RAF worked together to set up the Legal Aid Scheme in 1942, providing legal services to those under the rank of sergeant major on any civil matter, and if divorce was decided upon, the Services Divorce Department helped secure one. Women received no such help under this scheme.

The number of divorce petitions skyrocketed over the course of the war. In 1938, just fewer than 10,000 petitions for divorce were made. That number jumped to almost 25,000 in 1945, with the high-water mark of the period coming in the year after the end of the war, when a little over 47,000 petitions were logged. Whereas adultery was cited as the reason for the dissolution of marriage in 50 per cent of the cases in 1938, over 70 per cent cited adultery in 1945.

From these statistics, adultery would seem to have increased during the war. This may be true, but it is not as simple as the statistics suggest. When marriages broke down, the courts accepted only a few reasons for divorce. One could sue for divorce based on cruelty, insanity, desertion or adultery – there was no recourse to divorce simply on irreconcilable differences, which was only an option after 1969. If, as was the case so often in the *carpe diem* of wartime, marriages were hastily formed with little real knowledge of one's spouse, or separated couples found love elsewhere, it was difficult to dissolve the marriage once it was realized the two weren't really compatible.

In fact, some worked the system and employed the excuse of adultery in the absence of any other legal option to divorce. Stories abound of spousal collusion to create the illusion of adultery in order to escape an unhappy marriage. Individuals or couples could hire professionals to stage what was known as a 'Brighton quickie' – an artful ruse in which the name of one spouse was entered in the books of a hotel (usually in Brighton) with a person other than their spouse.[2] The bill for the hotel was then 'accidentally' sent to the supposedly wronged party, inquiries were made and someone would be produced to corroborate the story. Although Helen Mitchell never goes into details, it seems that one of her friends 'faked a divorce' in a similar manner. Helen was intrigued. Perhaps she toyed with the idea herself, but it seems unlikely that her husband would have entered into such intrigue or believed any ruse she might construct on her own. The courts did become wise to this type of judicial manipulation and often refused to grant a divorce if collusion was suspected.

Sometimes divorce was not an option because the costs were too high. This is certainly the case up to 1949, when Legal Aid was expanded to help civilians who could not bear the financial burden of divorce. Barring legal recourse to marital dissolution, however, individuals escaped unhappy marriages by moving out and setting up house with another person. This was often the case for those who could not afford divorce and for those who were denied divorce by the courts.

On the other hand, divorce was the pathway of last resort for many, especially women; there was a strong degree of commitment to marriage, even if they were dissatisfied with the relationship. Both in the home and in the media at the time, there was a sense that a woman's primary role in marriage was to ensure its success, regardless of personal needs or desires. In her 'Be a Success' column in *Woman's Own*, Rosita Forbes, a regular wartime columnist for the magazine, dealt with the issue of marital discord by answering one young 'frantic' wife's pleading question, 'Is there *any* life after marriage?' 'It's all so awfully different from what I thought,' the young woman complained:

... just cooking and cleaning and listening to a man grumbling and seeing him leave things about. I thought it would be fine to have a man to talk to and discuss things with, but it hasn't turned out like that at all.

Forbes responded with empathy, noting that, 'Wives, of course, do have a lot to put up with.' Husbands could be critical, demanding, and sullen, she acknowledged, but the solution to the problem ultimately lay in the young woman's hands. There was 'life after marriage', Forbes assured the young woman. The successful wife needed only to be adaptable. 'Change yourself to fit being married. It really is less trouble,' Forbes advised.[3]

Indeed, despite her discontent with being adaptable and 'changing' to fit her husband's needs and moods, Nella Last nonetheless believed she had a successful marriage. Hers was not a transcendent, intense love affair, but rather a practical one. Great love did exist, she admitted to M-O, but for 'ordinary' women like her, one had to rely on more than love. What made her marriage a success turned less on love, she figured, than on 'toleration' – hers alone. Alice Bridges also believed her marriage to be a success story. In her mind, once 'the glamour of love and physical attraction' faded, friendship was key, as was a 'mutual mental and spiritual intercourse'. On the other hand, she also believed that the successful marriage hinged upon a woman having 'affection, keep[ing] herself . . . fresh and always sweet' and maintaining a sense of humour. If this was done, 'She will always keep her husband's love,' Alice stated with confidence. Like Nella, Alice also believed that the responsibility for the success of a marriage lay almost entirely with the wife.

While wartime and the years immediately afterwards did see something of a breakdown of these notions and an increase in divorces, it cannot be denied that the war did create unique circumstances that threw men and women together and created the foundations and opportunities for infidelity. Long-term separations, like Natalie experienced, were one of the reasons for extra-marital affairs. Loneliness and the psychological stress caused by worry for loved ones or the physical and emotional pain of bearing the tragedy and destruction of blitzes alone provided the impetus for finding comfort in another's arms. But the call that brought women increasingly into national service, whether it be in factory work or voluntary work, also provided prime opportunities to mix with the opposite sex.

This fact underpinned many of the arguments against bringing women into what was then considered the male domain. Concerns abounded that women in factories were a distraction to the men with whom they worked side by side. In one factory, the management sent fifty-three women home for wearing tight sweaters. Although they argued that sweaters posed safety hazards because they might catch fire or become snagged on machinery, it seems likely that the sweaters represented more of a danger to the male workers than to the women. Those who disagreed with the dismissals noted sharply that, 'A small figure in a large sweater might be a threat to safety, a big girl in a small sweater was only a moral hazard to men.'

Shop rules were put in place to minimize such distractions as well-endowed women in tight sweaters. For instance, in one factory, women were required to wear trousers because the work involved stair climbing. Other factories kept women deemed 'virgins' – in this case young unmarried women, 'old maids' and widows – separate from other workers.[4]

While some saw dangers in the intimacy of the workplace, the blackout was also cause for concern, because it provided perfect cover for romantic trysts. Since night-time was the primary scene for fire watching and ARP duty, the mixing of men and women in these jobs came under particular scrutiny for those who saw families and the moral fabric of society disintegrating before their eyes. In September 1942, eligible women were required to participate in fire watching. Because of the moral panic stirred up by the mixing of men and women on such night shifts, the government soon took steps to ensure that men and women had separate sleeping accommodations when they were engaged on fire-watching duties.

It was precisely this wartime moral panic that prompted Alice Bridges to investigate liaisons between men and women in various mixed-sex situations such as ARP duty and dance halls. M-O's mission to observe and understand British society provided an excuse for Alice to embark on these investigations. She was never officially employed by the organization, but purely of her own volition dutifully reported her observations to them. Many Mass-Observers did report what they heard or saw others doing in the course of their daily routine, but Alice continually placed herself in circumstances that would allow her to study what she called 'sex life'. While she assured M-O that her investigations were entirely innocent, it is obvious that she soon became dangerously entangled in less-than-above-board situations.

Alice's investigations began in earnest after a row with her husband in March 1942 over her attempts to find a suitable wartime occupation. From the beginning of the war, Alice had fought her husband and her poor health to find ways to do her bit for the war effort. In fact, the need to do something for the country was so intense that the anxiety 'strained' her heart so much that Alice reported that she 'nearly went deaf' worrying over ways in which she could help.

She looked for volunteer work, considered paid employment and schemed various ideas to be helpful, but her husband continually thwarted her efforts. She complained:

> He wouldn't let me adopt a small Dutch evacuee . . . he didn't want me in ARP, too many men about, he didn't want me to do war work, it would knock me up and who would look after Jacqueline and him? . . . He didn't want me to adopt any one in the services, cost too much for parcels and they'd only want to visit. He didn't like it when I suggested we had a Canadian for the first Xmas as a guest.

Finally, however, despite his protestations, she did join the ARP and slowly became involved in the work. But Alice's intransigence irked her husband, and he insisted she give it up, and her newfound friends, so that she could focus on her family – on him, in particular.

If she were to give up her friends, Alice pressed her husband to tell her what he was prepared to offer her in return. 'He looked astonished and said "Nothing, what do you expect?"' 'The same old answer,' she quietly seethed, 'he soon asks me to give and to give but in no way in thirteen years has he ever given me anything.' He may have felt he had won the argument, but the issue was nowhere near being resolved in Alice's mind.

The next day, he stayed out late drinking on a cold and 'perishing' evening with his friends, despite the fact he had severe bronchitis. That night she paced the kitchen – walking past the supper going cold on the table – worrying over him, but becoming more and more angry each time she thought of his staying out late without telling her:

> 7.30 came and 8.30 came and 9.30 came and 10.30 came and no Les, I couldn't do "nothing" so I went in the kitchen and started washing a few clothes and as I stood at the sink the tears poured out of my eyes and never stopped.

When he finally walked in, he mumbled he was sorry, but Alice let loose a torrent of tears that broke forth so violently he became concerned and promised to be more respectful of her feelings in future. Several days later, when the two had apparently reconciled, she felt comfortable enough to ask him why he couldn't be more of a companion to her.

The issue was no longer just about her doing something useful for the country, it was also about the fact that he spent more time with his mates and kept her home alone, night in, night out. It was a sore wound, picked at over and over throughout their marriage, and the tenuous domestic peace once again evaporated. To her, their relationship would be perfect if only he would take her dancing, to the movies or spend more time with her. Alice told him she appreciated that he gave her enough money to run the household, and she had no complaints about their sex life, but there was more to a relationship than that. She complained that he was unwilling to go that extra step, to make the marriage '100 per cent': Les' patience now razor thin, he shot back, 'You can go out where you like so long as you don't ask me to take you.' This was the pass she needed. From this moment onwards, Alice decided to take her husband at his word. That very night, as he went to the local with his mates, she went out with her ARP friends and started her research for M-O in earnest.

On some nights she patrolled darkened Birmingham as an ARP warden. But after the last major blitz on the city in May 1941, there was relatively little action in the skies. The same could not be said about the streets.

On duty a few weeks after she volunteered, Alice and another warden walked alone through the black-out. Vic slipped his arm around her waist 'as though it belonged there'. Alice didn't balk: it was all in the interest of science. In fact, she had tried to meet Vic alone once before, but when he appeared at the appointed rendezvous point, with his wife in tow, Alice breezed by the couple as though nothing were amiss. This evening, as they walked together, she left his arm where it was, but told him she was only interested in him 'from the fun side'.

Alice was curious about men's behaviour under the cover of darkness, but since Les wasn't interested in going out with her, she was also searching for a companion to take her dancing, to the cinema or simply an ear to bend. When it was clear that Vic wanted more than a movie date and sparkling conversation, she told him she had no intention of becoming sexually involved with him. She was 'fun starved, not love starved'. Furthermore, she blasted, Vic could never measure up to her husband, 'who was an artist at lovemaking', in her eyes. As they approached the ARP post, she gave

Vic a kiss ('all he's ever likely to get from me') and bade him adieu.

A week later, she fixed Vic a cup of tea and flirted with him at the ARP post. 'I intrigue him, I tease him, I tantalize him, he gets worked up to fever pitch,' she boasted to M-O, 'and then I tell him it's time he went.' After he left, she went out on patrol with a Mr F, but his embrace reminded her of a 'jelly fish', so she shook him off and beat it back to the post. 'It just goes to prove how everything, the blackout . . . the wardens' hours . . . can and does make morals lax,' she mused in her diary. She, however, was entirely 'above board', she promised M-O. 'What fun I can get decently I'm going to.'

Alice 'tantalized' Vic all that summer, but when he failed to meet her one night, she slit his tyres. Just to make him squirm, she told Vic that she was writing about 'sex life in the area' and had committed their tryst to paper, expecting it would be published soon. He 'nearly passed out', she reported, pleased with herself for bringing him down a few pegs. But Vic had not seen the back of her: Alice confided to M-O mischievously, 'I haven't finished with his peace of mind yet.'

Although she continued to volunteer at the ARP and to taunt Vic, by 1943 Alice's curiosity about 'sex life in the area' led her to spend more and more time at the local casino. Here, she would eye the crowd from the balcony, make eye contact with interesting-looking men and await an offer to dance. Whether she danced or waited, Alice persuaded the men around her to talk about their private lives and about current issues so that she could report the conversations to M-O. She asked a Canadian soldier what he thought of Britain, and he responded that everything was out-dated and ran too slowly. Other men talked about their personal philosophies – most of which centred on the pursuit of happiness to the exclusion of all else. After dancing with a black GI, she learned from a 'large fat (let the war go on, I'm doing alright) man' that no American would ever ask her to dance if she danced with a black soldier. Alice wasn't worried. Americans had a reputation for being cocky and immature, she said, and she could do without them.

Some of these conversations led to long-term relationships. While she enjoyed mixing with various men at the casino, Alice preferred a reliable dance partner. Since some men were reluctant to dance, others poor dancers, and still others looked too shady for a turn on the dance floor, a dance partner ensured that she regularly danced, which – though she sometimes protested otherwise – as the war progressed, seemed more important than her scientific mission.

She met Fred at the casino in the spring of 1943, and since she liked him and he was an excellent dancer, he soon became her regular dance partner, but by October, the relationship had become serious. Fred turned up at her house when Les was at work, brought her gifts (many of which could only be appreciated in wartime, such as a No. 8 battery), and wrote letters professing his love to her. Alice resisted, telling him she did not love him, insisting all she wanted was a friend, and threatening to break it off. They continued to go dancing, but he was so sullen that Alice complained she could find no fun in it. Finally, she scheduled a meeting with him to discuss the relationship. She met him in town, brought him home and made him tea. If they couldn't be friends, Alice told Fred, the relationship was over. He told her his delicate state was her fault: 'Fred says it's the fact that I'm so darned good that's made him fall in a big way for me.' He then made vague remarks about ending his life, to which she responded a bit callously that she knew an excellent place where he could do so without raising suspicions.

When Alice appeared at the casino the next week, Fred was there, and they spent the afternoon together. He was still 'glum' and Alice was irritated that he ruined her fun. She came home late that night and met Les just as he was going out of the door for fire-watching duty. He was 'steamed up boiling pitch': tea wasn't ready, the blackout hadn't been installed and the fire hadn't been made up. He left without eating or changing out of his work clothes. Alice gave him a feeble lie to explain her tardiness, but she 'felt like a pig' for the intrigue. It made it worse that Les was drenched to the bone by a cloudburst after going out.

Les' misadventure in the rain caused bronchitis to settle in his chest, and on his birthday several days later, he was in bed. That didn't stop Fred from coming by to see Alice. She did tell Les that she had a visitor, but Alice explained to M-O that she wanted to spare Les the 'disadvantage' of being seen in his dressing gown by her dancing partner, so she didn't let on who the visitor was. With Les in bed upstairs, Fred watched Alice wash the dishes – 'not exactly conducive to romance', she admitted. When Fred did anything 'saucy', she playfully splashed him with water. Once the dishes were finished, she walked Fred down to the end of the street. He left without his usual kiss because Alice knew 'the eyes' of the neighbourhood were upon them.

'The eyes' watched Alice's intrigues – they knew when Fred stopped by, they had witnessed Alice toy with men at neighbourhood dances and they knew that Alice entertained more than one man while Les was at work. The gossip was scathing, but she told M-O she didn't care. The liaisons with Fred and with others at the dances, she reasoned, were mostly good copy for M-O, and the men who stopped in during the day were there for her advice.

For several years, she went to a weekly 'discussion group' led by a psychologist. They talked over common texts and debated current psychological questions. She took the knowledge gleaned from these discussions and counselled anyone who asked for help. In fact, while Les was kept generally in the dark about the dancing partners, he knew about the advice his wife doled out; he was sometimes present when the men called in the evening, and she was very open about it. She was not, however, forthcoming about kissing her dancing partners. Les was jealous of the various men in her life, but most of it was a vague jealousy, for she never gave him any solid evidence of what went on in private. He never knew the line that his wife had drawn in these relationships.

Fred was still involved with Alice in November 1943, when they celebrated his birthday. She bought him a pipe and a birthday card. By now, she told M-O, he knew her rules of engagement: the only form of affection she allowed was kissing. But even that was too much for Fred, who exclaimed, 'Good God, your kisses thrill me!' after he thanked her for his gifts. 'What would you be like if—' he contemplated aloud, and then sighed, 'Oh skip it, what's the use?'

Beyond some saucy stories to recount to M-O, there were a number of fringe benefits to these trysts. For one, Alice told M-O, they made her more affectionate with her husband. All the pent-up sexual tension of her daytime adventures was apparently saved for Les when he came home and 'went all romantic', as she called it. She also made new friends, went out more and became more empowered than she'd ever felt before. The men she met flattered her, and told her how beautiful and intelligent she was. But it was also clear that Alice held a certain power over the men: seeking them out, enticing them and creating boundaries that she seems to have policed with relish.

Her shameless flirting, though, had a particular edge to it, a fact that came to light when she confided to M-O that as a teenager she was nearly raped. The power to police those boundaries that had once only narrowly escaped being violently shattered remained intact as long as Alice didn't fall for her partners. She enjoyed Fred and Vic's company, but she didn't love them. She appreciated Les' trust in her, as 'He knew I would never do the unsporting thing.' But at the same time, Alice confessed to her diary, 'What a blessing I never *have* fallen really in love with another man.' What if she did fall for someone?

CHAPTER SEVEN

THE SUN NEVER SETS

Edie pounded the typewriter keys with ferocity. The nerve. Of all the 'dirty low down tricks', she fumed. Well, she reckoned, he was growing old. He had done some good in his time, but now, he was increasingly becoming a 'nuisance'. The British Empire would be better off without him. Best to let him die rather than give in to him, she thought.

It was 23 February 1943. Gandhi had been on hunger strike for thirteen days, but with eight days left in his twenty-one-day protest against his imprisonment and the rough treatment of prisoners throughout India, his kidneys failed. The crowds assembled outside the palace of Aga Khan in Poona, Gandhi's prison since August 1942, were allowed inside, and reverently filed past the ailing seventy-three-year-old. All were convinced this was the end. While his family and supporters steeled themselves against the inevitable, Rutherford's office mates in Sheffield were of the opinion that, 'He should be allowed to die if he persists in his fast.' Edie told M-O that, although she felt the British could not afford dissent during the war, and Gandhi's death would almost certainly unleash chaos, mass protest and the 'attendant killing' in India, she was nonetheless convinced, 'In the long run to be rid of Gandhi would be a good thing.'

Winston Churchill agreed. When Gandhi had been imprisoned six months earlier, in August, the Prime Minister was so jubilant to learn that the Indian leader was in custody and out of the way that his doctor overheard him singing gleefully in the bath. Churchill told Leo Amery, Secretary of State for India and Burma, 'If [Gandhi] likes to starve himself to death, we cannot help that.'[1] With Japanese forces at the gates of India and British losses everywhere mounting, Gandhi had given Churchill cause for much concern, for he led a movement of Indian nationalists who felt that the time was ripe to break away from Britain.

Gandhi's Quit India Movement erupted in 1942, a moment when Allied fortunes across the globe looked particularly grim. The Russians, who were now Britain's allies after the Germans attacked the USSR in June 1941, had suffered grievously in the first six months of the German invasion: at least four million Soviet troops had been killed or captured. By the summer of 1942, as Gandhi's independence movement gathered momentum, most Britons watched anxiously as the Soviets engaged in a desperate battle to defend Stalingrad. The Americans, drawn into war in December 1941, had yet to find their stride, and British interests were everywhere being rolled back by seemingly invincible Japanese and German forces.

On 7 December 1941, the same day that Japan launched its attack against the Americans at Pearl Harbor, Japanese forces were also moving on British territory in Hong Kong and Burma. In the early hours of the morning, even before the attack on Pearl Harbor,

Japanese forces landed in northern Malaya and began their trek south through supposedly impenetrable jungle towards an apparently indomitable 'Fortress Singapore'.[2] That evening, Singapore received its first air raids. It was an easy target: unlike the darkened cities of Europe, there was no blackout and the lights of Singapore glittered, creating an irresistible target for the night-time attackers.

A few days after Pearl Harbor, Britons were stunned to learn of their own naval disaster. Enemy aircraft patrolling the Gulf of Siam in the South China Sea had sunk two British ships, *Prince of Wales* and *Repulse*, sent to thwart the Japanese landings in Malaya. The ships were the pride of the Royal Navy – one, *Prince of Wales*, had recently hosted a meeting between the Prime Minister and President Roosevelt – and the commanding admiral was a personal favourite of Churchill. The incident was a significant turning point – one that signalled that Britain no longer ruled the waves. Japan reigned supreme in the east; the empire was now, according to Churchill, 'weak and naked'. Churchill later recalled, 'In all the war I never received a more direct shock' than when the First Sea Lord, Sir Dudley Pound, rang him with the news.[3]

Not long afterwards, Britain would lose its oldest possession in Malaya, the island of Penang. Under severe Japanese bombardment, European inhabitants of the island were given strict orders to leave behind local staff and servants and evacuate. Some were disgusted at the ignominy of the orders, but nonetheless they obeyed and boarded the ferries to leave the island, some of which were manned by the survivors of *Prince of Wales*. It fell to the Indian editor of the local English-language newspaper to lower the Union Jack;

no British officer had stayed to formally surrender. One woman who had tried to stay but was forced out recalled soon after that the evacuation was 'a thing which I am sure will never be forgotten or forgiven'.[4]

For Edie Rutherford, a native South African and proud supporter of empire, the imperial losses pointed out the 'farcical muddles' of the government, both at home and abroad. The loss of *Repulse* and *Prince of Wales*, for instance, constituted what Edie called a 'double blow' to the war effort. On the same day Britons learned the fate of the two ships, she reported that many women received an additional 'blow' – to their chances of lending their support to the war effort back home. The government had advertised important work for typists, yet by noon that day, Rutherford noted, it was announced that all positions were taken, leaving 'thousands' of women 'disappointed'. From her perspective, this proved that, although Britain was fighting on its heels, the government nonetheless refused to make use of the millions of eager women, like Edie, waiting to take a crack at Hitler, and now the Japanese.

As Edie nervously watched the empire unravel in the titanic struggles across the globe, she was plunged into her own battle to find meaningful war work. Back on the first day of war, 3 September 1939, Rutherford had resolved that she would do whatever was necessary to help 'push the ship along'. She seemed closer than ever to achieving that goal in March 1941, when the government decided that all women between the ages of twenty and forty (the requirements would eventually expand to include women between eighteen and fifty-one) had to register for war work. When she heard about the order, Edie thought that the government should extend the law to include women in their fifties and sixties. Many of them, she thought, could run circles around her because they were through the 'change in life' and were more healthy and energetic than someone like her, who 'still endure monthlies, getting faint indications of what goes with the change, and cannot help at times feeling under the weather, what with one thing and another'.

Like Nella Last, Edie was a skilled domestic manager, a master of rationing and ever vigilant in the battle against waste. But while she was serious about the domestic soldier's mission to keep her family and community 'fighting fit', she felt equally compelled to take on what she considered to be useful war work. Indeed, for her (and many others), paid employment was the most effective way to participate in the war effort and Edie, who was thirty-nine at the time, would now be officially required to register for work in 1942.

She did not, however, wait for the government to find her a job of national importance and instead immediately launched her own search. An occasional freelance writer for newspapers in her native South Africa and, therefore, a skilled typist, Edie felt certain that her talents would be needed by the government. But, as so many women found out, the job hunt was eminently frustrating, especially if one insisted that the job matched one's experience and skills, as Rutherford did.

Edie went to interview after interview and was sometimes offered work, but the wages were so paltry or the work so unsuited to her talents that she flatly refused. Despite the shock expressed by these employers at her seemingly unpatriotic rejection, she was steadfast, insisting that she was indeed patriotic, but would not be exploited, nor dispirited. 'I WON'T lose hope, nor believe my time wasted,' she resolutely told M-O. Still, it was difficult to be offered such low wages or, as often happened to Rutherford, to realize that her problems often had little to do with her qualifications.

The 'condescension' that interviewers took towards her when they learned she had not worked for ten years and had never worked for – nor had references from – a Sheffield employer, was, according to her, 'pitiful'. Nor did her age help matters. As she left one interview, she saw a long line of women – all much younger than herself – waiting. 'That's another job I don't get,' she thought bitterly.

The one bright light at the time was the American entrance into the war. Although Churchill fervently desired US help in Europe, many Americans were initially reluctant to go to war there. They much preferred to focus their efforts where they'd been hit: in the Pacific. Four days after Pearl Harbor, however, Hitler and Mussolini gave them no choice when both declared war against the US. Churchill was ecstatic. With the Americans in the war on both fronts, he later wrote, 'We had won the war. England would live; Britain would live; the Commonwealth of Nations and the Empire would live.'[5]

On Boxing Day 1941, Churchill addressed a joint session of the United States Congress. The Prime Minister charmed the chamber with his humour, as well as his sense of the historical gravity of the moment, and made multiple references to the newly forged ties between the two countries. One *New York Times* commentator pointed out that it was the first time that Churchill could speak of the two countries as '"We" – linked openly and irrevocably together in common struggle'.[6] As for the members of Congress, many thought it the 'greatest speech' they had ever heard.[7] The recent setbacks caught up with Churchill, however. No one but his personal doctor knew – until the truth came out after Churchill's death in the 1960s – but the Prime Minister suffered a heart attack that night.

The speech was broadcast back home on the BBC, and marked the first time the British public heard a prime minister address the American Congress over the wireless. Most back home cheered Churchill's speech. Irene Grant exclaimed with delight, 'Grand old boy!' and worried over his safe return. Edie Rutherford thought it a 'good speech' and believed it wise that Churchill exploited the 'emotional' connection he had with the US through his mother's American ancestry. But what Edie enjoyed most about the speech was that 'WC' delivered some nice jabs at the isolationists who had, until recently, refused to become involved in what they saw as European infighting. Although she knew the erstwhile American isolationists would now deny their past, she hoped, nonetheless, that Churchill's barbs made them squirm.

Natalie Tanner didn't mention the Prime Minister's speech that day. Her main concern was the surrender of Hong Kong, which had occurred the day before. As stories of Japanese atrocities filtered into the British press, and those around her waxed indignantly about them, Natalie remembered how apathetic people had been when the Japanese had invaded Manchuria in 1931. Back then, she had protested against Japanese aggression in China, but she was told to 'mind my own business' and was labelled a 'war monger'. Now, at least, she felt vindicated.

The triumph was hollow indeed, and Natalie could do little more than shake her head sadly at the devastation brought down upon the garrison at Hong Kong. Newspapers reported that lack of food and water forced the troops to give in, leading Natalie to worry that her beloved Gibraltar (where she'd been married nearly twenty years before) might also suffer the same fate. But there was more to the siege of Hong Kong than the official line. The Japanese had been casing the colony since at least 1934, sending in numerous plainclothes spies – such as the naval commander who worked as a barber for seven years, listening carefully to the conversations of the high-ranking British officers who patronized his shop. Japan had an intimate knowledge of the colony, its defence and the behaviour of the defenders before it began its concerted attack in December 1941.

Japan had also succeeded in winning over many locals to its cause and these fifth columnists created devastating unrest, especially in the first days of the invasion. Still, the defenders of Hong Kong – both the British and Chinese Nationalist forces loyal to Chiang Kai-shek – acquitted themselves better than can be said for their compatriots in other parts of the Far East, such as Penang. The British had been tasked with holding on as long as they possibly could, and this they did, as isolated islands of soldiers and volunteers fought off larger Japanese forces until their ammunition ran out. They were wholly outnumbered and outgunned on land, sea and in the air. On Christmas Day 1941, the Governor of Hong Kong, Sir Mark Young, became the first British governor to surrender a colony since the American War of Independence.

*   *   *

The news from the east made for a solemn New Year. Each year, Nella Last always suffered from what she called 'Hogmanay blues', but this year was particularly depressing. The stories of young British soldiers desperately retreating in the wake of swift Japanese action dredged up painful memories of Dunkirk, and Nella and her neighbour, Mrs Atkinson, were tearfully reminded of the loss of friends who had perished on the beaches at the beginning of the war. Their friend, Dorothy, whose husband had gone missing and was 'presumed dead', had spent the last eighteen months searching out anyone – even fortune-tellers – who could offer any shred of news.

In the sadness that pervaded that dark holiday season, Nella felt her resolve falter. She wondered if the soldiers were suffering the same malaise that seemed to permeate Barrow and descend over the entire country. As midnight approached on 31 December, the New Year 'blues' seized hold of her mind and set her thinking. Was it the food situation that made her so gloomy? Or the news in Asia? Was it that her husband Will continued to 'stop in' and stare dumbly into the fire? 'Is it the tension' of wartime, she wrote in her diary that night, 'the ceaseless undercurrent of conjecture if not real worry?' Perhaps her war work was becoming too overwhelming – 'the constant "keeping on" with no little break?' – she wondered. Whatever the cause, she confessed that she felt a 'curious "sapping of vitality", of stagnation'.

As the bad news kept streaming in, the cold chill of winter gripped the nation: pipes froze and snow and freezing rain snarled traffic. In Sheffield, Edie Rutherford picked her way through iced-over, muddy, 'black pudding' streets. Days like these made her long for the sun and warmth of her native South Africa – the letters she received from family and friends in Durban and Johannesburg hardly helped, since they complained endlessly about the scorching African heat! Amid the falling snow and freezing temperatures, Edie wondered how Russians and Germans could possibly wage war in such conditions. 'All my instincts are to hibernate when it is like this,' she told M-O. 'I can't summon up enthusiasm for sociable meetings let alone hostile ones!'

Coping with the cold in Barrow-in-Furness, Nella Last's thoughts were also of Russia. On 22 January, she reported that it was 19 degrees (-7 °C) in Barrow. Milk froze if it was left in the garage for an hour, but the Russians 'have thirty degrees below freezing [-17 °C]. I cannot imagine it twice as cold,' Nella admitted. It made her 'shudder' when she thought of bombed-out Russians with no shelter in such conditions. The next morning it rained, and Barrow's streets were night-marish with rivers of rain and puddles of slush, 'traffic skidded and slithered and piled up ... *What* a day!'

For Helen Mitchell at home in Kent, the snow and cold simply meant more work. Day after day, she 'lugged coal, coke and anthracite' from her stores into the house to stoke up the three fires necessary to warm her son and husband. Usually, the house in Kent was fairly empty – her husband, Peter, spent most of his time nearer his work in London and her son, William, was in the army. Except for the servants, Helen spent most of her time alone. But, much to her chagrin, Peter was home more than usual that January. Furthermore, William came home on leave unannounced at the end of the month. On the day he arrived, the pipes had frozen, there was no water and the plumber was nowhere to be found. But, despite the cold and its attendant problems, events in the east were never far from anyone's thoughts. Caught up as she was in her domestic drudgery, even Mitchell stopped to joke with an acquaintance that she had no idea how to keep her stockings up now that the Japanese had 'pinched all the rubber'.

Japanese victories were not only imperial embarrassments; they also meant significant shortages on the home front. With the winter victories of 1941/42, Japan had 'pinched' a large proportion of Britain's source of rice, sugar and tea – not to mention rubber and tin. Added to this, German U-boats were pummelling shipping in the Atlantic. Rations took a hit and food consumption in Britain was at its lowest during this period. Irene Grant complained, 'Our cupboard is bare.' To ensure that her husband Tom had enough to eat, Irene went without. 'No woman can eat less than I,' she told M-O.

It didn't seem possible, but the new year, with its food shortages, bitter temperatures and leaden snow clouds, soon became even more bleak. In early February Helen Mitchell noted that the government announced it would begin to ration soap. The news put her on high alert to watch the 'extravagance' of her housekeeper, Mrs Cripps, who was a perennial source of aggravation for Helen. She thought Cripps 'batty', and constantly found herself in exasperating struggles with her housekeeper.

Cripps always left such an unforgivable mess of the kitchen that, when the Mitchells bought a new cooker, Helen vowed never again to allow her near the saucepans or the cooker and swore to forever banish her to work in the garden. At least in the garden, she wrote, 'One hopes she will be less of a menace than in the house.' One morning, Cripps decided to take down the blackout curtains before the sun came up. Mitchell dashed madly behind her, frantically putting the curtains back in place while yelling at her to desist her crazy and dangerous behaviour. She was too late. 'The long arm of the law', an ARP warden, rang the bell to serve Mitchell with a fine. 'Haven't recovered from the horror of it,' she wrote, 'Cripps quite unable to see the enormity of the offence.'

Natalie Tanner thought the addition of soap to the ration was 'rather a blow' and found 'the news very depressing'. But days later, Britons suffered a calamity far more grave and depressing than this: Singapore had fallen. After the infamous retreat from Penang in December 1941, refugees had flooded to the safety of 'Fortress Singapore', but the fortress was an illusion. Air support had been knocked out in one blow when the Japanese air force destroyed every available aircraft in the nearby airfield. Furthermore, all defences had focused on a seaborne attack, not a ground assault: the powerful gun batteries on the island pointed out to sea. When, just one month before Singapore surrendered, British General Archibald Wavell finally imparted this fact to Churchill, who had sincerely believed the myth of the stronghold, the Prime Minister told the chiefs of staff that 'one of the greatest possible scandals' had been exposed.

As Japanese forces pushed further south into the city, European refugees flooded the causeway onto the island. On the island, they found 85,000 British, Indian and Australian troops, most of whom were demoralized from the fierce fighting on the mainland. One of

the soldiers in the garrison mockingly echoed Churchill
when he wrote of the situation:

> Never before have so many
> Been buggered about by so few
> And neither the few nor the many
> Have bugger all ideas what to do.[8]

On 15 February 1942, Singapore surrendered to a
Japanese force one-third the size of the Allied forces
left on the island. That night, Churchill addressed the
nation and gravely told them about the situation in the
east. 'I speak to you all under the shadow of a heavy
and far-reaching military defeat ... Singapore has
fallen.' It was a devastating defeat. Indeed, privately,
Churchill declared the fall of Singapore the worst
disaster in British military history. Nonetheless, the
Prime Minister attempted to rally the nation in the
face of such demoralizing news. 'This is one of those
moments', he stressed, 'when [the British race] can
draw from the heart of misfortune the vital impulses
of victory.' He reminded his audience of past victories
snatched from the jaws of defeat, as their ancestors had
done, so too, Churchill stated, 'We can meet reverses
with dignity and with renewed accessions of strength.'
Finally, he roused them, 'Let us move forward steadfastly together into the storm and through the storm'.[9]

The speech was unconvincing. As she was by most
setbacks, Helen Mitchell was 'very depressed' by
Churchill's address. She thought it 'weak and illogical', and 'wondered if we're sunk'. Even those who
were generally less apt to lose faith had genuine difficulty drawing any comfort from Churchill's words.
Edie Rutherford believed that the government was

covering up incompetence in the matter and found that most people she asked were not 'enthusiastic' about the speech. Most importantly, she wrote, 'The speech showed fear.' Across the country, it seemed that many agreed with this sentiment. The former canon of Westminster and Bishop of Durham Herbert Hensley Henson noted in his private diary that Churchill's 'voice and manner suggested a depression and even dismay, very unlike his accustomed buoyancy of carriage'.[10] Irene Grant's husband predicted that the debacle would bring down Churchill within six months.

The empire was staring into the abyss. Indeed, the Indians and Malays who witnessed the defeat felt sure that, 'The last days of the British Empire had come'. Edie Rutherford was dismayed. 'Singapore gone', she wrote in her diary when she heard the news. 'Oh, I do hope our men have made a getaway in time. Has it been worthwhile?' she wondered. Usually a confident and proud supporter of empire, her faith was shaken: 'I believe in our Empire but God, is it worth the price we are paying now?' It was difficult to escape the dark cloud descending upon what appeared to be the empire's imminent demise. She could find only uneasy comfort in day-to-day distractions and a constant faith in 'the invincibility of all that we hold dear'. 'There is no other way of keeping an even keel when things look black as they do now', Edie confessed to M-O.

If Japanese victories demonstrated that the British navy's control over the waves was slipping, an incident in the English Channel further undermined the nation's naval prestige. Three days before the Prime Minister's admission of the loss of Singapore, Britons learned that two German battleships had left port in Brest, on the coast of Brittany, slipped through British defences in the Channel and steamed, unaccosted, into the North Sea. It was a humiliating prelude that intensified the impact of Singapore's demise on the British psyche. Indeed, the proximity of this embarrassing episode to British shores exceeded the crippling loss that followed. Fears of invasion once again gripped the nation.

Within weeks of Singapore's fall, the Burmese capital of Rangoon was evacuated as Japanese troops closed in. British forces escaped north towards eastern India; the enemy was now perilously close to the jewel in the imperial crown. With Japan at the gates of India, no one was entirely sure if the Indians would fight the invader or side with them against the British. In fact, some dissident Indians had already gone over to the Axis, installing a pro-Nazi Hindi radio station, Azad Hind, in Berlin to counter the BBC (which Azad Hind called the 'Bluff and Bluster Corporation') and building an army to help oust the British from India.[11] In the hope of fostering loyalty against the Japanese at such a precarious time, Sir Stafford Cripps journeyed from London to Delhi on 14 March with the promise of independence.

Sir Stafford was the man of the hour. A teetotal, vegetarian ascetic, who exuded the very essence of austerity, he nonetheless had sparked the popular imagination after he was sent to Moscow as ambassador in 1940. Although it wasn't true, many believed that Sir Stafford was a confidant of Joseph Stalin, and this myth gained him much popularity. Irene Grant, who always championed the cause of the left, was thoroughly enamoured with Cripps. He was one of the few politicians, she believed, who was truly 'for the people'. He was a socialist who had spent some years in the political wilderness for radical views, but now he seemed to be Britain's greatest hope. Indeed, in 1942, he was the only politician who posed a genuine threat to Churchill's premiership.

In the spring of 1942, with disaster following disaster, the Prime Minister was in grave danger of losing his post. Twice, in January and July, Churchill fought off votes of no confidence in the House over the direction of the war. Several days after the first opposition, Sir Stafford Cripps delivered a wildly popular *Postscript* broadcast after the 9 o'clock news, summing up the general feeling of discontent with the war. A M-O survey concluded that many felt that the broadcast was 'sensational'.[12] Indeed, the broadcast scored a 93 per cent favourable rating – better than either Churchill or J.B. Priestley at their best.

Helen Mitchell wondered if Sir Stafford's mission to India was a political manoeuvre by the Prime Minister to dispense with a popular rival. But, despite the potential political benefit to Churchill of having him out of the country, Cripps did indeed seem like the perfect person to broker a deal in India. He was sympathetic to the cause of independence, a socialist like the leader of the Indian National Congress, Jawaharlal Nehru, and a vegetarian like Gandhi. He also had previous experience in working with the Muslim League's Mohammed Ali Jinnah.

When he arrived in Delhi, Cripps offered the Indian National Congress the opportunity to draft a constitution. After the war, he promised, independence would be granted. In a nod to Muslims, the Cripps Offer also allowed those who disagreed with the new constitution to opt out.

Edie Rutherford followed the proceedings anxiously. She expressed some sympathy for the Indian cause, and felt that the Cripps mission to India was the right step towards a fair deal for India. But negotiations began to stall. Rutherford wondered if Japanese bombs dropped on Indian soil might make them see reason and speed up the process. Despite the fact that bombs did in fact begin to fall on India (Calcutta received its first on 6 April), the Indian National Congress was angered by the stipulation that allowed Muslims the right to secede, and the Muslim League was incensed by Congress' reaction. Furthermore, with British fortunes down, Gandhi considered the deal to be a 'post-dated cheque on a failing bank'.[13] The Offer fell through.

Demoralized by the process, angered at Gandhi and alienated from Nehru, Sir Stafford left India on 12 April 1942. Edie Rutherford's faith in the righteousness of the Indian cause was in tatters; she thought vindictively that perhaps Britain should abandon India to the Japanese in order to teach the rebellious Indians what tyranny really was. Natalie Tanner remarked simply that if Cripps couldn't broker a deal, no one could.

So it was with the offer of independence in shreds and British fortunes in the east at their nadir, that Gandhi devised a plan to wrest India once and for all from the hands of the empire. Axis forces seemed irresistible that spring. The Japanese had closed the Burma Road, the Allies' crucial supply line to China, and now roamed the Bay of Bengal with impunity. In Gandhi's mind, the only way for both India and Britain to survive was for Britain to leave. 'Britain cannot defend India, much less herself on Indian soil,' he argued. 'The best thing she can do is leave India to her fate. I feel somehow India will not do badly then.'[14]

In August, the Indian National Congress agreed to support Gandhi's Quit India Movement. The next day, Gandhi declared 'open rebellion' against the British and told his supporters that this was the moment to 'do or die'. 'We shall either free India or die in the attempt,' he declared to the cheering audience.[15] That night, he and a number of leaders of the Congress were arrested. Once news of the arrests broke, waves of violence and arson erupted across India, which took over six weeks to quell.

Nella Last learned of Gandhi's arrest and the result-ing chaos while listening to the news over tea. A 'wee bright fire' burned in the fireplace as Will and Nella lingered over some wholemeal bread and a few poached eggs from her chickens. Neither one seemed particularly interested in doing much else but to stare at the fire, meditating wistfully about their son and the deteriorating situation in India. Cliff had recently been deployed overseas and all they knew was that he'd been sent 'east'. Now they wondered if Cliff was landing in India, perhaps helping to subdue the local population or fighting off a Japanese invasion.

To Irene Grant, the chaos in India was a direct result of years of 'capitalist' meddling and 'bad neglectful treatment at our hands', but she was more concerned with her own struggles with debilitating sciatica and arthritis. Over the course of July and August, she received nine gold injections that were supposed to heal her ailments. Unfortunately, the treatment did little to help, and she complained of 'pains very bad indeed', spending most of her time 'dazed and in pain'. It was a battle just to walk out to her garden.

Edie Rutherford received the news of Gandhi's arrest with satisfaction. Although she expected India

to erupt in rebellion, she also thought it would benefit the British to have him 'out of the limelight'. Edie
respected Gandhi and his stance on non-violence, but
she felt it was treacherous and unsporting to raise
opposition while Britain was in the fight of its life. She
hoped that his incarceration would give him time to
think over the fact 'that the freedom of India at this
moment was not worth exchanging for the freedom of
the rest of the free world'.

While Edie could be, and often was, quite critical of
the government, she nonetheless believed wholeheartedly in the righteousness of the war against the
Axis powers. As Churchill repeatedly reminded the
British people: not only freedom, but the very fabric of
civilization was at stake in this fight. For Edie, active
opposition to Britain at such a time was an unnecessary, inexcusable and dangerous diversion. Indeed,
she had no time for those who sat on the fence, either.
In a war of good versus evil, there could be no neutrality, she believed.

Reports of hardship in neutral countries failed to
move Edie to sympathy. When she came across an
article in the newspaper regarding Eire's difficulties
in wartime, her only response was, 'I hope we're not
expected to feel sorry for the mutts? Neutrals deserve
to suffer for their blindness.' In fact, Edie was so fed up
with Eire's neutrality that news from the island only
made her 'just spit and spit and spit and make rasp-
berries'. After an earthquake struck San Juan,
Argentina, in January 1944, leaving 2,000 people dead
and 4,000 injured, she wrote indifferently, 'Can't say
I have much pity for Argentina . . . they are neutrals
waxing fat on the war, faugh.'

Edie was a fierce supporter of the war effort and, as a daughter of empire herself, the performance of the Commonwealth and colonies in aid of Britain was a point of personal pride and significance. As such, she closely followed the happenings elsewhere in the empire, especially in her native South Africa, with great interest. The 'Boer Diehards' of her native country, who refused to fight for Britain, were a constant source of Edie's ire.

She did not write a M-O diary at the time, but one suspects that, had Edie kept one, there would have been a hearty cheer for Jan Smuts on 6 September 1939. It was then that Smuts had forced a parliamentary debate against anti-British and pro-Nazi Boers led by J.B.M. Hertzog, in order to bring South Africa into the war on the side of the British. The majority of the Union's parliament sided with Smuts, who became premier on the force of this debate. Still, there was a significant minority of South Africans who were never supportive of the British war effort – a fact that continued to exercise Edie throughout the war.

Edie's extended family, however, contributed wholeheartedly to the war. Between her own and her husband Sid's family, there were at least ten servicemen involved in the fighting, with whom she kept continual correspondence. Sid's nephew served in the RAF in Cairo, India and the Middle East and a cousin fought with the Cameron Highlanders in France after the D-Day invasions. Her brother and brother-in-law, as well as Edie's nephew, all fought in South African regiments. These volunteer forces saw action against the Italians in East Africa, the Germans in North Africa in 1942 and later were involved in the Italian offensive in 1944 and 1945.

It irked Edie that the British media, and Britons in general, rarely mentioned the significant events or endeavours of the empire. In order to balance matters a bit, Rutherford made a point of enlightening M-O on many Commonwealth efforts. In July 1943, she spent an entire week listening to the BBC for election news from South Africa to be broadcast, but when nothing was reported, she figured that the 'BBC considers [the] news not worthy of notice'. The next year, when the BBC mentioned South African Union Day on 31 May, Edie could hardly believe it. 'Hold me before I fall,' she quipped, 'the BBC actually mentioned our National Day!' But, when Anzac Day (a commemoration of Australian and New Zealand forces who fought in the First World War) was celebrated in April 1945, *she* made sure to mark it, but sniped, 'not that it means a thing to folk here'.

She was most proud by far, though, of the South African 'Springboks', and made sure their efforts were always reported in her diary, as when she reminded M-O that it was South African troops that helped recapture Bardia, on the Libyan border with Egypt, in early 1942. Edie compared them to others in the empire, noting with pride that, despite the 'wretched Boers', South Africa contributed more troops than other Commonwealth nations with similar numbers of whites. But although she applauded the bravery and participation of South Africa's volunteers, Rutherford was disgusted that the best of South African blood was spilt on foreign battlefields while, 'The anti-British Boers with all their narrow prejudices are safe at home breeding more youngsters to whom they can pass on their poisonous ideas.'

The 'poisonous ideas' refer not only to the animosity towards the British, but also their aggressive racism.

When racial matters cropped up in the news, Edie wrote with authority and sympathy, though not without a hint of racism herself. She held a deep conviction that the 'colour bar' should be abolished, not only throughout the empire, but globally. Early on in the war, Edie was happy to learn that the 'coloured children of my country', when given a chance, volunteered in droves. Military service was an excellent opportunity, she thought, to give them a good job, decent food and a chance to better themselves. Plus, it highlighted the treachery of Boers, demonstrating that colour was a poor indicator of loyalty.

When famed West Indian cricketer Learie Constantine was refused a room in 1943 at a hotel in Russell Square, London, Edie was delighted to learn that he sued them. Although Edie told M-O that she felt 'many English folk have no colour sense at all,' this was not the first time that racial discrimination had reared its head in wartime British society. Just two years earlier, the distinguished Indian jurist, poet, novelist and vice-president of Delhi and Nagpur universities, Sir Hari Singh Gour, had been turned away by another West End hotel. Even the Royal Navy's recruitment policy was questioned when George Price, a young man born in Edinburgh of a West Indian father, was refused entrance into the service in 1940.

The problem of racism in Britain, however, became exacerbated once American GIs arrived en masse. By July 1942, just six months after Americans landed on British soil, complaints of American mistreatment of black Britons began to filter through official channels. Indeed, Constantine's experience was directly related to this issue, for the hotel manager who denied the dynamic cricketer a room maintained that the

American officers who frequented the hotel disliked the presence of blacks.

Popular opinion in Britain seemed to be with Constantine. Newspapers covered the story and Parliament debated the issue, coming to the conclusion that, as Home Secretary Herbert Morrison put it, 'responsible public opinion' would 'condemn' discrimination against 'a fellow British subject on the grounds of race or colour'.[16] Learie Constantine won his suit. Still, this by no means solved the problems of race. Constantine, who also acted as a local Ministry of Labour welfare officer for Jamaicans in Liverpool, later complained to the ministry after being accosted by two American GIs in a pub that the government was unwilling to confront the issue with their allies. Indeed, it was a delicate situation, for Britain needed *both* American and imperial support.

To Edie, the hotel incident shed light on British rule throughout the empire. 'It is more than time that we decided if the coloured people in our Empire are to enjoy the privileges whites in it enjoy,' she argued. Otherwise, 'We should withdraw from their countries in favour of others who will afford them equality. We can't have it both ways.' Her openness towards 'coloured people', however, was tempered by an underlying assumption that they could not lead their own countries without help. They were, after all, as she put it, 'children' and according to Edie, it was therefore up to some other nation, presumably European or American, to *give* them equality.

Even if her feelings were fraught with contradictions, at base, Edie saw herself as a champion for justice and equality. This was especially true in the shifting sands of women's rights during the war. In August 1942, controversy flared on the home front when the government instituted compulsory fire-watching duties upon women. Women who were pregnant or who had children under the age of fourteen were exempt, but all others between twenty and forty-five years of age were required to either take turns watching at their place of employment or to register for local duties.

Objections to this new directive abounded. Letters to the editors of newspapers across the country registered the variety of those complaints. Some women argued that they were already pulling double shifts, working in full-time employment and coming home to take care of their families; the addition of overnight fire-watching duty was entirely too much to ask, they thought. Men chimed into the debate as well. One man who wrote to the *Liverpool Daily Post* felt that the order placed women in dangerous work that should be carried out by men only, and was thus a 'serious reflection on my manhood'. Others worried less about women's physical safety, and instead felt that the order put women's moral safety in jeopardy. In the darkness of the night, who knew what moral dangers women would face?

Edie thought the moral panic embedded in this debate ridiculous. First, she argued, women were already doing the work: she had served as a fire-watcher during Sheffield's Blitz the year before and understood the realities of the work. To her, the moral arguments against women's fire watching suggested that women could not be trusted in the presence of men under the cover of darkness. 'If my husband had so little trust in me when the country called on me to do a duty away from home at night, I would tell him precisely where he gets off,' she told M-O. She didn't doubt that there would be liaisons, but she felt that the debate also demonstrated the 'nonsensical' idea that women's transgressions were worse than men's. 'Does it not occur to men', she enquired rhetorically, 'who sleep with odd women that some man could be as indignant about them as they are at the thought of their wives doing it?'

What truly infuriated Edie about the compulsory fire-watching order, however, was its underlying inequality: a woman injured in the line of duty did not receive the same compensation as a man. Under the Personal Injuries Act for civilians, men were given 7 shillings more per week than women who sustained the same injuries during civil defence work. Labour MP Dr Edith Summerskill, who fought in the House of Commons against this discrimination, summed up the issue when she asked the Minister of Pensions, Sir Walter Womersley, 'Will the Right Honourable Gentleman say why a woman's arm or leg is not of the same value as a man's?'[17]

This was the core of the issue for Edie, and, she told M-O, for the men and women alike who she knew supported women's fire watching *and* equal compensation for injuries sustained during such work for the nation. When Home Secretary Herbert Morrison shut down Conservative MP Mavis Tate's attempt to ensure that equal compensation would be part of the fire-watching order before Parliament recessed in August 1942, Edie was furious. 'It would serve the Government right if women refused,' she told M-O. But, 'Fortunate for the government, women are not so base as Gandhi and Co.'

Things looked bleak that August for equal compensation, but soon the tide would turn. Fuelled by the efforts of Mavis Tate and Edith Summerskill, a committee was formed to investigate the matter in November. Based on their findings, the government reversed its stance on the issue, and in April 1943 equal compensation was granted for civil defence injuries.

As things began to turn around for women's rights in late 1942, so the tide began to change in the war. Rays of hope started to break through the bleak midwinter of the Allies' war effort. After the devastating spring losses in the Far East earlier in the year, the British also found themselves in dire straits in Northern Africa, where British forces had been forced by German and Italian troops into pockets in eastern Egypt and near the Libyan port of Tobruk. At the end of June 1942, Tobruk surrendered, along with 30,000 British and South African troops. 'Defeat is one thing,' Churchill said of the loss at Tobruk, 'disgrace is another.'[18]

After Tobruk, General Erwin Rommel's desert troops drove through Egypt to meet the British Eighth Army at El Alamein, about sixty miles west of Alexandria. Rommel would get no further. In late October 1942, British General Bernard Montgomery launched an attack that pushed the Germans 1,500 miles west, expelling them from Egypt and Libya. Two weeks after the attack began, British and American troops were landing west of the Germans on the shores of French Morocco and Algeria. Rommel now faced significant Allied forces on both the east and the west.

The situation in Russia was also beginning to improve that November. On 23 November, over 200,000 Germans found themselves surrounded at Stalingrad. Though fierce fighting would ensue until January, the Nazi advance into the USSR had reached its limit. Russia would not fall. In India, Japanese forces stalled in the eastern region of Assam. Still, it was only, as Churchill put it, 'the end of the beginning'.[19]

Edie's luck also began to change at the end of the year. As required, she registered with the labour exchange in March 1942 and for most of the year, checked-in regularly with the exchange, going on the interviews they arranged, but was never offered a position. Indeed, though (or perhaps because) she 'pestered' the exchange so often during this period, she could do little more than laugh and throw up her hands in disbelief when she received a letter from them stating that she needed to fill in another form, and answer the same questions she had done many times before, or she would be stricken from the register.

Edie complied with the order, re-registered and was given a New Year's gift when the exchange informed her she was to start an office job at a steel company in Sheffield on 4 January. The job was part-time and, though she was thrilled to work in a position that she felt used her talents and also had a direct effect on the war effort, she soon found that working and keeping the home going was not an easy task in wartime. Receiving a wage packet for the first time in years certainly was gratifying, but this was balanced by the sobering realization that, while the government continually urged women to find work, the home front was not set up for women who actually heeded that call.

Four days after starting the job, the thrill of her first pay packet adding bounce to her step, Edie made her way to the shops. The first stop was the butcher's, and it was there that the reality of the double burden of work and domesticity sank in. Though it was only

12.30, she was told there was no meat left. 'Where was our ration then?' she angrily queried. The butcher only blinked and stared back at her blankly. After a few heated comments about the uselessness of coupons and rationing, she left empty handed and vowed never again to patronize that shop. She 'traipsed around' town for two hours, but still came home with nothing. For dinner that night, she pulled together what little food she had left and made vegetables with dumplings and gravy, feeling a little triumphant that the gravy came out quite nice. But her husband baulked at the lack of meat on his plate. Incensed by his attitude, she took a 'firm line' – 'When I work full-time, I shall have even less time to shop . . . It is not my fault if I can't get things'– and told him he could very well go hungry that night. He did.

CHAPTER EIGHT

FIGHT LIKE HELL
UNTIL ALL ARE EQUAL

Irene stared out at the hill behind her home. Once, horses grazed and farmers ploughed the soft and verdant slopes, but they had long since passed into memory, now only a lifeless, gritty mound glowered back at her: 'Dull, black, low hedges' cut across the barren hill like scars, and a melancholy slag heap arose to dominate the view just to the left of Irene's back garden. As she turned away from the hill and entered the low mean building before her, she was utterly depressed; the hill view punctuated the gloomy, 'God and man forsaken hole' that Irene called home.

She resented that she had spent years there, 'wasting my talents', making do, mending and patching the old, decrepit structure. Increasingly she was confined to her home by a variety of ailments, including rheumatism and sciatica; the bleak walls seemed to smother her. To Irene's mind, what made it worse was that, with all its detractions, the cramped two-bedroom house wasn't even hers. Though most of their friends and family had managed to purchase their own homes before the Great War or afterwards, Tom and Irene simply could not afford to. Grinding poverty and unemployment in the inter-war years had wasted away all of their savings, and uncertainty made them loath to consider buying, even when Tom was in work.

The war changed all this. As early as April 1940, one journalist reported that Tyneside, where the Grants lived, was humming again after years of soul-rending, emasculating inactivity. Incomes began to increase as wages rose and the drive for more war materiel multiplied opportunities for overtime. By 1943, Britain was operating at near full employment: the 60,000 out of work consisted mostly of those who were moving from one job to another. In fact, the nation that only six years before had experienced nearly 70 per cent unemployment in some of its hardest-hit areas was now recruiting workers from abroad. In this atmosphere, Tom's work at the chemical plant seemed secure, and the couple once again began saving.

Chafing in the crowded, dingy and rented accommodation, Irene and her two daughters began searching for a new home that they could afford. Their search of the surrounding communities commenced in the winter and spring of 1942/43, as British and American troops were squeezing Rommel's troops into an untenable position in Tunisia, and Russian troops were driving Germans out of Stalingrad. On 15 November, bells rang across Britain to announce the first significant Allied victory of the war at El Alamein. Most felt the celebration presumptive. Helen Mitchell was 'appalled by the bells ... They are ringing the bells now, but they'll be wringing their hands soon,' she was sure. For Irene, the bells sounded joyous, if a little premature: 'It wasn't as if war was over ... Now let's get on and not rejoice until something bigger shows,' she thought.

Rejoicing could wait until a solid victory was achieved, but the house search could not. While she and her daughters were enthusiastic about the possibilities of owning a new home, Tom was deeply concerned and did all he could to dissuade them from their endeavours. The wartime economic boom simply couldn't last, he believed, and knowing how the peace had played out after the last war, the future looked bleak: all he could imagine was a replay of the hard times of the inter-war years. While Tom's job remained stable, the family was comfortable, still he feared that it was financially dangerous to become homeowners. He was determined not to 'be got into poverty again', but Irene assured him that they had enough money to comfortably afford a new home. Still, he continued with the argument he always used to shut down Irene's dream: high taxes, an economic slump and a worthless housing market would surely follow the war and ruin them if they made the move. 'Oh! the pessimist!' she exclaimed to her diary, 'I say we've waited twenty-seven years and have a right to move for the sake of the girls (and me).'

Quietly, she resolved not to give up despite Tom's fears; she knew the finances better than her husband and now decided to take control of all housing matters, knowing Tom would eventually come around. With a new determination, Irene retired to bed, dreaming of a new home.

Tom wasn't alone in his dreary vision of the post-war future. Most people worried that, in peacetime, the economic hardships and unemployment that had plagued inter-war Britain would return, and the government would once again turn its back on the people. Very early on in the war, however, many were determined that this time it would be different; lessons could be drawn, they believed, from the callousness of inter-war public policy and the greed of vested interests. In 1940, from Dunkirk until the Blitz heated up in the autumn, J.B. Priestley built his stunning celebrity on this issue.

In those uncertain and momentous days of 1940, hopes for a new world order abounded, and Priestley shaped the debate. In his Sunday night BBC *Postscripts*, he set the tone for the People's War, reworking Churchill's moving, but often officious and militaristic, rhetoric into a homely and uplifting chat, embracing everyone in the war effort, and, more importantly, mobilizing them for the People's Peace. After the last war, Priestley lamented, the very ones who won the war were abandoned: veterans and their families were left to 'take their chance in a world in which every gangster and trickster and stupid insensitive fool or rogue was let loose'.[1] This time, he hoped, the people would work together to build an equitable peace: no one would be left behind.

Most Sunday nights, after the nine o'clock news, that summer and autumn of 1940, J.B. Priestley introduced his burgeoning audience to 'ordinary people' and ordinary scenes he'd encountered on his travels across the country: cheerful, good-hearted people and the simple towns and countryside that were the backbone of the nation. For example, there was the young RAF pilot and his wife trying to cobble together a life during the Battle of Britain; the baker in Bradford who refused to close his shop after being bombed; the invalid who served up bubbly 'repartee' and spread cheer through the ranks as she was evacuated from a hospital on the Isle of Wight; even an indomitable mallard duck who bravely marshalled her ducklings despite the Blitz.[2] In these evocative and heart-warming tales of Britain, Priestley reminded the people of the very best that lay within them, of the humour, the bravery and the humanity that made them not only different from the 'automaton' Nazis, but that would ultimately help them prevail against the forces of evil.[3]

But the fight was not, according to Priestley, just against the Nazis. It was also against the politics of 'officialdom' and the greed and privilege that had prevailed in the inter-war period. 'We're not fighting to restore the past,' he argued one July evening, for 'it was the past that brought us to this heavy hour.' Instead, the fight against the Nazis was only an 'encumbrance' to be eliminated so that the real work could be done: 'so that we can plan and create a noble future'.[4]

That new future was a radical restructuring of society, steeped in equality, in which kindness and decency trumped bald-faced power, and community needs triumphed over the individual. Priestley urged the people to ensure that the post-war era prioritized community and creativity over power and destruction, asking his audience to consider the needs of all ahead of selfish, individualistic concerns corrupted by money and property. To illustrate this idea, Priestley told his audience of a large garden in his neighbourhood that had fallen into disuse because its owners fled to America at the opening of the war. Under the traditional conception of individual ownership the community was supposed to protect that property, but, he argued, that duty to protect the absentee owner's land made no sense when war workers in the area desperately needed land for vegetable allotments. The people had every right to take over that land for the larger good.

In order for a new dawn to break after the war, all ordinary individuals had to come together and stand up to the bureaucrats and vested interests that threatened to tamp down popular feeling and put things back the way they were. The failure of the inter-war years, he told his audience, was that they 'let the old hands, the experts, the smooth gentry' trick them into believing that ordinary citizens could not grasp the problems of the day, and certainly could do nothing about them. In the process, these 'old hands' put their hands back on the reins of power, abandoned the people and ultimately 'sold [them] out'.[5] Priestley's greatest fear, he made clear on his last regular *Postscript* appearance in 1940, was that the popular spirit of 1940 would evaporate, allowing the 'old hands' to enter once more and usher in the bad old days of the inter-war period.

Every time Priestley took to the air, he skilfully entwined his new vision of the world order and a call to popular action as he painted wholesome, kindly pictures of ordinary Britons and Britain. This radicalism increasingly infuriated the upper levels of government (including Churchill) and, though he assured his audience that it was entirely his decision to leave in October 1940, it was most probably his quest for a new world order that was behind Priestley's departure as a regular *Postscript* announcer. He appeared in the *Postscript* spot several times during the remainder of the war, but never with the regularity of his 1940 stint.

J.B. Priestley's 'people's peace' message resonated with Irene Grant. Rarely one to miss his *Postscripts*, she also devoured his newspaper columns with great eagerness. To one article, in which he insisted that the nation could easily get by without the aristocracy and bureaucracy, but would sink into oblivion without the honest workers, she exclaimed, 'Them's my sentiments!' On another occasion, she echoed Priestley's community-over-individual ideal in stressing that any vacant homes left standing after a blitz be given to the homeless. 'The poor homeless people are 100 per cent more value than . . . property,' she explained to M-O. The failures of the past that so concerned Tom as he considered buying a new home had transformed Irene into a crusader for a better peace, both for herself and for others. 'Won't I fight for the new order with Priestley and Co.! . . . Good old Priestley!!' she cried.

Irene felt closely connected to Priestley and his calls for a radical rebuilding of society: she felt that he had a special way of expressing her thoughts and feelings in words that she could never conjure on her own. Irene wished that she could be as articulate and persuasive as he was in advocating a world order in which she strongly believed. Though she humbly told M-O, 'My choice of words is so poor,' she regularly laid out her hopes for the peace in her writing.

As in Priestley's vision, Irene's ideal society emphasized hard-working, salt-of-the-earth, 'real people', like her and her family. 'Yes out goes my chest, I'm *real*,' she proudly told M-O when she declared that Priestley had the support of 'real people' across Britain. She believed that capitalists and 'Tories the world over' had lived on the backs of the common people and had hijacked the power of the state away from them. She was convinced, too, that these same Tories had started the war for their own selfish ends and forced working people around the world to fight one another. In the post-war future, Irene hoped to see a reversal of power through a national takeover of banking and industry, which she believed would undercut capitalist and corporate influence and greed. She also strongly advocated common ownership of land – 'It ought never to have belonged to any private person,' Irene asserted.

As she and her daughters went house-hunting, Irene personally confronted another problem of the capitalist basis of British society: the escalation of prices as supply became scarce and demand rose. Many profited from the housing shortage exacerbated by the Blitz; houses that had once gone for £400 were now selling for twice as much, Irene angrily reported. At the start of her house-hunt, she had believed that £600 would be more than enough to buy them a comfortable home, but after a few months' search, she found that £900 was more like it, a fact that priced her out of many previously affordable homes. 'Demand and supply is a wicked greed,' she fumed.

In the end, she hoped to see socialism established in Britain and across the globe. As George Orwell once wrote, 'The "mystique" of socialism is the idea of equality; to the vast majority of people Socialism means a classless society, or it means nothing at all.'[6] Equality was very much the core of Irene's understanding of socialism. Indeed, Irene was driven by acute memories of past experiences of inequality. Though her father had been a respectable, hard-working man who never drank or squandered his money, he never seemed to get ahead. The poverty of the father, too, Irene realized, became the burden of his daughters: Irene felt that she and her sisters had been held back because her family could not afford higher education. 'My decent brain and my good hands (plain truth, not swank)', she told

M-O, 'could never have a proper chance because of lack of money, though I come of hardworking people.' Instead, she watched while others whom she called 'nin-compoops' wasted a university education gained simply because their parents had money.

In the bitter cold of winter, with food increasingly scarce, Irene seethed with anger about the rich who were feeding on luxuries in cafes, while her diligent and respectable family went hungry. She sincerely hoped that, after the war, all 'ordinary people' would 'fight like hell until all are equal'. The chance for ordinary people to 'fight like hell' came not after the war, but rather during it, when Sir William Beveridge unveiled a plan that he hoped would be 'a contribution to a better new world after the war'.

In numerous public and private capacities throughout his entire career, William Beveridge constantly concerned himself with social reform. In addition to civil service work before and during the First World War, he worked in London slums as a young man and wrote one of the most important texts regarding the problems of unemployment in the early 1910s. In the 1920s and 1930s, he ran the London School of Economics, and during the early years of war was appointed to research and analyse various policy issues.

The plan that Beveridge introduced to the public on 1 December 1942 would become the pivotal document shaping social insurance in Britain for the rest of the twentieth century, but while he was working out the details of a comprehensive insurance scheme that year, he was also dealing with the more pressing wartime concern of fuel shortages. Early in 1942, the

Board of Trade commissioned him to solve the growing gap between coal supply and demand. More than six months before the plan that would make William Beveridge a household name and place him at the forefront of the crusade for a better future, he unveiled a coal rationing plan that was hotly criticized.

Fuel shortages and the quality of coal were a constant source of irritation throughout the war, but with Germans prowling the Atlantic and coal extraction suffering in Britain, 1942 was a particularly difficult year. Irene Grant complained incessantly about the quality of the coal delivered to her home, most of which consisted of less fuel than worthless stone and the cost was outrageous, especially in light of its poor quality. The fuel situation also hit Edie Rutherford hard that autumn.

In the wake of coal shortages that year, the Ministry of Fuel and Power called for a ban on central heating in all but industrial buildings. Edie's flats were soon freezing and she was furious. As the head of the tenants' association, Edie went on the offensive, writing to the BBC, her regional fuel controller and her MP about the injustice of the new fuel measures. The tenants also fought the management, who threatened to raise the cost of rent, in order to cover the rising costs of coal, if central heating was reinstituted. Edie stood firm. 'We shan't get the heat we used to have,' she told management and the fuel controller, but 'of course we don't expect it.' The tenants were simply protesting for their fair share, Edie argued; all they wanted was, 'One warm room which everyone else in the country has got.'

Her mission was ultimately successful and the ban on central heating was soon lifted, but the fight with management did not end there. In an interview with a local newspaper, the owner of the flats stated that he 'hoped [the tenants] could economise'. This angered Edie deeply, for it made them look 'greedy and extravagant with fuel'. The opposite was in fact true, she told M-O. Edie and Sid were committed to conserving energy: even before the fight over fuel erupted, they woke up with candlelight, draped themselves with heavy rugs to keep warm; Edie cooked pot roasts on the hob instead of in the oven and both used the stairs to save the fuel needed to work the lift. Edie simply couldn't imagine what else they could do.

Soon after the owner gave his initial interview on the central heating problem, he once again sought out the media to announce that, since workers were rarely home during the day, he would not stoke the central fires until 9 p.m. Once again, the tenants pulled together to combat this new measure – for, as Edie stressed, the elderly and young children were at home during the day and deserved warmth as much as the workers who came home late at night. With all the difficulties she faced that autumn, Edie agreed with Beveridge – rationing was the only equitable way to deal with the uneven access to fuel that kept her shivering in the dark.

Few were enamoured with this view. Although some accepted Beveridge's proposal to ration coal in the same manner as food as the only way to ensure that the dwindling supply of coal would be available for war industry, most recoiled at the thought of implementing such a policy. Some argued that restricting coal to homeowners was unfair and others (many from mining districts) worried over the potential impact on miners' wages. While some called for Beveridge's resignation from the Board of Trade, he doggedly hung on and took his cause to the media, stating that, like food rationing, the plan would actually ensure fair shares. But the original 'Beveridge Plan' was soon dropped.[7]

While working out the intricacies of a coal-rationing plan in 1942, Beveridge was also leading a committee that carried out investigations and deliberated over the issue of social insurance. The recommendations that flowed out of this process laid the foundations of the post-war welfare state, yet it was not certain at the outset that the Social Insurance Committee's work would ever see the light of day, let alone have any significant influence on government or social behaviour. Indeed, Sir William was known in governmental circles as having an unbending personality, and his placement on the committee may well have been a political tactic designed to sideline the irascible civil servant. Beveridge was initially upset when he learned of his appointment to the committee, which he saw as a 'kicking upstairs', placing him out of the way, on inconsequential research.[8]

But, within six months of work, it became clear that Sir William would not be quieted. Word soon got out that the committee was taking on such controversial questions that the government became worried, and Sir William was informed that the other civil servants on the committee were now only advisers who could not officially endorse any recommendations that resulted. The government washed its hands of the whole affair; henceforth, the committee's work was entirely Beveridge's.

Still, Beveridge's Social Insurance Committee carried out its investigations during the most dismal period of the war, and though many in government wished to tamp down the potentially revolutionary ideas bandied about by Beveridge, others saw the committee as a potential panacea for waning wartime morale. In fact, hoping for the maximum public effect, the Ministry of Information suggested that the committee's work be marketed as the 'Beveridge Plan' rather than its singularly uninspiring official title, Command Paper (Cmd) 6404.

Sir William himself also did his own marketing before the official rollout in December 1942. He appeared on the BBC's popular discussion programme, *Brains Trust* (the predecessor of today's *Any Questions?*), gave interviews about his work and wrote articles for various newspapers such as the Liberal *News Chronicle* (which Irene Grant, Edie Rutherford and Natalie Tanner all read) and *The Times*. While the public became more hopeful of the possibility of significant social insurance reform, the government became more wary that Beveridge was fomenting nothing short of revolutionary change. This was especially true after a journalist for the right-wing *Daily Telegraph* baited Sir William in November 1942 into agreeing that the implementation of his proposals would 'take the country half way to Moscow'.[9]

It was this fear of change that postponed the official unveiling of the command paper on the committee's work. Lord Privy Seal, Sir Stafford Cripps (the unsuccessful missionary offering the promise of independence to India earlier in 1942) wrote to a friend that the report was completed in October, but that it had not been released because the Cabinet thought it 'too revolutionary'.[10] Indeed, one of Beveridge's assistants wrote that the 'atmosphere' in official circles at the time was 'unpleasant' towards Beveridge and his plan.[11] Soon, Parliament and the press were abuzz with allegations of official suppression of the report.

On 1 December, however, the long-awaited 'Social Insurance and Allied Services – Report by Sir William Beveridge' was finally released to the public.

The plan was an instant popular success. When Sir William went on the BBC the day after his report was published, nearly 40 per cent of the British listening audience (more than 11.5 million) tuned in. Tommy Handley, the frontman for the popular comedy *ITMA*, was on the air a few days later joking about the new plan, calling it 'Gone with the Want' and, ever the artful schemer, conjuring up ways to get the best benefit for himself.[12] Within two weeks of the report's publication, a Gallup poll reported that 95 per cent of people surveyed had heard of the report and nine out of ten believed the government should adopt its proposals.

As the poll suggests, not all were enthusiastic about the plan. Edie Rutherford immediately cast it aside as a 'sop to the masses', while Mrs B, a tenant living with Helen Mitchell, nearly swooned when she heard the broadcast. 'Isn't the Beveridge Report dreadful,' she cried, 'we shall be just like Russia!' Always oppositional, Helen had to 'confess to a strong admiration of Russia' and a tendency to lean towards the political left. Yet, privately, she believed the plan to be at base 'defeatist – assuming universal misery and want'. In any case, tapping into her deep cynicism of all things political, Helen was convinced, 'If it's any good, it won't be implemented.' That was her husband's sentiment as well. During a 'violent discussion regarding Beveridge' on 6 December, he contended that the plan was a 'good thing'. The only problem, in his mind, was that it would never be properly implemented – the government and trades unions would 'whittle it down to nothing'.

Having mysteriously lost the use of her left arm, due, the doctors thought, to the violent concussions caused by the aerial bombings she had so often endured, Alice Bridges spent most of November in hospital dealing with various 'experimental' tests, treatments and recuperation. But when she finally returned home in early December, she was keen to continue the weekly discussion group she had been attending for over a year. The group debated the Beveridge Report and she 'flabbergasted' them with her view that the 'Conservatists' would have to adopt the plan if they wished to remain in power, for, she argued, the 'great Insurance Societies' would lead the post-war world. Natalie Tanner could not be so sure. She listened to Sir William's radio address and thought it 'sound' and full of 'pious aspirations', but ultimately, she thought, the government was too conservative ever to allow it to come to fruition. Furthermore, there was a fundamental flaw in Beveridge's plan: 'You can't build socialism on capitalist foundations,' Natalie argued.

Indeed, Beveridge did not propose dismantling capitalism, but rather he wished to simplify and humanize social insurance. Sir William's plan sought to rationalize and yoke together all earlier sources of social insurance under one umbrella. Previously, no less than seven government departments administered and paid out benefits to various populations such as injured war veterans, widows, orphans, old age pensioners, workers injured on the job, disabled civilians and the unemployed. The destitute fell back on demoralizing means-tested public assistance managed by local authority committees.

Beyond a single comprehensive system for social insurance, Beveridge also proposed paying out family allowances for each child born after the first, policies promoting full employment and the creation of a universal national health service, all paid for by the national exchequer. The system was to be universal and contributory: every individual and each employer, as well as the state, chipped in a third towards the benefits. The benefits were designed to provide a minimum – but supposedly decent – level of subsistence below which no one could fall and upon which to build for those able to save or pay for services beyond those offered under the official scheme. The basic rate was 40 shillings a week for each adult, which other benefits, such as family allowances, could top up. (40 shillings = £2/week or £112/year, was a lower working-class income. £250/year is generally considered the lower limit of a middle-class income at the time.)

Newspapers personalized the plan and devised scenarios illustrating how people's lives would improve if the 'cradle to grave' benefits in the plan were adopted. The *Daily Mirror*, for instance, carried an article on 'How to be born, bred and buried by Beveridge'. The readership of the *Daily Herald* learned about 'Life in Beveridge Britain' through a fictional working-class family. The story fast-forwarded to the 1960s, when the matriarch of the family, Mary Johnson, told her grandchildren grim tales of life before Beveridge. 'There wasn't any Social Security plan,' she explained to the children, 'people often hadn't the barest necessities of life, and if you had a baby you never knew whether you would be able to feed it properly.'[13]

Sir William played a significant role in shaping the symbolic power of his plan in the minds of the people. Throughout 1942, whenever he went on the air, wrote a newspaper column or gave an interview, he stressed his intention to resolve the mistakes of the past and create a better world in the future. He talked about 'equality of sacrifice' and his hope to eradicate poverty.[14] He propounded the possibility of the new system to foster national unity and social harmony in peacetime – to heal the old wounds of the inter-war period. He mobilized what the public already believed was the power of war – of the People's War in particular – to change society and governmental administration radically.

Change was already afoot: although more myth than reality, people nonetheless believed that the war was breaking down the barriers between the classes. The government was already making significant inroads in directing people's lives and labour, and if they could find millions to carry out war, why not spend millions to make the lives of Britons better? War, Sir William said, was 'abolishing landmarks of every kind'. There was no better time for change, and radical change at that. 'A revolutionary moment in the world's history is a time for revolutions, not for patching,' he argued.[15] The plan was the physical, printed manifestation of the hope for an equitable People's Peace. According to Quintin Hogg, a Conservative MP who supported the plan, it was not simply an official government paper, but rather a symbol, 'a flag to nail to the mast . . . a rallying point for men of goodwill'.[16]

In this 'revolutionary moment', Beveridge didn't want simply to tweak the already existing schemes that had proven wholly inadequate before the war. Sir William wanted to dismantle the demoralizing public assistance of the past; he believed it was a system that encouraged idleness and discouraged thrift in order to be paid benefit or that tore families and neighbourhoods apart by the hated means test.

Under the 'dole' and the means test, officials pried into the lives of the poor who needed government assistance. They visited homes, assessed the worth of property they found there (such as furniture, crockery and ornaments) and the worth of the resident workers to decide whether or not the family would receive benefit, and if so, the level of that assistance. The means test was a nasty and hurtful cost-saving measure that made sure individuals were absolutely destitute before benefits were paid. Many were too ashamed to take the assistance, as Alice Bridges remembered. Though her father was out of work much of the time when she was growing up, he refused to accept government money: 'His pride wouldn't let him,' she explained. The result was a deep poverty, softened only by her mother's determination to keep her children clothed and fed as best she could. In Irene Grant's eyes, the elimination of such a degrading system could only make people's lives better.

Sir William's plan would revolutionize, rationalize and humanize the system in order to slay what he called the five 'giants' that threatened to destroy Britons' happiness, health and freedom in the post-war world: the giants of want, disease, squalor, idleness and ignorance.[17] Furthermore, it would ensure the right of all citizens to an adequate income while also encouraging privacy, independence and thrift. In other words, individuals could be assured a basic minimum of security upon which they could build a better life.

As some, such as Natalie Tanner and the Mitchells, feared, many in the government saw the plan as too radical, and official resistance was unmistakable. Although hopeful for the change, many were also cynical about the government's commitment to the plan.

The legacy of the Great War was certainly no source of comfort; few who remembered that war's broken promises were willing to be burned once again by high ideals and impotent action. Irene Grant praised Sir William for his 'grand words' and was drawn by his ideas to 'Work as u [sic] never worked before for *your land, your industries*, your good time to come, *your material security*, for common ownership is here; no more dole – etc etc.' Still, '*Words mean nothing* if we see nothing done,' she told M-O.

Despite the scepticism engendered by past betrayals of the popular faith, the Beveridge Plan stirred up a great deal of hope when it was released. Irene Grant, ageing and hindered by declining health, was especially hopeful that old age pensioners' benefit would increase in order to allow some modicum of independence in old age. Nella Last was captivated by Beveridge's BBC speech on 2 December – not since she first heard a voice over the radio, she confessed to M-O, was she so interested in what anyone had to say. Listening to the broadcast, she began to feel 'more hopeful about the "brave new world" now, and . . . feel a *real* effort will be made to grasp the different angles of the many problems'. What intrigued her the most, however, was the fact that Beveridge had considered the welfare and position of women.

Sir William was careful to include housewives in his plan, as he believed that these women were doing work of national importance during the war and would continue to do so in peacetime. Furthermore, since his system was to be comprehensive and all-inclusive, provisions had to be made to include individuals who had 'different ways of life', such as those who did contract work, those unable to work due to age or infirmity, or housewives who rendered 'vital unpaid services'. Benefits for housewives included maternity grants, retirement pensions and provisions in the case of widowhood or 'marital separation'.[18] A woman would also receive benefits if her husband was disabled or unemployed and she herself were not gainfully employed. On the other hand, married women who were gainfully employed received lower unemployment and disability benefits, based on Beveridge's assumption that their husbands supported them. Still, women's magazines buzzed with excitement at the explicit provisions given them as mothers and housewives in the plan.

Beveridge 'recognizes women', *Woman's Own* magazine enthused, 'with their contribution to the national well-being as equals and partners of men', and the magazine pointed out that the plan formally acknowledged women's place as citizens.[19] *Good Housekeeping* called the report a 'Charter for Women' and noted enthusiastically how,

> The financial consideration of motherhood – the new status and rights of housewives – the free medical treatment even for those "not gainfully employed" – all these suggestions give the housewife's position a dignity it has never before possessed.[20]

The dignity of housewifery aside, Nella was thankful that someone had finally recognized the financial precariousness of married women's position and had proposed something to rectify it.

If her husband Will died, under the existing widow's pension scheme, Nella reckoned she would be entitled to only 10 shillings a week (about £28 a year – Seebohm

Rowntree's studies of poverty in York in 1936 postulated that a woman required nearly 23 shillings a week on which to live on her own). She had little savings of her own and Will didn't believe in insurance. She had managed to convince him to take out a meagre £200 policy, but that would soon expire. If her sons did not take her in, she would become destitute. But with Beveridge, she would receive 40 shillings a week (roughly £112 per year), plus free medical services.

Perhaps the best-received aspect of the plan was the provision of universal national health care. Many women were not covered under the existing insurance schemes before the war. Nella, for example, did not have health insurance. When she fell ill and required an operation in the 1930s, she recalled the 'bitter struggle' to survive due to the costs. Health insurance was available for contributing workers before the war through the National Health Insurance scheme, inaugurated in 1911, but this did not cover married women, children or the long-term unemployed.

Friendly societies helped fill in the gaps through contributions to help their members pay for medical care, while insurance companies also offered health care options. In some districts, community members and employers contributed to hospitals in order to gain access to care. Edie Rutherford's Sheffield and Alice Bridges' Birmingham had strong contributory schemes of this nature, which allowed people both community governance of and access to multiple hospitals in the area. Although it is unclear whether she contributed to them, it nonetheless seems likely that Irene Grant and her family may have received care at one of the thriving schemes providing Tynesiders access to a local hospital, such as Newcastle's Royal Victoria or Sunderland's

Royal Infirmary. Finally, voluntary and local authorities could also help poor and deserving individuals
gain health care. The system was cobbled together,
poorly coordinated and based on the ability to pay for
services. Beveridge hoped to change all of this through
his comprehensive National Health Service.

Irene Grant thought such a service would be a huge
improvement on the current system. People waited
'hours and hours in hospital, even when they only need
a ¼ hour's attention – and they sit on horrid hard cold
seats'. Furthermore, she complained, paying patients
received the lion's share of doctors' attention, leaving
others in the lurch. Nonetheless, despite a great deal of
popular support, in the months following the publication of the Beveridge Report it seemed highly unlikely
that any of the recommendations would ever come
to fruition. The Liberal and Labour parties both came
out in favour of the plan, but the government was
extremely reluctant to support it, and the BBC placed a
moratorium on discussion of the plan until Parliament
met in February 1943.

By February, many felt that the government was
purposely sidelining the issue. When Parliament
finally opened the debate on 16 February, the Cabinet
was given specific instructions by Churchill – gravely
ill but simultaneously coping with Gandhi's hunger-
strike – to make it clear that the decision to implement
Beveridge's proposals would not occur until after a
new government was elected when the war ended.
The ministers charged to relay this message tact-
lessly revealed their true feelings about the report
when they stood up in the House. The Chancellor of
the Exchequer, Kingsley Wood, argued the financial
shortcomings of the plan with such relish that the

depth of government resistance towards reform was patently clear.

Peter Mitchell was furious at the government's resistance to the report, but Helen could barely muster concern. Since Beveridge went public in December, she had been coping with the Bs, tenants that Peter had arranged to occupy half of their house since September. Although it meant some extra work – Helen had to whitewash the walls since the place looked like a 'slum dwelling' – she initially enjoyed the company. Helen and Mrs B worked out a schedule for the use of the kitchen and thus avoided 'stepping on each others' toes'. Helen was happy that the couple seemed to be 'considerate people' who were quiet and respectful of her space. By early November, she reported, 'They continue to be pleasant tenants, and I prefer them here than to be alone.'

Soon, however, she had tired of the Bs. On 16 November, Helen felt a 'nervous wreck' because the Bs' daughter, Anne, flitted around the house all day, raising a racket. The schoolchildren behind her home screamed and carried on for most of the day, and it didn't help that Helen's housekeeper, Cripps, added to the chaos by 'violently' cleaning the house from 9 a.m. to 4 p.m. After Cripps finally made her exit for the day, Helen took a sleeping pill and flopped into bed early.

The general din of the tenants and other annoyances continued to ratchet up through the holiday season until Anne began nightly screaming fits in mid-December. Anne was terrified by the face of a 'nasty man' she claimed to see floating about the nursery. 'Suppose ghosts are inevitable in these foul Elizabethan houses,' Mitchell huffed. 'Anyway, life is going to be impossible with the child; shall become neurotic from constant noise.'

Lack of sleep plagued Helen until finally, she fell ill with bronchitis. She went to hospital, where the doctor informed her that in addition to the poor state of her lungs, her heart was not strong. The doctor told her she 'mustn't do any hard work, quiet and rest indicated and no worries!' She stifled a sarcastic chuckle, thinking 'Doctors are innocent folk!' Avoiding chores and finding peace was a laugh, but Helen did take to her bed for several weeks in an effort to rebuild her strength. The pity of it, she thought, was that the rest only ensured that she would resume her daily round, which amounted to cooking breakfast for her family (when home) and tenants, washing up, doing housework and starting all over for lunch and dinner. 'Ridiculous life', she grumbled.

Life became a little more bearable for Helen in early March when the Bs finally departed. Even her son, William, was in a good mood when he came home at the end of the month because he'd received a commission and was now an officer. Nonetheless, as she read about the debates raging in Parliament over the Beveridge Report and listened to the war news, Helen couldn't help wonder whether the government was now committed to prolonging the war in order to avoid implementing the now wildly popular report.

In the weeks surrounding the debate, several pro-Beveridge parties, demanding its immediate implementation, won stunning by-election victories against the government in the spring of 1943. Mainstream parliamentary parties, such as Labour, the Conservatives and the Liberals, did not contest seats during the war; other parties, however, did not recognize this political 'truce'. One of those parties was Common Wealth, formed when a non-political pressure group called the 1941 Committee, headed by J.B. Priestley, merged with Sir Richard Acland's Forward March Movement in 1942.

Sir Acland was a wealthy aristocrat and former Liberal MP who was an earnest supporter of social, but bloodless, revolution. Many in the House of Commons laughed at his invectives, but he had an oratorical appeal that could pack halls across the country, fuelled by what an admirer once described as 'the burning sincerity of his enthusiasm, his obvious joy . . . in his "discovery" of socialism'. In his fiery speeches, he castigated the old order and called for a 'New Jerusalem' of classless equality.[21] Moreover, Acland was not simply a man of words: to demonstrate the strength of his convictions, he handed over his hereditary estates in Devon to the National Trust in 1943.

In addition to the creation of a classless society, Acland's party (Priestley, who had little time for organized politics, left in the autumn of 1942) advocated common ownership of essential land and resources, democratic reform such as proportional representation, and 'moral' political behaviour, including an end to backstairs diplomacy and lying to the public. These measures politically embodied Irene Grant's vision of socialism, and she followed the party with great interest, showering the highest praise on Acland, especially when he put his words into action and handed his lands over to the National Trust. It wasn't Acland's generous gift to the National Trust, nor Common Wealth's commitment to common ownership or moral political behaviour, however, that helped them gain seats in Parliament, but rather the party's insistence that the Beveridge Report be implemented immediately and in full.

On 21 March, Churchill finally responded to the growing public anger over the government's handling of the Beveridge Report. In a lengthy speech, he reminded his audience that he had 'framed' the first unemployment insurance scheme and had introduced 'my friend' Sir William Beveridge to 'public service' thirty-five years before (thereby hoping to associate himself with social reform). But this was the only explicit mention of Beveridge, and the Prime Minister never mentioned Beveridge's Plan by name. Instead, he promised what he called a 'Four Years' Plan' designed to 'maintain and progressively improve [Britons'] standards of life and labour'.

Beveridge's influence did appear in the speech, however, as Churchill asserted that he and his ministers supported 'cradle to grave' insurance schemes, a National Health Service, measures to maintain employment, helping parents with the care of their children and improving education. Nonetheless, Churchill spoke more about the war and the international situation than these domestic concerns. He chastised those who believed, after the victories in North Africa, that the war was over and that post-war planning could commence. 'I am not able to share these sanguine hopes,' he informed his audience, 'and my earnest advice to you is to concentrate even more zealously upon the war effort, and if possible not to take your eye off the ball for even a moment.' Although he was willing to 'peer through the mists of the future' and talk about domestic issues that night, he made it clear that he did not wish to be pushed into making promises that he did not intend to keep. Churchill's Four Years' Plan never truly took shape in his speech, but rather, seemed an ambiguous vision of some undefined, uncertain future – certainly *not* a 'plan' like Beveridge's.

It was a reasonable and quite rational speech, informing the people of a long, hard road ahead: the Nazis must be defeated, then the Japanese, after which the international landscape needed to be shored up. Furthermore, he warned his listeners, 'There will be famine to take care of,' Europe and Asia would have to be rebuilt and attempts at constructing a lasting international peace must be made.[22] It was a typical, sobering Churchillian speech and did nothing to excite in the people hope for a promising post-war future. Despite his nod to a nebulous Four Years' Plan, the Prime Minister fooled few about his agenda. He was a bulldog with a bone – the war, and only the war, was his concern.

Irene Grant followed the political debates of 1943 closely, but she was also still actively fighting Tom over buying a home. In February of that year, Irene fell in love with a spacious home in a better neighbourhood. At every mention of the new home Tom argued vehemently against it. He tried every line of defence to dissuade Irene, but he could not dampen her enthusiasm. During one argument, her husband told her that she would regret the move once it was made, but she shot back,

> Tom, you hate change. At ninety you'd love your name in the papers as the old duck who lived in one spot for 90 years. I loathe this inconvenient hole.

The cost of the home was much higher than she had hoped, but Irene finally convinced Tom that they could afford it. However, when she thought all was settled, the deal fell through, and once more she and her daughters began house-hunting. Irene was devastated, but would not swerve from her mission to find a new home.

Taking time out of her schedule to catch Churchill's speech, Irene reported to M-O that she was convinced he was solely a war leader and she didn't trust him in the peace, since 'He's not for the People.' Still, she liked the speech and seemed to grasp at anything positive in it. Remembering her own abridged education, she was probably most attracted to his inclusion of education reform, in which he stated, 'No one who can take advantage of a higher education should be denied this chance.' Friends of Irene were less accepting of his speech, however, and thought that the Prime Minister made a poor showing and had even faked his illness because he did not want to face the issue.

Edie Rutherford made an informal poll of her new workmates for M-O and found that less than fifty per cent had tuned into the Prime Minister's speech. Those who did listen had 'expected something sensational', but were 'disappointed' because he said nothing that interested them. 'Can you believe that?' she wrote to M-O in disbelief. As for herself, Edie cheered Churchill. A successful outcome to the war was also her priority, and additionally she believed his Four Years' Plan had gone a good way to undermining communists who, she feared, were gaining support in the wake of the Beveridge Plan.

For most, however, Churchill's speech stuck a pin in the debate, deflating the growing hopes for a better peace, and a sorrowful disillusionment seemed to creep into society. Listening to Churchill that night, Nella Last sadly wondered whether talk of reform would have any real results; would it, she wrote in her diary, 'change people's minds, give them ideals, a new standard of "living" which will lift them and enable them to "lift others"? Or when the "shouting and the tumult dies" will things be "as they were"?'

CHAPTER NINE

DON'T LET'S BE
BEASTLY TO THE HUN

Edie Rutherford stood in her kitchen preparing tea, ruminating over the recent BBC news reports about RAF raids on Berlin. A number of bombers had been lost the previous evening – 5 September 1943. Echoes of Wynford Vaughan Thomas' BBC broadcast from a Lancaster bomber under heavy fire two nights earlier (replayed several times, on popular demand) danced relentlessly in and out of the fears she harboured over the lost airmen.

A knock at the door jolted Edie from her thoughts. As she opened the door, a young woman from a nearby flat thrust a telegram into her hand. Before Edie had a chance to read it, Ethel managed to muster a stammered, 'Mrs Rutherford, Henry's missing'. Edie drew Ethel in at once and wrapped her arms around the young woman, who broke down in sobs. Edie held her like this for some time, softly cursing 'this blasted war' as Ethel wept.

'He isn't dead,' Ethel kept repeating, 'he was home only last Wednesday.' Ethel looked at Edie and attempted a rational explanation, 'I'm sure he isn't dead ... He's alive somewhere and worrying because he knows I'll get this telegram to upset me.' Edie read the telegram. 'Regret to inform you your husband missing operations night Sept 5/6.' She felt as if her 'inside had fallen out': Henry was one of the missing airmen she had heard about only that morning; she could hardly believe it. Edie did her best to comfort Ethel, but, she confessed, it was difficult to know what to say.

Two days later, still reeling from the loss of Henry and the grief of Ethel, Edie was cheered by the arrival of a parcel from family in South Africa. The package was full of hard-to-find rationed treats: tea, sugar, choco-late and plump, juicy raisins. She set aside some for herself and Sid, then divided the gift into small pack-ets for friends and neighbours. Soon, the dark cloud of Ethel's recent loss began to recede to the edges of her heart. The sun shone and the weather was glorious; so was the news.

Over the six o'clock news that night, Edie learned that Italy had surrendered. Immediately, her mind sped to South Africa, where she knew her countrymen and women would be rejoicing, knowing that the release of South African troops, or 'Springboks', captured in fighting in North Africa must now be imminent. The Ethiopians, who had been ruthlessly bombed into submission by the Italians in 1936, also had much to rejoice, she reflected. The British 'on this island', however, took the news very 'soberly'. Indeed, she thought that the BBC made a 'rather pathetic attempt' to celebrate the victory. Helen Mitchell, on the other hand, thought the celebrations went a bit overboard. Her take on the BBC's coverage was 'cheap as usual' – she hated premature triumph, and the ceaseless playing of patriotic songs annoyed her. She was especially chafed by what she thought was jingoistic gloating by the BBC, knowing in her bones that something sinister must lurk just around the corner. Bad news had been so much a part of day-to-day life during the war that it took time, Edie explained to M-O, for many to accept that Italy had actually 'packed up'.

The road that led to Italy's capitulation was built earlier that year, after Allied troops had forced the Germans out of North Africa. Once ensconced in North Africa themselves, the Allies embarked on an invasion of Europe – through Sicily. Churchill believed that Italy was the 'soft underbelly' of the Axis in Europe and pushed his plan with the Americans.[1] It was not the 'second front' in the west for which Stalin had been calling ever since the Germans had attacked the Soviets in the summer of 1941, but it would eventually leach important resources from the Nazi war machine in the east, and it would prove integral in the downfall of Hitler's ally.

On 10 July 1943, Allied troops began the largest seaborne assault of the war – larger than the Normandy landings a year later, with much longer distances to overcome. Two weeks later, Mussolini fell from political power and was replaced by the king, who installed a new leader, former Commander-in-Chief in Ethiopia, Marshal Badoglio. Edie listened in and read the news with her usual piqued interest that summer, but the image became ever more vivid as she learned first-hand about conditions on the ground from her nephew who flew sorties for the RAF, ferrying injured soldiers – both Allied and Axis – to treatment in Africa. The rations in Sicily, he complained, were 'pommy' rations, not the generous issues he was used to in the Middle

East or South Africa. Luckily, he told Edie, the Sicilians were willing to trade bully beef for fresh fruit and eggs.

By the end of August, Sicily was comfortably in Allied hands, and on 8 September the new Italian government under Badoglio announced an armistice. Helen Mitchell noted in her diary that she was glad Italy was out of the war, for now, 'It [and its artistic, historic and religious treasures] would not be smashed to pieces.' But the battle for Italy was hardly over. German troops flooded in to shore up their erstwhile ally's defences, presenting a shocking and bloody resistance to British and American servicemen, who had expected a friendly reception by cowed Italians, when they attempted landings on mainland Italy on 9 August. Instead it took three weeks for the troops to reach the initial objective of Naples, less than forty miles up the western coast of Italy.

The Germans fell back in a measured retreat towards Rome, putting up a ferocious defence in the mountains south of the city. The Allies had expected to be in Rome by the end of October, but that triumphal entrance would have to wait another eight months, until the eve of the D-Day landings in June 1944. By November 1943, the usually optimistic Edie Rutherford sighed, 'I don't believe we'll ever reach Rome.' Churchill summed up the depressing stagnation that autumn and winter on the Italian peninsula as 'scandalous'.[2] Newspapers back home blamed the slow progress on the weather, but that was hardly convincing or comforting, as the Russians were advancing in their theatre.

While the Allies were establishing a bridgehead to Europe through Italy, and fighting their way north in 1943, Allied air raids on Germany also intensified. At the Casablanca conference in January of that year,

British and American leadership decided that Sicily would be the target for an Allied invasion of Europe. The Allies also resolved to bring about the

> . . . progressive destruction and dislocation of the German military, industrial and economic system and the undermining of the morale of the German people to a point where their capacity for armed resistance is fatally weakened.[3]

This translated into a large-scale bombing campaign against Germany, with Americans flying daylight raids on significant enemy installations while British flyers hit cities at night, a policy that Churchill referred to in the House of Commons as 'saturation'.[4] The campaign fuelled competition between the British and American air forces to wreak the most devastation on their foe – the competition in which Edie's neighbour, Henry, was lost over Berlin.

The RAF proved its aerial ascendancy in this deadly and terrifying war game, especially after the devastation wrought on the German port city of Hamburg in July and August 1943. Every other night in the last week of July, over 750 British bombers attacked the city with horrifying effect. On the night of the 27th, incendiary bombs whipped up hurricane force winds in the city that fed a firestorm, covering over six miles and reaching temperatures of 1,000 °C. Those in the path of the storm were suffocated to death before the fires incinerated them. Between 40,000 and 50,000 people were killed during the RAF's weeklong bombing campaign (code-named a sickeningly apt Operation Gomorrah) over the city.[5] *The Times* estimated that the operation was nearly 100 times more devastating than the Coventry raid in November 1940. In just four nights of bombing the RAF had exacted retribution for two-thirds of all British air raid fatalities.

Word of the 1943 bombing campaigns over Germany filtered back to Britain on a regular basis, in newspapers and over the air. Nella Last was horrified by the reports of aerial destruction. Since June 1942, her attention had been focused almost solely on setting up a Red Cross shop to raise funds for prisoners of war. By 1943, the work had become daunting, 'The shop is taking more time than I thought,' she confessed to M-O. The morning after a particularly hard day at the shop, Nella lingered in bed for some time, dreaming of her idea of 'heaven'; lying 'on a sunny beach' wallowing in 'books, oranges, grapes, thinly cut bread and lots of country butter on it, lots of milk for my food'. In her fantasy, she would 'let peace and quiet soak into me . . . no reminding myself I was a soldier, no hurried scramble round with a duster with an eye on the clock'.

Although she was 'dreadfully tired' most of the time, she fought through it because she believed in the shop's mission. Every shilling, every pound raised was a triumph, for she knew that '10/- means comfort to a poor forgotten man.' The dreadful tiredness of her efforts were rewarded in the Red Cross packages sent to prisoners of war across Europe and Asia, little packages of hope for a prisoner, of 'food to eat and the knowledge that someone is still thinking of him although he is shut away like a savage beast'. She thought of the death and destruction wrought in the air raids across Germany and declared that she 'could never work so hard for "bombs to drop on Berlin"'.

The Times reported the Hamburg attacks with a characteristic objectivity steeped in statistics that belied the true devastation, citing, for instance, the 2,300 pounds of bombs dropped on the city on 25 July and the pillar of smoke that rose four miles into the sky as a result. Nearly a week later, it was reported that the city was still alight, while bombers continued to hit targets that had so far escaped the wrath of the RAF – 'dropping bombs at the rate of more than 50 tons a minute'.[6] *The Times* focused overwhelmingly on the tactical significance of the bombings – the docks, the factories, the U-boat installation. Only later was the human tragedy finally revealed, when the paper reported that 'chaos' had ensued in the city; refugees were flooding towards Denmark, and panicked inhabitants were 'senselessly throwing furniture and other possessions through the windows, causing injuries to many persons who were rushing along the streets in search of shelter'.[7] For those individuals back in Britain who had experienced similar enemy onslaughts, such news reporting was unnecessary: the reality of the 'collateral damage' visited upon the citizens of these important targets could hardly be forgotten. Despite the statistics and attempted objectivity, the inevitable human impact underlying these actions was highly unnerving for Britons who themselves had braved enemy bombings.

According to a Gallup poll taken near the end of the worst of the Blitz in 1941, many people who never or rarely lived through bombings were the most keen to exact reprisals on the Germans, while those who actually suffered from the Blitz were less likely to do so. Having experienced air raids first-hand and having suffered great psychological trauma from them, Helen Mitchell understood, and felt deeply, the conflicts that the question evoked. As with so much else in her life, the bombing of German cities made her 'too miserable for words'. As she listened to the planes drone over her Kent home, Helen admitted that she 'loathed the RAF for what they were going to do', but she could not help but valorize them for their bravery in defending Britain (and thus thwarting German bombs from landing on her house). Still, she concluded that aerial bombing was 'despicably cowardly as a form of warfare' because more innocent people were victimized than the guilty were punished.

There were those, however, who did harbour vindictive feelings of righteous retribution, such as Alice Bridges, who was convinced that the war had demonstrated that *all* Germans were incapable of living peaceably, and therefore, 'It's time they were wiped out sufficiently to stop them becoming a menace.' Others, like Mitchell, were not so willing to tar all Germans with the same brush. Many considered there to be a difference between Nazis – who started the war, spread hatred and inflicted suffering and death – and the ordinary Germans who were apathetic victims of the Nazi regime and did not actively seek wholesale destruction. Irene Grant was happy to have 'Hitler and Company . . . torn limb to limb' for their war crimes, but she had difficulty assigning such a fate to the rest of Germany.

Nella Last believed that Germans were just like Britons – some were good and others evil. Wholesale punishment for all Germans could not be the answer, and Nella worried that bombs did not discriminate. 'If we could kill Nazi SS and Gestapo, I'd glory in the bombing and think it just retribution,' she reasoned. At the same time, she was deeply concerned for the 'innocent little children and frightened people who are as sick of war as we are', and who would necessarily become collateral victims of such reprisals.

As air raids over Germany heated up in 1943, the playwright, singer and songwriter Noël Coward added a satirical edge to the debate with his song, 'Don't Let's Be Beastly to the Hun'. His style was to sarcastically emulate those 'humanitarians' who were concerned about being too hard on the Germans or gathering them all in the Nazi camp. 'It was just those nasty Nazis who persuaded them to fight,' he sang, 'And their Beethoven and Bach are really far worse than their bite.' The BBC sought to ban the song, convinced that it was seditious, and afraid Coward's song might be interpreted by the public as pro-German. But that was going too far. It was clear from his tone, the rollicking melody and the content of the song that Coward was expressing the moral conundrum of fairly punishing the appropriate Germans without setting the stage for a future war, as so many felt the terms to end the First World War had done. In every verse, he alluded to failures of the Treaty of Versailles and the inter-war period – allowing the Germans to rebuild their fleet and occupy the Rhineland with impunity, for instance – and linked them to the current conflict. Tongue-in-cheek, he offered to be nice to the Germans, but also to 'remind them that "sterilization" *simply* isn't done'. As the melody lightly rolled along, Coward jokingly encouraged making 'them feel swell again' so they could 'bomb us all to hell again'. 'But don't', he gibed, 'let's be beastly to the Hun.'[8]

There were no clear solutions, and individuals struggled to find a judicious solution that would end the war quickly, while simultaneously harbouring an irresistible desire to lash out at the enemy who destroyed lives, homes and businesses with wild abandon. Irene Grant's attempt to wrestle the problem of bombing

German cities illustrates the complexities and contradictions felt by many in Britain. She admitted feeling 'all ways about' the issue and listed out her thoughts for M-O as they occurred to her. Her first impulse was that massive bombing of 'the brutes' would end the war sooner and thus, ultimately, save lives on both sides. Yet, she could not ignore 'the horrors and miseries' that must come with such action. Furthermore, the damage that committing such 'savagery' wrought upon the young British bombers themselves was particularly disturbing.

It was a common feeling, with which many of the women agreed. Both Edie Rutherford and Natalie Tanner felt the raids were ineffective at undermining German morale, and they considered the impact on the British air crews a horrific experience that would most likely inhibit their ability to become useful members of society after the war. Others, with more millenarian predilections accepted the bombings – and sometimes revelled in them, viewing them as necessary for the second coming of Christ – but, despite their part in God's grand plan, felt that the fighters would have to account for such sins in the final reckoning.

After pondering the miseries attendant on both sides, Grant felt the sharp stab of vindictiveness and impulsively wrote 'Serves Germans right!!' Struggling with the issue, she then pulled back, recognized her generalization and, perhaps feeling embarrassed by it, admitted that one couldn't tar all Germans with the Nazi brush. She even noted that many Germans themselves had been victimized by the Nazis. Yet, once again, Irene was overcome by the feeling that it was 'better [to] wipe Germans out than decent peace-loving folks'. Then, she turned back to the British bombers themselves and, like Rutherford who noted losses regularly, confessed that her 'heart misses a beat' every time she learned of missing and downed RAF fighters. In the end, she felt no nearer to finding an answer to the problem and threw her hands in the air, telling M-O she didn't know what to think, and cursing 'the wickedness and cruelty' that made such dreadful contemplation necessary.

The complex moral questions surrounding the destruction wrought upon the German people by their own 'brave lads' continued to exercise many Britons until the end of the war, and indeed was exacerbated by the atomic bombs released in August 1945 to end the war with Japan. Still, in the summer and autumn of 1943, everyday life went on.

Edie Rutherford took her yearly holiday to Bakewell during the week that the RAF burned Hamburg. Helen Mitchell flitted from friend to friend, trying to escape the never-ending grind of housework and the evil drone of aircraft overhead at home in Kent, relishing in the delirious 'pre-war life' of her friends' tidy maids and refreshing mid-afternoon cocktails, all the while lazily dreaming of a better life from the comfort of lawn chairs and gently swinging hammocks. Nella Last fretted over Cliff's latest deployment and tried to negotiate the politics of the local WVS. Natalie Tanner's son was home from school until mid-September, so the two spent much time together, as they always did on his vacations: at movies in town, train spotting (his favourite activity) and leisurely exploring north-east England. Meanwhile, Irene Grant was moving into her new home, and enjoying the joys and frustrations of home ownership. And, characteristically, Alice Bridges was deeply involved in dance hall intrigue: teaching new 'chappies' the tango and precariously balancing her signature risqué flirtation with a paradoxically confident moral rectitude.

Ensconced in their own personal lives, the women also watched the international and domestic events closely. Imperial problems were manifest, and debates over both significant and trifling domestic issues abounded. Many, for instance, were intrigued that autumn with the Prime Minister's crusade to establish Basic English across the globe.

Developed in the 1920s and early 1930s, Basic English was supposed to improve international relations through a commonly understood, and easy to learn, method of communication; it pared the English language down to just under 1,000 of the most necessary words, which could, theoretically, describe anything. An altercation between Edie Rutherford and an Esperantist (one who expounded a different form of international communication) illustrates the core of the Basic English debate: '[the Esperantist] said in Basic English I cannot be called a wife, but a married woman.' Unruffled, Rutherford replied, 'that was OK by me, "kept woman" would be all I'd baulk at, having worked most of my married life!' 'Then you can't say eyebrows, but hairy arches above the eyes,' the Esperantist shot back. 'Well . . . I'd know what was meant and that is all Basic English intends I suppose,' Edie retorted.

That is indeed what Basic English was supposed to do. But there was more to it, and Rutherford astutely perceived the underlying significance of the movement. She told M-O, 'Churchill is artful. He knows what he is doing.' 'If we can get Basic English established over the face of the earth,' Edie argued, 'it will be a grand thing for all'. Edie saw Basic English as a manoeuvre to assure the predominance of the English language across the globe, and hence the hegemony of English-speaking nations. Furthermore, Churchill believed that the special relationship between Britain and the US was effectively built upon a common language. If this ability to understand each other (if only in a limited fashion!) could be extended, the implications for peace, Churchill stressed, were astounding. Noble and crafty as were his intentions, many nonetheless had a good laugh at the Prime Minister's expense.

In November 1943, the issue of Basic English came up in Parliament. Churchill was asked jokingly if the BBC would be required to adopt the new standard, or if they would continue with 'Basic BBC'. Willie Gallacher, Scottish Communist MP, asked the Prime Minister, 'Would the Right Honourable Gentleman consider introducing Basic Scottish?'[9]

Even the American President, Roosevelt had his own fun with Basic English. When Churchill approached him with the idea, he replied, 'I wonder what the course of history would have been if in May 1940 you had been able to offer the British people only "blood, work, eye water and face water," which is the best I understand that Basic English can do with five famous words.'[10] Churchill was miffed by the playful banter surrounding his pet project. To those in Parliament who asked similar questions about the impact upon the beauty and emotional depth of the language, he responded, 'Basic English is not intended for use among English-speaking people but to enable a much larger body of people who do not have the good fortune to know the English language to participate more easily in our society.' Those who did not see that Basic English was not a 'substitute for the English language' were, he stressed with a rhetorical flourish unimaginable within the corpus of Basic English, 'quite purblind'.[11]

Basic English sparked a bitter debate between Helen Mitchell and her husband, Peter. He could see the benefits of its usage, but she hated it. The one thing they could agree on that night was another issue that came up in Parliament that cycle: something that struck closer to home. Earlier that year, a judge in Oxford had ruled that the savings laid aside from a woman's housekeeping money were, in fact, her husband's property. In this case, a jilted husband claimed, and received, the £103 his wife had saved over the course of their marriage. The woman in question, Mrs Blackwell, had put aside the excesses of the housekeeping money her husband had given her over the years, as well as earnings from taking in lodgers, in a Co-operative Society savings account. The judge ruled that Mr Blackwell was entitled not only to the housekeeping money (which had come from his earnings), but also to the savings accumulated from the profits his wife made in her boarding business, since he had paid for and provided the home.

The case, and the unsuccessful court appeal of the wife, sparked a firestorm of anger from married women across the country. Dr Edith Summerskill, MP, claimed that she had never received such 'a deluge of correspondence' over any other issue raised in Parliament. The overwhelming message from this correspondence was that the judge, and the legal system that upheld his decision, made marriage 'a mockery': housekeeping money and the home should be shared, they argued, and urged the government to make explicit changes to the law.[12] Indeed, The Married Women's Property Act of 1882 had ensured that a married woman's wages were hers alone – not her husband's, as had been the law until that point. Still, *Blackwell v. Blackwell* revealed an obvious loophole that angered many women, includ- ing Edie Rutherford and Helen Mitchell.

Helen reported that even her husband, Peter, felt the ruling 'a bit thick'. Household expenses – from rent to food to paying domestic servants – were often paid out of the husband's pocket, but from the woman's hand. Most women managed household matters with what- ever money their husbands gave them and felt it their right to keep any money they managed to save. Nella Last was proud of her domestic management and skill in saving, and announced to M-O that despite the fact that she had not once asked for a rise in her housekeep- ing since the war began, she nevertheless was able to save. There wasn't much left, though; she complained,

> I've often wished I had a little more money – to travel,
> to have good holidays and not to always plan – to buy
> a new hat because I liked it and not because I needed it.

The root of the problem lay in the fact that full-time housewives did not earn wages, a fact that Edith Summerskill lobbied strongly against; to mitigate this problem, she and her Married Women's Association argued that wives should be paid for their work in the home. William Beveridge disagreed with Summerskill on this point, but nonetheless recognized the precari- ousness of women's financial security in his 1942 report and therefore suggested that housewives be insured under his schemes. While such a scheme would help housewives if they became widows or if their husbands were unable to work, it did not change the fact that much of their independence was nonetheless often subject to the whim of their husbands.

For Natalie Tanner, this fact was no problem, as Hugh seemed very generous with his earnings. At least from January 1943, Edie Rutherford earned her own wages; otherwise, it seems she and Sid had a financial agreement that rarely chafed Edie's sensibilities. Irene Grant and her husband, Tom, also enjoyed similar congeniality, while Alice Bridges made her own money through seamstressing. But for Nella Last and especially Helen Mitchell, the financial constraints of housewifery were palpable.

If Helen's husband thought the result of the Blackwell case 'a bit thick', it was also a bit ironic, because Helen felt Peter never gave her enough housekeeping in the first place. Indeed, from her perspective she had little property or savings of her own, beyond a piano, which she often played in order to recapture some semblance of peace and sanity. If she had wanted to leave her unhappy marriage, it was painfully clear that she had nothing and would, therefore, be destitute if she struck out on her own. And, after the ruling in the Blackwell case, in the event that she actually had been able to save something, it would obviously be returned to Peter if she left him.

The furore over the case lasted until November 1943, but then soon ebbed away. The Blackwell decision stood, and beyond a few moments of levity in the House now and again (when a similar issue came up in 1951, members laughed it off, saying that the 'supposed' problem of women's inequality had gone so far that men were in danger of becoming women's 'chattel'), little would be done to resolve the issue subsequently.[13]

Not long after the Blackwell case faded from the newspapers and parliamentary debate, a new political controversy sparked indignation and anger across British society. In late November, the Home Secretary,

Herbert Morrison released Britain's most infamous Fascist couple from prison. Sir Oswald Mosley, the leader of the British Union of Fascists (BUF, renamed BU in 1939), and his wife, Diana, had been thrown in jail three years earlier because of suspicions of the BU's Nazi sympathies. Indeed, the couple had strong ties to the highest echelons of Nazi power, including the Führer himself. The two had been married in Joseph Goebbels' drawing room in the presence of Hitler, and Diana's sister, Unity, spent much time in Hitler's entourage before the outbreak of war. (When Unity learned of war in 1939, she attempted suicide, but failed, suffering instead severe brain damage.) Mosley's fascist union – attracting perhaps 9,000 members by the beginning of the war – had stirred up violence and hate in pre-war Britain, but never gained the political power it craved.

Nonetheless, once the German war machine began rolling in earnest after Dunkirk, the BU came under close scrutiny for its likely fifth column tendencies and its obvious links to the Nazi Party. By July 1940, when the BU was officially shut down by the government, the authorities netted over 700 BU members, most of whom were interned on the Isle of Man. For fear that he might stir up rebellion amongst the internees, however, Sir Oswald was kept at Brixton, while his wife spent her days in Holloway. But by 1942, Sir Oswald and Lady Diana were doing time together. Tom Mitford, Diana's brother, had successfully lobbied Winston Churchill (on the strength of Mitford's relation to Churchill's wife, Clementine, who was a cousin of Mitford) to allow the Fascist couple to live together. The two were given a home in the grounds of Holloway Prison, complete with a little vegetable plot and their very own servants – fellow prisoners – to wait on them.

If this arrangement was too much for the British public, the Home Secretary's decision to release the couple conditionally in November 1943 seemed entirely unacceptable. Morrison defended his actions, stating that Mosley was gravely sick, suffering from thrombophlebitis (blood clotting and inflammation of the walls of veins). More than the disapprobation of the British public, Morrison feared that Mosley's death while in custody would most certainly create a martyr – a possibility the Home Secretary did not wish to face.

Demonstrations protesting at Mosley's release erupted around the metropolis and across the country that November, culminating in a mass protest in Trafalgar Square that attracted thousands. Some MPs, such as Sir Richard Acland of the Common Wealth Party, swore publicly that they would support a vote of no confidence against the government over the issue. This threat did not come to fruition; however, certain members did register their displeasure with the Home Secretary's decision in the House. The MP for Finsbury, Reverend George Woods, moved to tell the King that the House, 'humbly regret the decision of Your Majesty's advisers to release Sir Oswald Mosley, which is calculated to retard the war effort and lead to misunderstanding at home and abroad'.[14]

To Helen Mitchell, who encountered an angry mob protesting at the Mosleys release in London, however, the entire controversy was rather surprising. 'Seems a lot of fuss about nothing. Shouldn't have thought he mattered,' she told M-O. Natalie Tanner hated Defence Regulation 18B, which sent Mosley and his Fascist friends to jail in 1940, for its blanket repression of anyone deemed an enemy of the state and its suspension of habeas corpus, yet she found Mosley thoroughly repugnant. Still, she thought, the street demonstrations over his release were less ideological and more a 'Roman Holiday' because boredom was the pervasive mood in the autumn of 1943.

For her part, Irene Grant didn't care if Mosley walked free; she was certain that the British people would censure Mosley on their own, 'Let him and pals get on soap boxes if they dare!' Irene exclaimed. Of course, Sir Oswald's release did not allow him such freedom of expression. He was under a strict gag order – he could not publish any statements, give interviews to reporters or otherwise speak publicly. Furthermore, he was not allowed outside a 7-mile radius from his home. Despite the Home Secretary's concerns over his health, Mosley made it through the war and died in 1980.

Edie Rutherford was less concerned that the old Fascist was let out to spew his hate another day than about the humanitarian crisis erupting in the empire that autumn. One year earlier, a massive cyclone had struck East Bengal (today's Bangladesh), decimating the rice crop for forty miles inland. Rice slated to be sown for that winter's crop had been eaten by the peasants, and by May 1943, a severe crisis was taking shape. Burma – India's largest source of rice – was in Japanese hands, and too much rice had been shipped to British troops. By mid-October, more than 2,000 people a month were dying in Calcutta alone. The streets of the city were littered with dead and starving skeletons, while birds of prey circled above. 'What a queer race we are,' Rutherford reflected to M-O:

Thousands can die of starvation in Bengal . . . and as far as one can see, no one gives a damn. A puppet and pipsqueak like Mosley is moved from prison to some secret place (where you bet he'll be well watched) and the protests are so public and emphatic that even the BBC has to mention them in their news.

Initially, the Secretary of State for India, Leo Amery, was unconcerned about the growing numbers of starving Indians (in his view, India was 'overpopulated' anyway), but the mounting crisis soon became a public relations nightmare and also threatened to destabilize India with the Japanese enemy at the gates. Help began to pour in that autumn, and an inquiry into the famine was launched in the summer of 1944. It was too little too late: by that time at least 1.5 million people had perished.

Nearly one year after Sir William Beveridge went to the people with his plan to slay the five giants of want, ignorance, idleness, disease and squalor, Churchill's government had done little to implement any of his ideas. Indeed, many believed that Churchill had effectively scotched the whole idea. Although he had gone to the people in a BBC broadcast in March of 1943 with his Four Years' Plan, it was clear he resented being strong-armed into focusing on reconstruction policy, considering, he said, 'We had nothing like won the war. People were always getting ahead of the events.' [15]

Furthermore, the man of the hour, Beveridge himself, had been ousted from official participation in bringing his plan to fruition. After the glowing reception of his report, he had hoped to be allowed to carry out further investigations – especially on the possibility of full employment – but no invitation to do so was forthcoming. Sidelined from official channels of government,

Sir William therefore embarked on his own personal investigations with the help of private funds put up by publisher Edward Hulton.

When Beveridge appeared on the BBC panel discussion programme *Brains Trust* in September 1943, his frustration with the government was palpable. While the panel argued that the people should 'fight with a unity of purpose for the very things in England that they want in England,' Sir William pointed out that 'the people who lead' must also effectively plan and organize for the future. When, later in the programme, a question was posed regarding the government's position on a National Health Service, Beveridge stuttered, 'I can't answer this question because I don't know what the government's proposals are – er – at all.' The entire panel that day seemed frustrated with the lack of concern exhibited in government circles over Beveridge's proposals. In fact, the final word on the subject was a slightly paranoid and thoroughly humorous jab at the government. To the presenter's summation of the debate, 'We're not really in a position to issue a statement because the government's position is not yet known,' Julian Huxley, biologist and popular regular on the programme, nervously responded, 'They aren't here, are they? The government?' The audience roared with laughter.[16]

The frustration and anger which that laughter thinly disguised eventually pressured Churchill into action. On 12 November 1943, he created a new ministry focused on reconstruction, with the popular Minister of Food, Lord Woolton, at its head. At last, it seemed, something might be done to make a better future. Still, scepticism regarding Churchill's true motives was never fully erased. As Irene Grant confided to M-O, 'I don't trust him in the peace.'

CHAPTER TEN

CAN YOU BEAT THAT?

On a clear and frosty February morning in 1944, a middle-aged woman stood before a magistrate in Barnsley, South Yorkshire, accused of seriously defrauding a local colliery. Nicknamed 'Lady Bountiful' by the press for her free-spending ways, Dorothy Elliott had almost got away with an elaborate scheme embezzling thousands from her employers, the Wombwell Colliery Company and Wombwell Coking Company. The chairman of the colliery, who also happened to be a director at the bank, by chance discovered Elliott's misdeeds in a bank meeting at which he learned of an overdraft that had been granted to the colliery. Believing his company was financially sound, he was 'surprised and horrified' at the discovery and immediately launched an investigation into the matter.[1]

The trail soon led to Dorothy Elliott, a secretary who had worked for the companies in various capacities for nearly thirty years. As secretary (a position she had held for over a decade), she was responsible for managing both the colliery and coking companies' bank accounts, handling payments and deposits. The investigators soon learned that Miss Elliott – who made

£500 a year – was notorious for her odd and extravagant spending habits around town, such as paying out huge sums (£1,100 in one instance) in £1 notes. Since customers often paid for their coal deliveries with such small bills, it was not long before Elliott became the prime suspect. Further investigation turned up a cheque from the coking company to the colliery which had been altered significantly. Knowing the coking company's accounts could not handle a £37,000 transfer of funds, Lady Bountiful lowered the cheque by £10,000 to cover her tracks. But, after ten years of cooking the books and defrauding the companies of over £90,000, she made a mistake in her reckoning, and the overdraft that started the investigation eventually led to her arrest.

That winter, Yorkshire was abuzz with the Lady Bountiful trial. In Sheffield, not far from Wombwell, Edie Rutherford followed the case with interest, and the story even broke in Gateshead, raising a few eyebrows in Irene Grant's household. As details of Miss Elliott's exploits filtered through the media that February and March, Natalie Tanner discussed the case with friends over cups of coffee at her usual haunt – the Gambit cafe in Leeds. The crowd at the Gambit was unanimous in their amazement that no one in Barnsley had ever questioned Elliott's source of income. An unmarried secretary of Elliott's stature might live quite comfortably, but Lady Bountiful lived lavishly: the press reported that she had recently bought a farm and several expensive paintings. Furthermore, she had a reputation for tipping handsomely (£100 in one case). A secretary's salary could never handle such free-spending ways, and Tanner figured that enough gossips trawled through the newspapers to see who had landed windfall inheritances to know that Dorothy Elliott had never been so lucky as to grace the news columns in such a way.

But the real question, according to the newspapers, regarded Lady Bountiful's motives. Dorothy Elliott's defence argued that she was mentally unbalanced and pressed for a psychiatric evaluation. The consulting doctor affirmed the defence and told the jury at Leeds Assizes that Dorothy Elliott was indeed 'hysterical and had two personalities'. Asking for clarification, the justice wondered if Lady Bountiful was a 'sort of Dr Jekyll and Mr Hyde?' The doctor answered that she was. On one level, he claimed, she was quite normal, but on the other, it was clear Elliott had no 'moral sense' that altering cheques was wrong.[2] Edie Rutherford, who followed current events voraciously, kept abreast of the developments in the case. She sincerely hoped Elliott would get the psychological treatment she needed, but wasn't convinced the plea would work. Indeed, it didn't.

Natalie Tanner's friends, or 'cronies' as she called them, were absolutely captivated by the case. The Gambit cafe cleared out during the trial, as Natalie's cronies flocked to the Leeds Assizes to hear the case unfold. Rarely moved by such public spectacle, she, on the other hand, drank her coffee in silence and later learned from her friends that the jury was unmoved by Elliott's plea of insanity. Lady Bountiful was sent down for six and a half years. Tanner was satisfied with the verdict, convinced that if the insanity defence had been successful, it would have cleared the way for abuses in the future – especially for big-time white-collar swindles. What was perhaps the most galling about the entire case, Tanner complained, was the fact that

such a defence could be entered in the first place. To
her, it was a matter of class inequity: no explanation
was needed when the poor steal, but when well-off
individuals do, Natalie argued, there *must* be some
underlying psychological defect. Indeed, she thought,
'If a poor person pinches things in a shop, it's plain
stealing – if a rich person does, it's kleptomania.'

The war provided many opportunities for the crim-
inally inclined, and – especially in the case of black
market trade – even for those who would be the most
upright of citizens in peacetime. Wartime shortages
of goods, rationing and coupon schemes, and other
government aid programmes, as well as a shortage of
manpower and oversight, extended a welcoming invitation for criminal activity. Furthermore, there were
many more potential crimes to commit in wartime,
as Parliament deemed a range of normally innocuous
behaviour – from gossiping or complaining to wasting
food – to be harmful, and therefore criminal, in a society plunged in total war.

In the initial eighteen months of the war, when the
home front atmosphere was tense in anticipation of
German invasion and the uncertainty of victory, pros-
ecutions for defeatist talk or behaviour soared. In March
1942, one elderly woman was fined £50 and sent to jail
for a month's hard labour when she struck up a conversation with a soldier at a cafe in Hove and expressed
pro-German sentiments. Simply acting depressed in
public could bring upon one a heap of indignation.
Nella Last was admonished when she came into the
WVS centre looking tired and a little depressed after
the news of the Belgian defeat in the spring of 1940.
She was quickly reprimanded that such behaviour
was a 'crime', especially since her usual contagious

'cheerfulness' was integral to the overall morale of the women at the centre.

In the first nine months of 1943 alone, Home Secretary Herbert Morrison informed the House of Commons that fifty-four individuals were found guilty of offences under Defence Regulation 3, 'the unauthorised obtaining and communicating of information useful to the enemy'.[3] These individuals were prosecuted for what the average Briton on the street in 1943 might call 'careless talk' – a phrase coined by an early propaganda campaign ('Careless Talk Costs Lives') aimed at thwarting the spread of rumour, defeatism or any sensitive details that might benefit the enemy.

As essential products and food became scarce or under the control of the government, an individual or business could be found guilty of the crime of wasting these items. The squandering of food, paper, rags and fuel, for instance, were all considered wartime crimes.

Although considered criminal behaviour in wartime, participation in the black market occurred along a continuum. Some people attempted to gain more than their fair share while others sought out the huge profits that could be gleaned on the black market. Some of the most common of these crimes occurred in the 'grey market', in which proprietors rewarded their best customers by offering them scarce commodities 'under the counter'.[4] Sometimes proprietors nudged prices above the government's controlled levels or fudged weights and measures to make extra profit, and there seemed little one could do upon encountering such deceptive practices, as Edie Rutherford found out one cold November day in 1941. 'Paid 2/8d for a small rabbit,' she related to M-O.

It was slapped on and off [the] scales so fast that even
my quick eye could not see what it weighed, but
anyway, it is afterwards relieved of its fur coat, so one
cannot check up whether one has been overcharged.

She would have complained, but decided against it,
as she had already waited half an hour in the queue,
and did not want to cause disruption for all the other
women queuing behind her who were ecstatic simply
to be given the chance to buy even a skinny overpriced
rabbit.

Scarce items might be had under the counter for a
wink, a nod and a little extra cash. One undercover
Ministry of Food inspector was able to buy a rabbit for
well over double its government-controlled price and
to pay an exorbitant rate for half a dozen eggs, a few
stockings and a coat – all without surrendering one
coupon. The butcher in question was given six months
in jail and fined £120. As in this case, one could always
find ways of sidestepping proper procedure – of paying
more than the allowed price without surrendering the
necessary coupons. (The butcher had told the inspector that coupons 'don't matter' and did not accept them
when offered.)[5]

Although there were penalties for engaging in this
illegal activity, some had no qualms disclosing that
they did so. Edie Rutherford and her office mates
'pounced' on the foreman when he told them that he
'buys clothes on the Black Market whenever he can,
as coupons are inadequate'. Furthermore, he informed
them, he refused to pay the high prices in the shop.
'These overalls I'm wearing cost 10/-. They'd be 35/-
AND coupons in a shop!' he proudly declared. But
Edie deflated his pride somewhat when she pointed

out that the only way he could spend so little was if the overalls were stolen, 'which means', she concluded, 'that you connive at theft as well as buy illegally'. She then warned the foreman to refrain from divulging any more tales of illegal activity, as she did not want to feel compelled to report him.

On another occasion, an acquaintance told Edie that the government regularly issued her ten clothing coupons for work overalls, but since the original ones had not yet worn through, she simply used the allocation to purchase other clothes. Rutherford was exasperated at such abuse of the system, and at the fact that people were not duly ashamed of their behaviour. 'Why such folk calmly tell others this sort of thing', she said incredulously, 'beats me'. Of course, some of Edie's annoyance probably stemmed from the fact that she did not receive extra clothing coupons for her work, despite the fact that she thought she deserved them.

The diarists were usually either indignant at such abuses, protesting their moral superiority in such matters, or – not wanting to admit wrong-doing – simply silent about it in their writings to M-O. Nonetheless, it is likely that Natalie Tanner, despite such silence, probably dabbled somewhere along the continuum from grey to black market during (and after) the war. Natalie rarely complained about shortages, and when her son needed or desired new clothes, there were rarely any problems. Over the course of the war, she bought her son at least two new suits, numerous pullovers, socks and other clothes that were difficult (if not all but impossible) to procure with such regularity under the strictures of clothes rationing and coupons.

Natalie also did quite well for herself, managing to feed her cigarette addiction and her shoe addiction at a time when both were quite scarce. In May 1942, for instance, she 'fell in love with [and bought] a pair of red wedge heeled shoes for 55/-'. Since her husband's business was thriving, it's not surprising that Natalie used the family fortune to purchase what she or her loved ones desired – it was a simple wartime fact that those with money could always find what they wanted, for a price. Furthermore, Natalie did most of her shopping in Leeds, which was notorious for its thriving black market. Indeed, the *Evening Standard* proclaimed in January 1945 that, 'You do not need coupons in Leeds if you are prepared to pay the price.'[6]

Professional thieves adapted to the exigencies of war and often shifted their focus from big-ticket items such as furs and jewellery to the more mundane but now high-demand and scarce items that could be easily moved on the black market, such as food and clothing. Rationing coupons also provided a lucrative trade for both big-time criminals and amateurs alike. Some defrauded the government by passing fake coupons, while others stole massive hauls of ration books and unloaded them on the black market.

On the other hand, there were those individuals who sold unwanted personal coupons or ration books simply to get by. Edie reported in the spring of 1944 that some women in Sheffield had been arrested for selling their coupons to store clerks. Edie was not offended by these women's actions, but instead sided with them. The incident, she thought, only pointed out the significant problems endemic in a system in which poor women were forced to sell coupons because they did not have enough money to purchase legally the necessary clothing for their families. Rather, these women had to sell their clothing coupons for money in order to buy the 'cast-offs' of the well-to-do. Furthermore, according to Edie and her neighbours, the women's actions were not harmful to others: they did not flood the market with coupons or steal coupons. 'Why don't they [the police] find the real lowdown people and prosecute them?' Edie wondered.

The workplace also provided prime opportunities for both small-scale and large-scale theft. Pilfering was commonplace, be it a worker lifting a few tablets of soap to sell at a local market, overloading delivery lorries in order to sell the surplus, or pinching cutlery from the canteen (the London Transport Board reported 66,000 missing forks, spoons and knives in 1943 – a loss of £8,000). Edie's integrity was tested one day at work when she came across three boxes of 'Royal Sovereign pencils – Husband's favourite', and impossible to buy in wartime. The temptation to lift them passed, and Rutherford reported that she asked the management if she could buy a box for Sid's birthday, which she was allowed to do.

Bombed-out homes provided easy pickings for amateur thieves; professional thieves generally tended to stay away from blitzed areas where police, firefighters and other volunteers rushed to the scene, instead preferring to target unoccupied and unwatched homes in the countryside. Although many volunteers did their best to protect and store the property of bombing victims safely, sadly it was often those first on the scene or those responsible for clean-up who had the best opportunity to loot. In February 1941, six men from a rescue squad in Sutton were found guilty of looting and were sentenced to six months' hard labour for stealing 'a rug, clock, sweets, chocolate, sardines, salmon and corned beef'. Though perhaps a trivial haul of goods, what made this act particularly heinous was the fact that the men had 'robbed the dead' – four individuals had died in the blast.[7] Several demolition teams were also caught stripping valuable lead from damaged buildings: twenty-eight soldiers and the metal merchant who bought the lead were found guilty of this offence while clearing a railway station in March 1941. Police officers were not immune to looting while on patrol, either. The fact that those entrusted to public safety were not beyond reproach led the Birmingham Police to caution the public that many blitz larcenies were in fact perpetrated by firewatchers.

While some incidents of looting were obviously reprehensible, a great deal of moral ambiguity clouded the numerous crimes of opportunity produced by the Blitz. Two firefighters were charged with looting when police officers discovered them picking up items apparently ejected from a blitzed building. Although one pleaded with the police that he had a wife and children to look after and the other had a spotless reputation as a hardworking volunteer, the two were given four months' hard labour for three lighters and a couple of pipes found on the scene. American news reporter Edward R. Murrow felt that such individuals were hardly criminals. He told his audience how the Blitz distorted the notion of private property:

> One has a strange feeling . . . in looking at the contents of a bombed house or shop, that the things scattered about don't belong to anyone . . . Picking up a book or a pipe that's been blown into the street is almost like

picking an apple in a deserted and overgrown orchard
far from any road or house.[8]

Perhaps the most pernicious and egregious of wartime
criminals were those who siphoned off a system
created to help those desperately in need. Government
schemes to aid evacuees or blitz victims were ripe for
abuse. Those who billeted evacuees were entitled to 10
shillings and 6 pence for the first child and 8 shillings
and 6 pence for each child thereafter. One billeting
officer took advantage of this and made over £1,000 in
one year by claiming allowances for fictitious evacuees
before he and his partner were caught. The government
also provided aid to repair bomb-damaged homes and
to resettle those blitzed out of homes, leading some to
falsely claim hundreds of pounds of financial assistance for bomb damage that was never sustained.
Unclaimed furniture and other household goods from
blitzed homes were kept in council stores to help those
who had lost everything through bomb damage, but at
a time when such commodities were rarely found on
the open market, some council employees took advantage of this source of ready inventory to line their
pockets.

Britons felt a palpable 'crime wave' wash over the
country in the last two years of war. Incidents of
larceny, burglary and shop break ins soared during
this period and into the first years of peace. Edie
Rutherford was deeply concerned when this statistic
hit close to home.

Throughout the winter of 1943/44, numerous thefts
and break-ins were reported in Rutherford's block of
flats. Laundry left unattended in the hallways went
missing, and household items were lifted from flats.

The crime wave at Prince Court that winter prompted a resident serviceman to install an alarm in order to soothe the fears of his wife while he was away on duty. The burglar was soon tripped up by this precaution and caught red-handed.

Edie knew the offender. He lived on the first floor and 'looked the type who would do a dirty deed like that'. The offender's family was obviously not what Edie considered respectable: his wife had recently left him and three daughters ('all by different fathers, so 'tis said!' she told M-O) to live with a Canadian serviceman. Once the thief was apprehended, Edie understood how the unemployed collier was able to live for months without work. Though the police found many of the stolen goods tucked away in his flat, she feared that most of her neighbours would never see their property again.

Edie was later incensed to learn the blackguard had been let out on bail after he appeared in court. 'He is going about now brazen as brass,' she huffed. In fact, the flats' caretaker told her that the burglar had shown up at the police station after his release, brandishing an electric iron and had apparently told the constable, 'This is the iron I pinched – you took mine away!' 'Can you beat that?' Edie marvelled.

As the war languished into its fifth year, a dark pall of gloom descended on Britain as people continued to cope with austerity measures and waited for the war to enter its final phase, which they knew would not come until, as Rutherford put it, 'We jump onto the Continent.' In that uneasy malaise of early 1944, the war seemed interminable. In February 1944, Irene Grant cried, 'I never never see an end to the war', and lamented the heaps of 'misery and trouble' that stalked the earth. Edie Rutherford proclaimed that she was 'impatient of slackers, black marketeers and dodgers – mad at injustices to people who serve the country well and then get handed a raw deal'. Quite simply, 'War is making me very weary of war,' she announced to M-O. Furthermore, the future after the war seemed very far from promising. Increasing tensions between the Soviet Union and the Polish government-in-exile in London over the placement of the eastern border of Poland that January made Rutherford confide to M-O that she 'dreaded the aftermath of this war'.

The weariness and malaise might explain the rise in crimes of the period – from the white-collar antics of Lady Bountiful all the way down to stealing laundry out of baskets left in the hallways of Edie's block of flats. It also goes a long way to explain the furore that developed over Spanish oranges that winter. In January, Britons learned that a shipment of oranges from Spain had been apparently sabotaged. Time-delayed bombs stuffed inside the crates went off on their journey to Britain; luckily, there was no damage done to the ship or the crew, but the precious cargo was destroyed. Expectant mothers and children had been entitled to cheap or free orange juice since 1942, but it was a rare and happy occasion when others were blessed with the fruit. The Ministry of Food, however, had made provision with Spain and Palestine in December 1943 to provide everyone on the island with a veritable windfall of oranges – one pound per head every month from January to April 1944. This warm and hopeful promise, announced to the public in an otherwise cold and dreary winter, made the destruction of the orange shipments all the more disappointing.

The sabotage kicked off a firestorm of personal and diplomatic fury aimed at Spain. Irene Grant and Edie Rutherford, for instance, let fly several choice statements of hatred towards the Spanish and their leader, Francisco Franco, while *The Times* insisted on calling the event an 'outrage'.[9] Spain reacted quickly by promising to bring the saboteurs to justice and implementing preventive measures, but Parliament was not easily convinced. Although Natalie Tanner, who had lived in Spain for five years in the 1930s and knew how the Spanish government worked, thought that the bombing was orchestrated by Franco to cover up huge shipments of rotten oranges, the event soon escalated beyond citrus. Instead, it provided an opportunity to air numerous complaints about breaches in Spain's neutrality during the war. Accusations surfaced that Spain harboured German spies, delayed Allied shipping and extended generous credit to Germany, especially for important armament materials such as tungsten ore.

Britain and the United States reacted swiftly to the orange 'outrage' by withdrawing shipments of oil to Spain at the end of January. Nonetheless, oranges made it to the shelves in fits and starts that winter. Indeed, some even complained that Newcastle received so many Seville oranges that they were rotting in the stores. Irene Grant, who lived near Newcastle, however, protested that she couldn't find any. When Edie Rutherford received her first allocation of oranges that winter, her husband was so shocked he wondered jokingly whether Edie had 'robbed someone's children'. By May, the air had cleared somewhat between the Allies and Spain, after Spain agreed to address the issues of spies and shipping, as well as to reduce significantly the delivery of tungsten ore to Germany.

When the orange controversy erupted in January, an MP from Heywood and Radcliffe questioned the parliamentary secretary to the Ministry of War Transport, Philip Noel-Baker, regarding an incident in which some dockers reportedly refused to unload cargo from Spain. Apparently, the dockers argued that the potential danger involved in such work warranted a rise in pay. Noel-Baker dismissed the claim as untrue. Instead, the secretary asserted, dockers were never asked to do such work; rather, he claimed, special- ized bomb-removal personnel and supporting troops unloaded the cargo. Whether the MP's version of events or the official version was true, the conversa- tion in Parliament highlights the very real problem of industrial action in the waning years of war.

Although strike action was officially illegal during the war, the considerable challenges of enforcing such a law meant that there was very little the government could do when workers downed tools in numbers. The simple logistical problem of where to incarcerate hundreds, let alone thousands, of illegal strikers was only the start of the difficulties inherent in such legisla- tion. Furthermore, all available workers were essential to the war economy – the government simply could not allow able-bodied workers to languish in prison for months under such circumstances. Nor could the government risk a general strike in sympathy for workers who had been sent to prison or slapped with hefty fines.

When 4,000 miners walked out of a Kent colliery in 1942, the supposed ringleaders were thrown in jail and the rest were handed the choice of a fine or a four- teen-day prison sentence. The tension created by this hard line forced Home Secretary, Herbert Morrison, to commute the sentences. Afterwards, prison sentences were never again handed out, though some offenders were given significant fines.

Strikes occurred on a regular basis for the rest of the war. Although industrial action had lessened in the early years of war, by 1942 the number of days lost was back to peacetime levels of nearly 1.5 million. The years 1943 and 1944 saw an even higher number of days lost (1.8 million and 3.7 million, respectively), and 1944 set a record for the total number of actual strikes. Although war industry, transport and dock-yards produced important strikes during the war, coal-mining experienced by far the majority of walk-outs throughout the war. And in the cold spring of 1944, a major strike from the coal industry seriously threatened the warmth of homes and the productivity of factories across the country.

Since the beginning of 1944, Irene Grant had complained about the abysmal quality of coal. Even the best quality was mostly stone and ash that Irene had to wash off in order to reveal a pitiable amount of usable coal. If the quality of the coal was poor, so too was the quantity: an outbreak of influenza, low pit product-ivity and transport problems coupled with stringent limits on coal deliveries introduced by the government that winter meant there was little to go around, even if it was mostly useless stone.

In the south-east, deliveries of coal to consumers were down to a stark shadow of what they had been the previous year. In Kent, Helen Mitchell was bitten by depressingly cold weather and a coal shortage. Always concerned to act patriotically in theory, but rarely in practice, she admitted feeling 'worried by intense cold of sitting room conflicting with desire to save fuel'. And in the damp, foggy chill of a Kentish January, it was her misfortune to spend hours coping with 'this strange wartime fuel' that continually clogged her anthracite stove. The winter of 1943/44 was not as bitter as the record freeze of 1940/41; nonetheless, gale winds blew, damp chill settled in the bones and snow flew in fits. With the coal shortage, it was an absolutely miserable winter.

In Sheffield, a virginal blanket of snow christened the beginning of March 1944. Despite the fact that the sun blazed and danced upon the snow as Edie had never before experienced, the chill of early March stubbornly refused to diminish the snow for well over a week. 'Seems to me more like Switzerland,' the native South African marvelled to M-O.

That March, against the backdrop of this dazzling winter landscape, nearly 200,000 men walked out of mines in South Wales and Yorkshire. It was a devastating blow to a nation already suffering coal shortages and preparing for the final push of the war. By the end of the month, Edie Rutherford reported that factories were shut down due to lack of fuel; nearby towns suffered gas and electricity cuts; and her block of flats was eking out the very last delivery of coke they could expect to see until the strike was resolved.

It seemed resoundingly unpatriotic for the miners to down tools that winter, and indeed many owners, officials and consumers cried foul. But for all the accusations of shirking, radicalism and general indolence levelled at the miners, the true problem was much more complicated than simple laziness or treachery. The economic slump of the inter-war period had ripped the heart out of the coal industry. Many miners had been thrown out of work for long periods of time and, furthermore, the poverty and decline of the coal-mining villages meant that these communities often failed to reproduce the next generation of workers. When the war came, with its insatiable lust for coal, experienced miners were middle-aged and had suffered from years of privation and inactivity. In addition, equipment was antiquated, and many of the abundant coal seams of the nineteenth century were exhausted.

The industry, therefore, limped along during the war with inadequate numbers of workers, poor investment and poor coal reserves. The government tried to ameliorate some of the problems by allowing conscription-age men to 'opt' out of military service if they agreed to work the mines. Some took up this opportunity, but not as many as the government would have hoped. Additional shifts were created, and experienced miners worked well over a full shift on a regular basis to make up for the shortages. (The frequently voiced term 'shirker' must have rankled with these miners.) Extraction of coal from thin and less-prolific seams with out-dated equipment was also dangerous, and nearly a quarter of miners suffered severe accidents during the last years of the war.

With coal production well under what the war economy required, the government decided to send more men down the mines. In December 1943, the Minister of Labour, Ernest Bevin, enacted a plan which would send one in every ten men eligible for National Service to work the seams. Many of these so-called Bevin Boys resented being directed to the coal industry, and many of the miners themselves held little love for the unwilling amateurs. Those who patently refused to do the work were packed off to jail, while others were regularly lax in attending work. Aside from the danger and solitude of the work, one of the largest detractors to Bevin's scheme was the fact that his 'Boys' were paid the dismal wage of a miner. Work in war armaments was far more lucrative.

The massive walkout that left families shivering and factories gasping for coal in March and April 1944 was ignited by the poor wage levels in the mines. Strikes and arbitration during the war had lifted the minimum wage of miners to £4.3s in 1942, and in early 1944 this was raised to £5. While this was well above the pre-war minimum, grave miscalculations in the pay structure that was set with this new minimum drove experienced workers to the edge, for the new guidelines wiped away wage differentials. Miners with years of experience could now expect to make the same wage as the volunteer workers who had opted for the mines over the military as well as the Bevin Boys. Moreover, soon after the minimum was implemented, it was announced that manual workers were making on average well over £6.

In this light, the anger levelled at miners was perhaps a bit unfair. And, indeed, despite the gravity of the situation, some Britons seemed willing to apply understanding to the situation. Though one of her conservative friends spewed forth condemnation on the miners (and the working classes in general), Natalie Tanner was very sympathetic to the miners' plight. Pinched by the cold, Edie Rutherford nonetheless also registered her support of the strike, feeling that the miners had been abused for long enough. To Irene Grant, the continual animosity and inefficiency in the mines only pointed to the fact that the industry must be nationalized. Indeed, Grant felt most industry and land should be handed over to the people, as they should 'belong to everyone'.

On Friday 7 April, the same day Rutherford noted the closure of several factories for want of fuel, Edie also announced that the miners had agreed to return to work the following week. Differentials were put back in place, and the miners emerged from the strike with the highest minimum wage of all industries. Angered at the intransigence of the miners at a critical period in the war – when the nation prepared for the invasion of Western Europe – Ernest Bevin wanted revenge. He was convinced that Trotskyites had orchestrated the strike, and to stave off future agitation the Minister of Labour would not rest until draconian anti-strike legislation was enacted. Under Regulation 1AA, convicted agitators could expect a prison sentence of five years or a fine of £500. Although the creation of the regulation resulted in a firestorm of criticism from the left in the Labour Party (led by Welsh MP, Aneurin Bevan) and nearly split the party just one year before its great electoral win, Regulation 1AA was never used.

The elevated rates of crime and industrial action of early 1944 were symptoms of the deep malaise into which the nation had descended in the fifth year of war. Despite the official Italian surrender less than six months before, in September 1943, the conflict now seemed to drag on endlessly, and the bleakness of austerity measures seeped into the fabric of day-to-day life, leaving many desperately dangling at the end of their tether.

CHAPTER ELEVEN

WORST RAID EVER LAST NIGHT

Helen Mitchell lay awake cursing the German bombers buzzing over her Kent home on 22 January 1944, as a 'foul raid' raged well into the morning. After the raiders cleared out, there was still no sleep to be had, with RAF bombers en route to the Continent for retribution humming and growling overhead, shaking the windows and foundations of Helen's home. Bleary-eyed from lack of sleep and an enervating cold, which made her temporarily deaf in one ear, she switched on the radio. Helen caught the morning news just in time to hear the BBC 'gloat' over the damage that those very same British bombers, which had kept her awake earlier, had wrought over Germany. The BBC's behaviour was no better than Germany's vicious crowing in the early years of war, Mitchell thought angrily.

At least Helen had someone with whom to endure the raids, and to whom she could grouse about what she called the BBC's 'childishness'. Helen normally lived alone since her husband, Peter, worked closer to London, and usually slept at a flat near his work. But recently, a houseguest had come to stay for a few days. A week before the 'foul raid' on the 22nd, Peter had arranged for a friend of his sister's to stay with Helen for company and to help with household chores during his wife's illness. Caroline would also help keep Helen's mind off the renewed blitz, Peter reasoned.

Since the beginning of the year, the raids over Kent had once again assumed the familiar drumbeat of the 1940–1 blitz. In early 1944, Hitler embarked upon a new bombing offensive, entitled Operation Steinbock, aimed at the capital. London and the south-east would now endure the so-called 'baby blitz', a four-month onslaught that would stretch nerves to breaking point.

After a relative period of peace, Londoners once again descended underground to the safety of the Tube. Although new deep shelters had been constructed in the capital since 1941, none was ready in 1944, and once again the Tube reopened and old bunks were reconstructed to accommodate the nightly migration of nervous city dwellers. In the countryside, people stole away to the protection of their outdoor Andersons, indoor Morrisons or other makeshift precautions. Helen usually sheltered downstairs on a divan placed beneath a doorframe. When she had company over, Helen heaved a heavy kitchen table into the living room, 'amalgamating it with grand piano as air-shelter'.

As the raids increased, Helen was initially happy that Peter had arranged for Caroline to come; however, it was not long before Helen tired of her guest. Certainly, it was a comfort to have someone nearby, but Caroline had a penchant for sleeping late, leaving the ailing Helen to wake early to start fires throughout the draughty 'medieval' home. After early chores were completed, Helen would tumble into bed, utterly exhausted, fed up and muttering at the laziness of her houseguest. Mitchell quickly wrote off Caroline as thoroughly useless: Helen complained to M-O that Caroline's idea of '"Nursing" consists of sitting on her bottom and sending out "healing vibrations"'. 'Feel a spot of dusting would be more useful,' she quipped. Conversation was hardly sparkling either. 'Have rather forgotten what a dreadful bore a really unintelligent woman who makes vapid remarks can be, but have so far managed to be polite,' Helen caustically remarked. Within a week, Helen was bored and Caroline was disappointed at the lack of things to do in the village; Helen was glad to see her guest off at the train station.

The renewed bombing campaign strained nerves in Helen's village, yet people pulled together the best they could to provide comfort during the tense nights. Husbands living and working away from home – like Peter and the husband of another friend of Helen's, Joan – did their best to be home when they could. When no help was forthcoming from husbands or others from the outside, the women in Helen's circle sometimes visited each other at night. They brought along bedding and a few rations, offering conversation and companionship, hoping to sleep through the night, but often huddling together as bombs crashed to the earth all around them.

Margaret, the owner of a local cafe with whom Helen had become friendly as a frequent customer, seemed the most wits-shattered of Helen's tiny village circle. In late January, Helen visited the cafe to find Margaret in an 'awful state about raids'. Helen offered Margaret a place to stay if she needed comfort from the raids. The easily flappable Helen, however, soon regretted her kind gesture. 'Alas!' she told M-O, Margaret showed up that very night, with cat in tow, no rations and then proceeded to blither non-stop the entire night.

Though the raid was only a 'minor' one and did not last long, Margaret failed to leave when the All Clear siren sounded. With each passing moment of Margaret's unwanted presence, Helen's silent rage increased, but she could hardly move herself to ask her guest explicitly to leave. Instead, fearing a future imposition on her already strained hospitality, and hoping Margaret would get the hint that she'd outstayed her welcome, Helen steadfastly refused to offer her guest tea. 'Was tough about tea', Helen told M-O, 'as I fear there will be much of this.' Later in the day, Margaret came back to announce that she had offered boarding to a Canadian soldier and, much to Helen's pleasant surprise, would not need to come in the night.

That evening, 29 January, with Peter just returned home for the weekend, the village had yet another 'foul raid'. It was so fierce that the blackout boards in the windows were blown out. The two tried to brave the raid by playing card games. Helen tried valiantly at stoicism, but she failed: her hands shook uncontrollably. Deeply disappointed with herself, she told M-O, 'Am becoming more and more cowardly!'

The next morning, a Sunday, Peter woke early and went to his weekly Home Guard drill. The Home Guard was created in 1940 under the Secretary of War, Anthony Eden. Originally named the Local Defence Volunteers (LDV), the Home Guard mobilized (mostly) male citizens to defend the country against a possible German invasion. Peter joined the Home Guard early, as did Tom Grant (Irene's husband) and thousands of other men after the call was made for volunteers in the spring of 1940. Between the initial announcement on

10 May and the end of June, over one million men had heeded the call.

In January 1944, when Peter went to drill, the threat of a German invasion on British soil was decidedly minuscule, but the Home Guard had by then been mostly absorbed into Civil Defence and Anti-Aircraft (AA) duties. Other than preening his equipment for 'ridiculous inspection', Helen never revealed the details of her husband's involvement in the Home Guard. Considering the number of heated air raids in the area, however, it seems reasonable to assume that Peter was involved in either AA work or recovery and other defence duties.

Typically, Helen awoke early to prepare breakfast on mornings when Peter was on Home Guard duty. However, that morning she slept late and left her husband to 'turn the knobs' on the cooker himself for breakfast. Though she needed the sleep, she confided that she 'felt like a pig' for being so lazy. When Peter came home after the Home Guard that day, the two took a walk together and enjoyed the waning sunlight of a crisp January afternoon. Later, Helen played card games with Peter and read P.G. Wodehouse aloud (possibly *The Code of the Woosters*, her favourite Wodehouse, which she'd picked up 'prewar paper and print' in London only two months before). In an otherwise stormy relationship and during a particularly fearful period of the 'baby blitz', where Helen reported raids almost every night, it seemed a refreshingly tranquil moment.

The next day, Peter went back to work, and after morning chores Helen retired in the early afternoon, drifting off to sleep as she listened to Jane Austen's *Sense and Sensibility* on the radio, 'alone again'. Margaret visited a day later, and though she was still boarding the

Canadian soldier, offered to stay with Helen during air raids. Despite feeling desperately lonely, Helen turned Margaret down flat.

The next morning, with an 'excellent gale blowing', Helen dragged old clothes out of storage to air and inspect for the telltale signs of moth damage that often plagued her wardrobe. 'No moth casualties', she happily informed M-O. As she sifted through the garments, she stopped to eye the old costumes and party clothes of bygone theatre productions and social evenings strewn about the room, nostalgic tears dropped gently off the edge of her lashes. 'Am glad I did not know ten years ago what "life" would be like now,' Helen thought miserably.

Later, she was stirred awake at 5 a.m. as German planes visited her village, bringing 'new and terrible bangs and house shaking including self'. When she stumbled into the kitchen, fatigued from lack of sleep and too much living in the past, Helen discovered that one of the pipes had burst in the raid. Day and night, Helen emptied buckets in a relentless battle against the water torture that sprang from her 'dear old house'. 'Too much of water hast thou poor Ophelia,' the former Shakespearean actor and producer lamented as she recalled the drowning of Ophelia in *Hamlet*.

In between the rattling raids that winter, Mitchell continued her daily grind and grouse of housework. In addition to the bombing, the house and the routine were, if possible, even more debilitating than ever for Helen. 'Drooled through the day in usual manner,' summed up her day's experience in one terse January diary entry. Throughout the long winter, a variety of repairmen appeared to patch windows blown out from raids, fix plumbing, remedy the dreadful dampness

that seeped from the walls of the old place and tune her
piano (which, in addition to Mitchell, was also suffering from the damp). All agreed with her: the old wreck
of a home should be condemned. Even the doctor, who
came to treat her cold, said it 'was the most depressing
place he'd ever been in!'

In the beginning of February, the raids over Helen's
village slackened off a bit. She was even able to sleep
one night in her upstairs bedroom with the blackout down and windows wide open. Though it was a
'pleasant change', it didn't last long: she was woken
by machine-gun fire early in the morning. That morning, when she switched on the radio, she learned of
a 'new form of horror'. The BBC now spewed forth
casualty statistics and 'calculations' of the damage that
Allied bombing had wrought upon Germany. This
'new entertainment with endless possibilities' churned
her stomach all the more as planes passed overhead.
Helen understood the fear of bombing too deeply to
glean any satisfaction from the BBC's tales of RAF
successes. And she knew all too well that Allied bombing sparked German retribution, which meant that her
village would inevitably become a target once again.

Indeed, on Valentine's Day, Helen and Peter experienced 'the worst raid ever'. The two lay on the floor,
shaking in terror while plaster and dust fell down all
around them. Helen trembled uncontrollably as she
heard the unmistakable clack-clack of incendiaries and
the chilling rip of the air as high-explosive bombs fell
to the ground. When morning came, Peter left for the
week, leaving Helen distraught and worried about
enduring the next horrible raid alone.

Five days later, on 19 February, London had its heaviest raid since the monstrous bomber's moon bombing

of 10 May 1941. Luckily for Mitchell, the raid wasn't too bad in Kent. Still, the siren went early that night, and – fully expecting a repeat of the Valentine's Day raid – Helen cowered beneath her kitchen table, waiting for the worst. The raids were taking their toll; 'Have descended to lowest depths and took bromide,' Helen confessed.

As the raiders continued their bombing runs – flying west to London or east in revenge – Mitchell's friend Joan stopped in one cold February morning and invited her to come to her house for the evening. For the remainder of the month, Helen divided her time between Joan's home and her own, pulling together rations for an evening away and tidying up in the morning before heading home to do her chores. On occasion, Margaret would appear during the day, complain about the raids and announce that she was staying the night. Helen much preferred spending the evenings at Joan's, since she seemed to get a restful sleep and found Joan 'very nice to be with, as doesn't grumble like Margaret'. But, with Helen's seeming inability to refuse anything that smacked of 'duty' or sacrifice, this invariably kept her at home, with the attendant cleaning and airing of a room that having a guest necessitated. Much as she hated the imposition, Helen could not refuse Margaret when she appeared at her door.

After a nice evening at Joan's, and an invitation to stay again that night, Margaret stopped by to tell Helen that her boarder would be late and she couldn't possibly get through the night alone. Helen felt obliged to cancel with Joan when she learned of Margaret's misfortune and, predictably, the night was spent in agony: Helen proclaiming to M-O that her houseguest was 'most upsetting, grousing and reiterating interminably'.

By the end of February, Helen stepped up efforts to flee the torment of the 'baby blitz' and made plans to stay with friends near Oxford in March. She had been planning an escape from Kent for quite a while. In fact, she spent a great deal of the war trying to break free either of the old house or from the constant bombing that plagued the south-east. On numerous occasions, Helen went on short breaks to friends in Tunbridge Wells, Epsom or London, or took a train to the west for the tranquillity of Minehead and the Quantock Hills. But on this occasion, if she thought she was going to also escape the noisome Margaret, she was sadly mistaken. Once Margaret got wind of Helen's plan, she asked to accompany Mitchell to the greener pastures beyond the capital, out of harm's way. 'Blimey!' exclaimed Helen when Margaret elbowed her way in to Helen's plans; nonetheless, she made arrangements for them both.

To judge by the numerous renters and boarders that showed up at Helen's own door, many people lived peripatetic lives during the war. In the periods when she was in Kent, one of the (many) banes of Helen's existence was the numerous callers wanting to rent or buy her house. From men and women moving jobs voluntarily or through government compulsion, to bombed-out families searching for accommodation, to evacuees and individuals like Helen and Margaret trying to escape the terrifying pounding of enemy bombs, hundreds of thousands of Britons were on the move during the war.

On 28 February 1944, as Helen prepared to move to Oxfordshire, her friend from Tunbridge Wells appeared, 'to talk over taking half of house'. 'Says they may have to go back to their flat in London, as tenants have fled, and they may not be able to let it, but wants to come here,' Helen recorded in her diary. Since she was on her way to Oxford, this was less of a problem for Helen than the interminable interruptions of expected and unexpected enquiries that plagued her during the months when she was determined to stay in Kent.

On 6 March, Helen caught a train to London, where she and Margaret then switched to the 'slow train' at Paddington. Later that day, the two were finally installed at Francine's, Helen being thoroughly fed up with Margaret and hoping her tagalong would soon disappear. Perhaps Margaret had also tired of Helen, for she did indeed move along with surprising rapidity. Within two days, Margaret had found a job and began to move her belongings to Oxford. 'Devoutly thankful', Helen wrote in her diary to mark the occasion. Margaret 'has fed on me emotionally for the past month and am fed to the teeth', she complained to M-O.

Without Margaret, the Oxfordshire countryside was a pleasant getaway from the continual air operations over Kent. The village where she now lived was much more lively than her home in Kent, and, though she felt compelled to do housework to earn her keep at Francine's, the stay was enjoyable. Nonetheless, Helen could still hear the air-raid sirens of London at night, and it sent her into 'much vicarious suffering, as know London was getting it'. As she lay in bed, listening to the sirens and distant gunfire, she thought of her husband and felt pangs of concern, knowing he was in the midst of the raid, worrying he was working too hard (as she thought he often did) and wondering if he was getting enough sleep.

Although the distant sound of raids cut into her own sleep, she bitterly contrasted those around town who looked 'so full of sleep' with the 'drawn tired faces in Kent and London'. The next day, she took advantage of the quiet and wallowed in the '1st *really* quiet afternoon I've known since I left Scotland 6½ years ago.' Still, Helen felt unsettled: Francine's family was descending on the farm for the Easter holidays and, although her friend insisted she stay, Helen couldn't bear the thought of being a burden. So, once again, she made arrangements to flee – this time to her beloved Minehead.

German bombers darkened Kentish skies during Operation Steinbock, which lasted from January to April 1944. While this period certainly tried Mitchell's nerves and, indeed, got the better of her, the 'baby blitz' of 1944 was only a spike in the horrifying air traffic that continually buzzed overhead throughout the war. Indeed, in the months leading up to the concerted effort of Steinbock, Helen marked numerous air raids in her village.

Although the 1940–1 blitz is the best known, and most intense, of the bombings over Britain, many – especially those in the south-east – endured an almost continual prospect of death and destruction from the air throughout the war. In the relatively quiet month of January 1943, for instance, thirty-eight children and six teachers were killed when a bomb hit their school during a raid on south-east London. And those living on the coastline were never safe from the so-called 'tip 'n' run raids', where one or several planes materialized out of nowhere, rained bombs down and evaporated as quickly as they came. In May 1943, twenty-three young women working ack-ack in Great Yarmouth were killed when a tip 'n' run raid dropped bombs on their hostel.

In mid-October 1943, the local air raid damage assessor came to look over the damage done to the Mitchells' carpentry shed. Helen often retreated to the shed to read, as, compared to her dark dungeon of a home, it had good natural light. Despite the fact that she essentially lived in the shed during the day, the assessor informed her that there were no available funds to patch up damaged outbuildings, much to Helen's chagrin. He also reported that thirty-two bombs had dropped around the village during the previous week. Although windows were blown out across the district and 'filth' shaken from the rafters of Helen's 'dear olde place' – requiring extra elbow grease to clean up – luckily there were no casualties.

In February 1942, the newly appointed Commander-in-Chief of Bomber Command, Sir Arthur 'Bomber' Harris, had decided to strike at workers' morale in Germany, selecting Lübeck, a beautiful and historic city on the Baltic. Harris didn't think the town 'a vital target', but it was better, in his estimation, to decimate an 'industrial town of moderate importance than to fail to destroy a large industrial city'.[1] On 28/29 March, British bombers destroyed half the city.

The Lübeck raids initiated another phase of the blitz on Britain. In retaliation for the bombing, Hitler ordered raids on tourist towns chosen from *Baedeker's Great Britain: A Handbook for Travellers*. It was Hitler's desire to attack civilians and centres of cultural and historical importance aggressively and thus exact the most severe damage on home front morale. 'Terror attacks of a retaliatory nature are to be carried out against towns other than London,' the order stated.[2] Goebbels noted in his diary that,

There was no other way of bringing the English to their senses. They belong to a class of human beings with whom you can talk only after you have first knocked out their teeth.[3]

From April to June 1942, Exeter, Bath, Norwich, Canterbury and York were all targeted and suffered damage to medieval and Georgian buildings, as well as loss of life.

It was during these so-called Baedeker raids that Natalie Tanner and her family came the closest to experiencing the blitz first hand. She awoke in the small hours of 29 April 1942 to sirens and distant thuds that rumbled the foundations of her home just outside Leeds. In the morning, she gathered that York had been hit. When she went with Hugh to collect his belongings from the mental hospital, where he'd spent the previous eight months because of his breakdown, she was shocked at the damage done to the train station. Other than that, nothing else seemed particularly out of place to her. She never mentioned the nearly 10,000 homes and businesses damaged, the destruction of the mid-fifteenth-century Guildhall, or the two hundred wounded and ninety-three left dead by the bombers.

Sporadically between 31 May and 3 June 1942, approximately eighty bombers visited Canterbury, damaging buildings in the cathedral precincts, but causing little damage to the cathedral itself: some bombs fell on the roof, but failed to explode. Though she was not far from the cathedral town, the damage to Canterbury was not in the forefront of Helen's thoughts. Tired of being cooped up inside, Margaret knocked on the door when the sirens went on 2 June, pleading with

Helen to roam the village lanes with her. Helen bluntly refused and 'got rid of her at the all clear'.

That night, Helen's thoughts strayed not to Canterbury, but across the Channel. 'Can't sleep for misery of thinking what it must be like in Germany with these raids,' she noted in her diary. The night before the raids on Canterbury were carried out, 1,000 RAF bombers visited the historic city of Cologne in Germany, dropping 1,500 tons of bombs and causing significant damage. The so-called 'Millennium' bombing rendered over 40,000 people homeless, killed nearly 500 (on a par with the recent Baedeker raids carried out on Bath) and destroyed Cologne's public transport, numerous factories and many buildings of historical importance.[4]

Several months later, in July 1942, raiders visited Birmingham once again. For the first time in months, Alice Bridges and her family rushed down to the Anderson shelter in her garden. The sirens woke the family at 2 a.m.; Bridges scooped up her daughter and, laden with clothes, gas masks and her key to the shelter, she dashed through the backyard. Once Jacqueline was safe, Alice realized, 'I had nothing to keep my reputation up.' Back to the house she ran, returning to the shelter with her hair tidied and stockings on. By this time, the bombers came, 'pouring across hell for leather' on their way to the Rover works.

Though Helen escaped to Oxfordshire during the 'baby blitz' of 1944, the war was never very far away. She had met her first Americans in Oxford and thought them quiet and a little too loose with their money. When she finally settled in Minehead after her stay with Francine, she saw more of them, training on the hills outside the town by day, and loudly socializing below her window at night.

The 'friendly invasion' of Americans started in early 1942, but began to build rapidly in late 1943 and early 1944.[5] Just prior to D-Day in June 1944, American soldiers and support staff in Britain numbered over 1.5 million. Americans brought with them money, cigarettes, gum and easy smiles. Much to the dismay of British soldiers and moralists alike, they wooed giddy girls and, despite the fact that many ordinary Britons, like Alice Bridges and Helen Mitchell, had seen more bloodshed and destruction than the Americans had, they acted as if they were heroes and saviours. It wasn't long before American arrogance, affluence and ebullience touched a raw nerve. 'What's wrong with the Yank Army?' a friend asked Natalie. The answer was the oft-heard sentiment, 'They are overpaid, overdressed, oversexed and over here.'

As the gradual build-up of American troops suggests, talk of a possible invasion of Western Europe had been in the news and bandied about in pubs for some time. After Hitler reneged on the Nazi–Soviet Pact and ordered troops into Russia in the summer of 1941, Stalin implored the Western Allies to open up a front in the west to take some of the heat off the German onslaught. Many at home agreed, and a great cry of 'Second Front Now!' erupted from communists and Conservatives alike in Britain. The slogan was scrawled on walls around the country, and mass demonstrations gathered to call for action on the part of the government. In the event, the opening of another front came not in France, as Stalin had hoped, but rather in Africa in 1942, in the action that eventually allowed for the invasion of Europe through Italy in

1943. While this did alleviate some of the pressure on Russia, it was generally accepted that occupied France must be invaded and liberated to knock Germany out of the war.

In the summers of 1942 and 1943, M-O questioned their diarists about their feelings regarding the possibility of invading the French coast. The overall tenor of the response was one of anxious fear surrounding the inevitability of impending, but necessary, doom. This fear was especially palpable at the nadir of British fortunes in 1942, while the country was still reeling from the losses of Singapore and Tobruk. The fall of Tobruk in Libya to the Germans – and the capture of the 33,000 British soldiers garrisoned there – was, as Churchill admitted, a disgrace that nearly cost him the premiership. In the wake of such stunning defeats, Nella Last was frightened by the very words 'second front', but her mind told her 'timorous heart we *must* go sooner or later'. Helen Mitchell felt that 'We should only make a mess of it,' and thought it was better to do nothing and let the Germans tire themselves out. Edie Rutherford tried not to think about it. 'I just can't bear . . . it,' she admitted. 'My blood runs cold because I feel that if we do it we shall have to do it in such force that the slaughter will be worse than anything yet seen.'

After a raid on Dieppe in August 1942 decimated a trial invasion force of 6,000 troops, mostly Canadian, the women's fears seemed validated and the 'Second Front Now!' movement lost some of its exuberance. For the diarists, Dieppe was a 'confusing' and impotent jab at a seemingly impervious foe. 'The Germans seem so dreadfully strong,' Nella Last worried. Helen Mitchell was simply 'depressed' by the raid, and they all wondered why the military would attempt such an ill-planned and costly adventure.

There was more confidence in 1943, especially after the victory at El Alamein in November 1942, the Soviet victory at Stalingrad in January 1943 and Rommel's surrender in the sands of North Africa in May, the very month that M-O put the question once again to its writers. But still, everyone dreaded the massive loss of life that they knew in their hearts – and for which the government braced them – was coming. The novelist and a fellow Mass-Observation diarist Naomi Mitchison perhaps struck the tone best when, anticipating D-Day in May 1944, she wrote,

It's at the back of one's thoughts all the time, like a wave, a tidal wave coming in from the horizon blotting out everything. In ten years' time, nobody will know . . . what the word [second front] meant emotionally to all of us.[6]

In the spring of 1944, rumours percolated and bets were placed as to when the much-talked about second front would begin. Churchill himself fuelled speculation when, in March, he alluded to the impending invasion and beseeched the people to prepare for the 'hour of our greatest effort', when the Allies would 'hurl themselves upon the foe and batter out the life of the cruellest tyranny which has ever sought to bar the progress of mankind'.[7] Around Minehead, American training operations intensified as guns blazed continuously that spring. Everyone anxiously awaited the much-anticipated, but dreaded, opening of the second front. On a beautiful summer-like day in late April, Helen Mitchell sat by the sea and tried to rest. Though everyone around her seemed happy, she nonetheless felt as though 'We're on edge of volcano.'

While rumours about the invasion were spreading rapidly in early 1944, the most important social reform to be enacted during the war was being piloted through Parliament. The desultory state of education and its deeply classed structure had been an issue for debate since the beginning of the war, especially when evacuation and army recruitment laid bare the problems of the system. In the first year of war, as schools evacuated in droves from the cities, thousands of children found there were not enough classrooms or teachers to educate them; by January 1940, a million children had been out of school for four months. Not only were educational resources obviously lacking, but the realities of the class system came under scrutiny when it was learned that many army recruits had a very limited education, some being illiterate or having extremely low literacy. These recruits were the product of an education system that offered secondary education only to those who could pay the fees. Most working-class children left school at fourteen with only an elementary education.

The Education Act (also known as the Butler Act) sought to redress these issues. With this new act, a minister of education was created, with the power to implement nationwide education policies and to balance out discrepancies in resources and skills in schools across England and Wales. The Act would also raise the school-leaving age to fifteen, and eventually to sixteen (which did not happen in actuality until 1971). More importantly, the Act made access to secondary education free, thus theoretically providing equality of opportunity. Furthermore, university education was made available to qualified students, regardless of their ability to pay.

Learning of the new Act, Alice Bridges reflected on her own educational experience. She 'bitterly regretted' that she had been denied an opportunity to attend university. All her life, she pursued intellectual endeavours – such as the weekly discussion group she attended – but often felt inadequate when she mixed with others who had had access to higher education. With the Butler Act, though disappointed she herself might not benefit, she was happy that the university provision might in future help others like her (and particularly her daughter). Furthermore, she thought that a general raising of academic standards would affect the standard of living positively for all. And she hoped that, with a more educated populace, war might eventually be eradicated. 'Shall we with education be able to keep our own country from war?' Alice wondered, 'Shall we be able to climb high enough to see the futility of wars and that inevitably it is the common man who saves us in dire need?'

The Norwood Report, which informed the new Education Act, proposed three types of learners: academically inclined scholars, the technically or mechanically inclined, and the 'modern'. Out of this reasoning developed three types of secondary education, or a tripartite system: grammar schools offered a liberal education that was preparatory to university; technical schools provided education for practical occupations such as technicians or engineering; finally, secondary modern schools were to provide a rounded educational experience neither too academic nor too technical. Which of the three paths a student would take was determined by the 11-plus exam.

Former teacher Irene Grant was a keen supporter of the Butler Act, even if it was too late for her or her family to capitalize on. She and her husband Tom were life-long learners who had both inherited the thirst for knowledge from their fathers, despite the fact that their time at school had been so short. 'How they'd [Tom and Irene's fathers] love to have stayed on at school,' she mused. In Grant's estimation, raising the school-leaving age to fifteen, and eventually sixteen, gave respectable and upwardly mobile working-class individuals (like her) an opportunity to continue to learn before being shoved off to work. Additionally, based on her own experience in the classroom, she hoped that the new system would allow students to 'pick and choose what subjects they wish to learn' and, more importantly, '*to change their minds*'. After children learned the basics, which to her included basic darning and dressmaking for girls, students should be allowed to 'get on with the jobs they are interested in'. While some of the flexibility of which Grant dreamed would not come to fruition until the advent of comprehensive schools several decades later, the Butler Act did lay the foundations for a better and more equitable educational experience, a fact Irene seemed to recognize very early on.

While wide-ranging support was given to the Act as a step towards a better future, the passage of the Butler Act also made a statement about the limited extent to which the war affected women's rights. During the debates, Clause 82, which stipulated that male and female teachers receive equal pay for equal work, was narrowly passed. Edie Rutherford noted this event with glee. She saw the amendment as 'the thin end of the wedge'; if equal pay was adopted in teaching, trades and professions would soon have to implement equal pay, she reasoned. After all, Edie told M-O, 'Sex distinction is entirely artificial and man arranged, and when I say man I mean MAN not mankind!'

But Rutherford's excitement would not last, for Churchill killed the amendment by forcing a vote of confidence. He moved that Clause 82 be stricken from the bill and, further, stressed that any opposition to such a move would be seen as an act of defiance against the government. Edie was incensed at Churchill's actions, especially as the Allies prepared to wind up the war with Germany, and called it a 'low down trick' to make a domestic issue a matter of international importance simply because 'He can't have things his way.'

Amid the buzz over the opening of a new front in Western Europe and the domestic debates over education and equal pay, few noticed the significant turn of events in the east that spring. To Edie Rutherford, it was 'the Burma scrap' and it was 'incredible'. Despite her extreme concern over all matters imperial, however, Rutherford made no other mention, and certainly none of the others felt it worthy of note in their diaries. Nevertheless, the action that began in the north-east corner of India on 17 April 1944 would ultimately prove to be the worst military defeat in Japanese history, and would also illustrate the strength of Indian loyalty – or at least, their commitment to ousting the Japanese from their land. That spring, Indian forces, courageously fighting alongside British soldiers, fought a fierce jungle battle against the Japanese. Over 80,000 Japanese were killed. Days later, Gandhi, who had since recovered from his 1943 hunger strike, was released from prison.

Back home, everyone seemed focused exclusively on the Western Front. Any lull in news was taken as a sign of the impending push. People tried to divine the meanings of mundane military orders. Was it significant that leave had been suspended? Did it matter that soldiers were redirecting their mail?

Edie Rutherford had a bet of 1 shilling with her husband that 'we jump on to Continent from this side' on Whitsun weekend. She lost the bet. Conversations Edie overheard in Sheffield suggested that the invasion would happen when Rome fell, which seemed likely to happen any day that May. But her husband, Sid, figured that the military simply needed time to build enough 'jet propelled aircraft' to overwhelm the enemy before it could launch the offensive.

In Newcastle that May, the Home Guard waited anxiously for the impending invasion of the Continent. Irene's husband, Tom, and other members of the Home Guard were issued supplies to thwart possible German retaliation when the Allied second front was opened – Tom believed that German paratroopers would attempt an invasion on the north-east coast. As for Irene, the anticipation was maddening. 'Waiting, waiting, waiting and yet how terrified that there'll be hell-let-loose on second front,' she wrote in her diary. Still, she told M-O, 'I hope we have news tonight that second front has started and Germany has collapsed.' By the end of May, regardless of the necessary death and potential retribution, everyone in Britain seemed impatient for the push to begin.

CHAPTER TWELVE

OH! WHAT A LEISURELY WAR

Natalie and Hugh Tanner were up early on the morning of 6 June 1944. Hugh's regular business trip to firms in the north-east was scheduled for that day and, as usual, Natalie was to accompany him. Every month, Hugh visited clients and suppliers in Darlington, Middlesbrough and Newcastle. As they prepared to leave, Natalie switched on the wireless and caught the 8 o'clock news. The details were unclear, but it 'sounded as though we were going places at last'. Hugh was positive that the much-anticipated second front was underway, while Natalie, on the other hand, decided to reserve judgement until further news came through.

Later that morning, Natalie and Hugh stopped in at Darlington and had coffee before moving on to Newcastle. As they approached Chester-le-Street, south of Newcastle, Natalie knew that her husband's instinct was right. Numerous lorries had been stacked along the dual carriageway leading into the city for months, but now, save a few being worked on by female mechanics, they had disappeared.

Preparations for D-Day had been in the works for some time on both sides of the Channel. Everyone seemed to realize that the impending invasion would be the decisive moment of the war, and overall victory hinged upon its success. General Erwin Rommel, once head of German forces in Northern Africa, was now in charge of building the 'Atlantic Wall' to defend against the massive Allied force that was expected to invade the Continent. Labourers, forced or paid by the Germans, beefed up defences along the French and Belgian coasts. Steel and concrete gun nests sprang up along the coast, while obstacles to both ground and air invasion troops were strewn across the beaches and countryside.

Across the English Channel, build-up for invasion was evident nearly everywhere. Thousands had been employed in constructing the specialized support equipment necessary for fighting on the beaches of Normandy. Shrouded under a veil of utmost secrecy, workers built huge floating harbours, code-named 'Mulberry harbours', designed to help transform the Norman coastline into usable ports.[1] The size of the port of Dover, the Mulberries were built to ride tides over twenty feet high and handle thousands of vehicles and 10,000 tons of supplies for the invading forces daily. As the Mulberries took shape, huge concrete structures began slowly to dominate the skylines of Merseyside, Southampton, Portsmouth and Goole in the spring of 1944. Sixty feet high, over fifty feet wide and two hundred feet long, these massive, hollowed-out, concrete caissons (code-named 'Phoenix') were built to float initially, but when in place, doors were opened and the structures sank, creating instant breakwaters to shelter the Mulberries and landing operations.[2] Most of the necessary 4,000 landing craft ('landing ships, tanks', or LSTs) designed to carry troops onto the shore were constructed at factories located in the eastern half of the US.

With artificial ports and breakwaters to tame the seas, and landing craft to ferry soldiers ashore, Major General Percy Hobart used his technological savvy to create vehicles designed to overcome the various obstacles troops were expected to encounter on the beaches. Hobart's 'funnies' certainly raised a few eyebrows, especially American ones (US commander Omar Bradley refused to use the silly-looking contraptions at Omaha Beach). But aesthetics did not matter in battle – functionality did, and Hobart's 'funnies' helped to ease British landings on D-Day. The 'funnies' included vehicles designed to clear mines, fill in bomb craters and anti-tank trenches, lay canvas across soft terrain to provide footholds for assault troops, blast concrete pillboxes with powerful mortars (nicknamed 'flying dustbins') and belch fire from the mouth of the 'crocodile' – a flame-throwing tank capable of incinerating anything within 360 feet.[3] 'Swimming tanks', or DD Shermans, and US-designed DUKW (nicknamed 'ducks' and used primarily for landing equipment on shore) rounded out the innovations which gave landing troops an edge in their harrowing mission.[4]

While thousands of workers set about building the necessary equipment for the assault, Allied troops needed to prepare. Troops descended on quiet villages and fertile farmland across England to train on terrain similar to what was expected to face them in France. In April, Helen Mitchell escaped the domestic drudgery and the aerial operations that drove her nearly insane at home in Kent. Searching for solitude and quietude in her beloved Somerset, she instead became caught up in these Allied training manoeuvres. Troops swarmed the town of Minehead and overran the surrounding hills that Helen so enjoyed rambling. American GIs loitered below her window at night, beaches were cordoned off, and paved roads were cut through the hills ('the worst bit of vandalism ever', according to Helen). Locals seemed excited at all the activity – a novelty for them, but a well-worn nuisance for the seasoned Mitchell.

Late that spring, as the wit-shattered Helen Mitchell coped with her own Allied invasion in Minehead, her son was involved in a secret operation to support the invasion. At the same time that troops and workers across Britain prepared to invade the beaches of Normandy under Operation Overlord, William Mitchell and thousands of others were engaged in an elaborate subterfuge designed to throw the Germans off the true invasion scent in Normandy. The deception plan, code-named Operation Fortitude, paralleled Overlord, spinning a multitude of believable lies about the invasion and feeding them to the Germans.

Fortitude operatives led the Germans to believe that a build-up in Scotland, which was in reality little more than radio chatter and double-agent misinformation, signalled an impending attack on Hitler's U-boat installations in Norway. Other hoaxes pointed to potential diversionary landings in the west and south of France, all the way through the Balkans. Allied secret operations pressed double agents and resistance movements into action in order to distract and pin down Axis troops all across Europe. The Red Army also agreed to hold off offensives in the east until the opening of the second front. The objective of such complicated and widespread machinations was to divert German resources away from the targeted landing beaches in Normandy, thus increasing the probability of Allied success, and saving lives.

The most important ruse to this end was the one that confirmed what many Germans thought was the most strategically viable invasion site: the Pas-de-Calais. Calais was the sensible choice: close to England and a straight line to the heart of Germany. The reinforcing deception of Fortitude made the German command confident that Allied forces would indeed land on the coast around Calais. Accordingly, Rommel spent most of his time in the area, strengthening defences and awaiting his enemy.

Helen's son, William, was recruited to assist in the Pas-de-Calais deception. As an architecture student and amateur carpenter, he was well-suited to help pull off a staged build-up of forces in the Thames Estuary and on the Kent and Essex coast closest to Calais. Dummy landing craft, wooden gliders and inflatable tanks sprang up throughout the area. Even a massive wooden model of an oil dock, complete with fighter defence and fog machines to shroud the illusion, was constructed on site according to the specifications of Basil Spence (the architect who would later rebuild Coventry Cathedral and design Sussex University). William and his team built and camouflaged the fake equipment to look realistic, yet the camouflage could not be too effective: the point was for the Germans to see it.

Equipment was important, but to lend even more credence to the deception, armies had to be created. Thus Fortitude operatives conjured American and British army groups out of thin air. With the help of cleverly constructed radio communications, news 'leaks', high-level visits to the area and other actions, the non-existent First United States Army Group (FUSAG), supposedly commanded by General Patton, occupied the area around the Thames Estuary in preparation for the supposed invasion at the Pas-de-Calais. The British Twelfth Army, complete with motorized infantry and armoured divisions, was also deployed and equipped, but only on paper. Allied bombers disabled many of the German radar and listening stations on the French and Belgian coasts, allowing British intelligence to control most of the information flowing to German command. Discreet radio noise was piped out over the east coast, while the ionosphere over the real D-Day port of Southampton remained silent; this silence was assisted by the laying of radio cables directing communications miles away from Southampton. Furthermore, double agents in Britain fed the Germans intelligence that supported the Pas-de-Calais invasion route.

From the air, the elaborate ruse made the area look as if it was bustling with activities associated with an impending invasion. Workers trudged through the long grass to create the illusion of troop activity in the area. Clothes lines and laundry hung on the fake landing vehicles, and disabled and older soldiers loitered on the decks of ships to provide human evidence of the build-up for the benefit of German aerial operations. To add to its authenticity, the King and Queen, as well as Supreme Allied Commander Dwight D. Eisenhower, made periodic inspections of the site.

But in May and June of 1944, as Natalie and Hugh Tanner had witnessed on their business trip to Newcastle on 6 June, vehicles and convoys began to descend on the south coast. Hampshire turned into a massive military store, military vehicles and ammunition shrouded from above by the canopy of the New Forest. Schools, homes and businesses in the real embarkation point of Southampton were requisitioned for the military, and the roads leading into the city were choked for miles with war materiel as the day for invasion rapidly approached.

Two days before D-Day, on 4 June, Allied troops captured Rome. 'Hurrah ... and beyond Hurrah', Edie Rutherford exclaimed when she heard the news. Although relieved, when Natalie Tanner learned that Rome had fallen, she was also quite bitter about the Italians' 'easy' defeat. When so much had been destroyed across Europe, why should Rome get off 'scot free?', she wondered. After all, Natalie thought, 'The Italian fascists are just as bad as the German Nazis only less efficient and I think less sincere.' Furthermore, she reasoned, they were largely responsible for the devastation loosed upon Europe. 'Without Mussolini,' Tanner was convinced, 'Hitler would never have got where he has, but would have spent his time in a lunatic asylum'.

Regardless of the relative reprieve handed to the Italians and their capital, there was little time for rejoicing over the fall of Rome; all activity rolled inexorably towards the invasion of Western Europe. Helen Mitchell's first indication that something was afoot was the sound of gliders overhead on the night of 5 June, and stillness in the morning – the guns had gone silent over Minehead. Her instincts were confirmed at noon by the BBC. Still, so few people talked about the invasion around town that she 'wondered if I had dreamed it'. 'Six intelligent females talking of this and that but no mention of invasion,' she told M-O of her D-Day experience in Minehead. 'Walked about streets and listened, but only talk among crowds personal affairs or grumbling about supplies. Went to 3 shops – no one mentioned it!' Helen exclaimed.

Desperate for information, she spent the evening in an 'orgy of listening', awaiting news, and was appalled to hear the BBC present the invasion in the 'usual happy picnic atmosphere' that she felt inappropriate to the gravity that the death and destruction of war dictated. Mitchell went to bed that night fearing German retribution. 'But not a plane to be heard.'

All around Britain, everyone was, as Edie Rutherford reported, 'glued to the radio as at Dunkirk time and as never since'. Alice Bridges listened in at 7 a.m., but had no indication that anything was brewing until later in the morning, when she was dusting. The radio next door seemed to be louder than usual, and 'the insistence of the radio voice' floating through the walls encouraged her to 'switch on', at which she 'heard the great news'. 'Exhilarated and pleased', she looked out of her window and expected to see everyone rushing out into the streets to 'make whoopee' and celebrate together. But not a soul could she see, so she turned back to her work and then took a nap.

Later, it occurred to her that she needed to find out what others were thinking for the benefit of M-O. Alice got dressed, put on her face and went into downtown Birmingham. Everything was 'bustle and business' down at the Bull Ring in the centre of town, but, as Helen had experienced, no one talked about the invasion. She walked up New Street and Corporation Street and found everyone was going about as normal. Unsuccessful in judging the tenor of the people, she breezed into the 'amusement place', set up specifically, she told M-O, to entertain 'Yanks' and take their money.

Finding only a young American airman who didn't seem too intelligent in Alice's estimation and worse, had no money, she moved on to the casino nearby. There, she asked a few women their feelings, but got very pat replies. Later, a man asked her to dance; he wasn't a good dancer, but she spent two and half hours talking to him about his rocky marriage. 'The human case book, that's me,' she said. When she left him at the end of the night, she advised him to be firm with his wife or leave her. There was no talk of D-Day.

At work in Sheffield, Edie and her office mates listened in. Tears streamed down the faces of some of the 'girls' who had brothers, sons, husbands or fathers 'in it'. Some simply could not bear to hear the reports and left the room. As the news came through, Edie wondered 'How many wives at 6 a.m. are by now widows???'

In the pre-dawn of 6 June, the main contingents of British troops landed at the beaches code-named Sword and Gold – Ouistreham and Arromanches respectively. Those who fought their way across Gold Beach were expected to take the town of Bayeux that day, while soldiers at Sword were supposed to make it eight miles inland to the town of Caen. By midnight of 6 June, 150,000 Allied soldiers had come ashore at designated beaches on the Norman coast. (Americans landed west of British troops at Utah and Omaha beaches, and Canadians at Juno, between Sword and Gold beaches.) Although none of the troops made it to their objective that first night, an important foothold was established in German territory and casualties were much lighter than feared. Churchill expected at least 10,000 casualties that day, but fewer than 5,000 perished on the first day of action. To illustrate the success of the operation: approximately

350 Canadian soldiers died on 6 June, whereas in the ill-fated debacle at Dieppe in 1942, nearly 1,000 died. To answer Edie's musings, back home in Britain, over 1,600 wives, mothers or sisters would soon learn they'd lost their loved ones.

When the Tanners reached Newcastle on 6 June, they had lunch and caught the 'fag end of the one o'clock news', confirming their hunch: the second front had indeed begun. Afterwards, Hugh left Natalie in town while he went to his business meeting, and as usual on her trips to Newcastle, she caught a tram to the Odeon theatre. The tram was empty, so Natalie chatted with the conductress, who agreed with her that though necessary, the invasion must be 'wicked' for the soldiers. On her way to the theatre, Tanner passed a crowd of onlookers who, despite the biting wind and rain, stopped to watch respectfully as a convoy of soldiers passed. There were no flags waving or cheers of excitement, only grave anticipation. Natalie paused for a moment, then carried on to the theatre.

The movie, Alfred Hitchcock's *Lifeboat* starring Tallulah Bankhead, she thought particularly well done – better by far, she thought, than the much-touted (all-male) Noël Coward film, *In Which We Serve*. Afterwards, Natalie waited for her husband and read in the hotel's lounge until the King spoke on the wireless. Hotel guests gathered round to listen and everyone stood up when 'God Save the King' was played at the conclusion of his speech. Natalie felt sorry for George VI; though they all raved about the BBC's coverage of D-Day, no one in the group mentioned the King and she personally found him particularly uninspiring.

The next day, a little frayed at the edges from a rough night's sleep (not so much from worries over the mortal conflict across the Channel as from the trains, trams and buses that scurried along beneath her window all night long), Natalie went down to the theatre to buy tickets for that evening's production of 'Is Your Honeymoon Necessary?' The Tanners were entertaining Hugh's clients, the Williamsons, and Natalie was tickled that she managed to get four well-positioned stalls for a little less than £2.

Later that day, Mrs Williamson met Natalie in town and brought her home for the afternoon. It was a nice stone terraced house that the childless couple had only just moved into – a 'family house', Natalie imagined. Mary Williamson and her mother were entertaining and accommodating, but Natalie felt somewhat out of sorts. Mary was easily in her early thirties and Tanner was nagged by the fact that Mary hadn't been 'roped into National Service'. It was odd, Tanner reflected later, to spend the afternoon 'with two women who were doing nothing apart from running a home ... positively prewar'.

Natalie's reaction to Mary and her mother can only be described as an amusing case of the pot calling the kettle black, for Natalie's own situation was hardly different from Mrs Williamson's. At forty-four, Tanner was fit enough herself to be 'roped into' war work. Since her son was under fourteen, however, she was exempted from official conscription. Still, as her son was away at school near Manchester, he was rarely at home, and one would think Tanner capable of volunteering, as she thought the Williamsons should have done.

Natalie may have thought that the difference lay in the Williamsons' close proximity to the large city of Newcastle. Tanner kept up with the events of the war and wrote about them for M-O, but there was little else she could do but take care of her home, her husband and her son, she explained to M-O, because she lived too far outside a major town. And yet, Natalie regularly found her way to nearby Leeds or Bradford for shopping, lunch and/or dinner, and usually a play or film. In fact, Natalie's war was rarely spent at home, but rather more often in these two towns or in London.

At least twice a week, and always on Fridays, Natalie – sometimes accompanied by her mother, who lived up the hill from their cottage – hitched a ride with Hugh into the nearest village. Here, Natalie ordered coal and her groceries for the week, and exchanged library books. On occasion, she ate at the local British Restaurant – non-profit, self-service cafeterias originally named Communal Feeding Centres, where one could get a cheap and generally filling meal.

There was little else to do in the village beyond the usual weekly errands and so, once these were done, Tanner usually caught a bus into Leeds or Bradford. In Leeds, she spent her mornings in the cafes at either Lewis' department store or the Great Northern Hotel. Here, Natalie sipped coffee and wrote letters or read until noon, when she moved on to the Gambit cafe for lunch and conversation with other regulars. Some of the Gambit grazers were politically conservative and Tanner, a communist and staunch supporter of the USSR, took great joy in crossing ideological sabres with them. Others were socialites, conscientious objectors and actors. After lunch, Natalie frequented a bookstore where she debated political issues with the bookseller, a member of the Communist Party, and picked up her regular *Daily Worker*, except from January 1941 to September 1942, when the communist paper was suppressed by the government.

Next, Tanner usually stopped at the cinema for a movie or two. Because of fears of mass casualties, cinemas and football stadiums had been closed during the first weeks of war, but, after raids failed to materialize in that time, and once people began to complain, cinemas and sporting events soon reopened. George Bernard Shaw called the closures 'a masterstroke of unimaginative stupidity' that could only be disastrous to morale, leaving people to 'cower in darkness and terror'.[5] From then on, movies were a popular wartime diversion. Despite the fact that an entertainment tax was levied on seat prices, attendance grew from 1939, when about nineteen million people a week went to the cinema, to 1945, when thirty million allowed themselves a few hours of weekly escape.

When M-O asked its writers to list their top six movies of 1943, Tanner duly responded with seven. The number-one spot on her list was a tie between two American films: Orson Welles' follow-up to *Citizen Kane*, *The Magnificent Ambersons*, and *Mission to Moscow*, a movie that was part of President Roosevelt's strategy to garner more popular American support for Russia. Tanner saw *Mission* twice and liked it because, 'I am always glad when the case for Russia is put by the Capitalist.' Further, she thought the movie 'authentic' and 'beautifully acted'. Though she felt the story was 'rather trite', *The Ambersons* offered a nice break from war-related films and was well-directed, produced and acted. *Casablanca* also made her top seven, as did the Russian film, *Alexander Nevsky*. The M-O directive must have been difficult to answer for Natalie the film buff, who intimated that, 'Actually I could make the list much longer,' and proceeded to add another 'memorable' seven to her response, such as the British war films *Went the Day Well, We Dive at Dawn* and Noël Coward's *In Which We Serve*. Tanner's movie-going went far beyond most during the war. About a third of the population said they went to cinema at least once a week, but she easily saw at least two films a week during the war, if not more.

Although she had seen several films in 1943, and said she enjoyed going to the movies, Nella Last could barely conjure more than three specific film titles for her M-O list: *Penn of Pennsylvania* ('I like "pioneer people" . . . and my forbears [sic] up to my Gran's time were Quakers'), *Yankee Doodle Dandy*, and her favourite actress, Greer Garson (of *Mrs. Miniver* fame) in *Random Harvest*. Stuck at home, suffering from arthritis, Irene Grant did not see any films in 1943. Edie Rutherford went to the movies very little, but said she enjoyed *Bambi* because 'It was good propaganda for animals and against man with his blasted gun.' She also saw *Two Yanks in Trinidad*, which 'infuriated' her because it underlined the ignorance and indifference of the Americans, who 'didn't think there was a war before Pearl Harbour'. Alice Bridges did not go in for movies, but enjoyed dancing and socializing instead. Unsurprisingly, the lonely and isolated Helen Mitchell had 'not seen a film for three years'.

Natalie Tanner, the upper middle-class Cambridge-educated housewife, hardly fitted the profile of an avid film-goer during the war, who tended to be younger, urban and working class. She was, in fact, a film connoisseur – a woman who might have had her own film critic's column in a newspaper, women's magazine or high-brow film journal. Instead, she reserved her criticism to her social circle and M-O. Like a film critic, she enjoyed, or endured, almost every production that hit the silver screen during the war.

On one of her usual Friday excursions to Leeds in 1944, she caught the American film, *The Hour Before Dawn*, an adaptation of the Somerset Maugham novel in which a Nazi spy marries an English pacifist to help Hitler plan his invasion of England. Despite the fact that she 'knew it would be bad', she went to see it nevertheless. 'The whole thing was bogus and preposterous,' she wrote, and the lead actor 'definitely miscast'. As might be deduced from this commentary, her criticism often went beyond storyline to casting and frequently to direction, lighting and camera angles. For instance, she thought the French film, *Le Jour se lève* (*The Day Rises*), 'well done', and her analysis of it led her to remark that some British films were equally impressive, if at times they looked 'poverty stricken'. The problem with British films, she mused, was, 'They never seem to realize that there is any other position for the camera except bang in front.'

It is unsurprising that Tanner's film criticism extended into the art of casting and production, since she and her husband were also intimately involved in the dramatic club at the Civic in Bradford. Her trips into Leeds often included a jaunt into Bradford, where she sometimes took in a rehearsal, a play reading or production at the Civic and then topped the night off with a few beers across the street at the Junction with the theatre set. When Hugh's busy schedule allowed time, and when the petrol ration allowed for daily drives into Bradford for rehearsals, he sometimes acted in Civic productions. Natalie dabbled in acting herself, taking lessons in December 1939, but it seems that she enjoyed being entertained rather than entertaining.

In order to have time to shop, discuss politics, graze and drink at local establishments and criticize movies and plays, Natalie was generally unfettered by the obligations of domesticity. In her diary, days spent at home were given short shrift. Diary entries on these days usually mentioned the book she was reading, made reference to the weather and finished with a curt, 'Cooked. Cleaned.' On the other hand, when she ventured away from the cottage, Natalie's writing was much more detailed. Clearly, these excursions were more interesting and important to her. She enjoyed connecting with others, shopping and engaging her mind through film, theatre and the mountain of books she borrowed from the libraries in the nearby village and Leeds.

Though she could, and on occasion did, cook, Tanner ate many of her meals out. This is especially true during the times when her son was away at boarding school. When he was home, a flurry of domesticity – cooking, ironing and constantly tidying in James' wake – took over her routine. Still, his presence did not interfere with Natalie's trips into town. She simply brought him along, treating him to ice cream at Lewis', lunch at the Gambit and a movie (or two) of *his* choice. On occasion, he attended plays at the Civic with his parents and acquired the family penchant for dramatic commentary. When the weather allowed, the family walked the four miles over verdant rolling hills to the village pub for lunch and sometimes stayed for dinner and drinks. The beer flowed easily and locals' tales of the harvest and town history made for interesting amusement, as, for example, on the night when a good-natured argument broke out over which village installed the first electric light.

For those with money, eating out was a way to stretch rationing. Individuals were not required to give up rationing coupons when they ate at restaurants, and though the government tried to limit abuses by placing a maximum of five shillings for all meals (except in classy establishments, where such a low-cost meal would never cover their costs), there were ways around this restriction. In theory, restaurants, tea shops, cafes and pubs were given the same level of rations as the ordinary housewife received. In reality, the shortages felt keenly at the local grocer's or butcher's were rarely perceived in eating establishments. Indeed, although Natalie sometimes complained about rationing, her family never wanted for much during the war because they frequently ate out. While other people were counting their coupons for a can of salmon in the stores, Natalie could find a delicious Dee salmon off-ration in a restaurant.

Those with less money who ventured out to restaurants might also find good deals on such delicacies, as Alice Bridges learned bargain hunting after Christmas during the Blitz. Taking a rest at a soda fountain, Alice savoured a 5d Horlicks, which was so rich it 'tasted like a milk shake', and indulged in a fresh salmon sandwich for only 2d. It was a rare delight for someone who made do to feed herself and her family on the rationing scheme.

Many others resented people such as Tanner, who enjoyed themselves regularly at restaurants and cafes. When Nella Last went for a short holiday to the seaside town of Morecambe in 1943, she was shocked to find diners wasting the lavish plates of food served to them. Mentally she reckoned the wastage left by the couple next to them in a restaurant:

There was a full week's ration for one – I could not have bought them in fact for 1/- at my butchers. I thought of what could have been done with them – the fat cut off and chopped for a 'suet' pudding and the chops braised with vegetables and made into a good lunch for the two of us.

Edie Rutherford believed that a scheme that allowed such wastage to occur without rationing was patently unfair. Restaurants, she argued, bought up most of the food, leaving the ordinary housewife to feed her family on what was left over. Furthermore, since rationing only guaranteed that certain necessities were available and one still needed to purchase rations, the poor were at a distinct disadvantage. While the rich feasted on game and salmon off-ration, Edie's sister struggled simply to purchase the rations allotted to her family. Indeed, though the government spent millions yearly in subsidies to keep food prices low, the cost of living had risen by 35 per cent by the end of the war. The rise left Rutherford with little expendable income beyond what went into her larder. The problem was acute for city dwellers, like Edie, who lived in flats without allotments. Unlike Last and Grant, who also felt the pinch of increasing costs, Rutherford could not supplement her diet with home-grown vegetables. Grant had a small back garden that produced some greens for salads, while Last grew various vegetables and kept chickens to ensure a steady supply of eggs.

Natalie Tanner rarely felt squeezed by rationing. She tended a garden that produced an abundant supply of vegetables and fruit, and nearby farmers provided the Tanners with plenty of eggs and the occasional holiday goose. The only economizing she had to endure was as a result of shortages in the supply chain. Since her husband made out very well from government orders during the war, she had plenty to buy whatever was available, which, she complained, was not much. Therefore, she could afford to spend more on restaurant dining, movies, books, stockings, suits for James, or whatever she found in the stores.

On the second day of the invasion, 7 June, Edie Rutherford noted that things continued to go well. She went to hospital and found a queue waiting to give blood. The wait was long, but, 'It is little we do compared to the men who fight.' On the way home, she stopped in her favourite shoe shop and enquired about lined boots for the winter. They had two pairs of Glastonburys left for £4.8s. She balked at the price, which reflected the 100 per cent purchase tax tacked onto luxuries. 'I never heard such rubbish,' she exclaimed. 'A lined boot is a wise purchase in this foul climate.' At the greengrocer's, Edie complained of the exorbitant prices and left the broad beans and new potatoes 'till they get within reason'.

Later that week, the military operation across the Channel continued to go well, 'If one can forget all the men who die and fall hurt.' As Edie waited for her tram home, a convoy of tanks passed, and tears welled in her eyes as she watched the 'lads'. By 10 June, over 300,000 troops were on French soil, all beaches had been linked and the first Mulberry harbour installed offshore at Arromanches. The Allies now commanded fifty miles of French coastline. Slowly, inexorably the Allies fought their way inland.

In Natalie Tanner's circle, conversation revolved around the ongoing action in Normandy. The bookstore owner in Leeds, who had already lost one son two years before when his transport sank, had one son 'in it' and another awaiting deployment in England. An acquaintance at the Gambit was waiting for his papers, and another woman spent all night driving casualties from Dover to Huddersfield. Only the young, it seemed to Natalie, could enjoy the excitement of the invasion. James wrote from boarding school saying, 'It is very good about the second front. It is the eighth wonder of the world.' 'It must be nice to be 11½ years old,' Natalie remarked.

After D-Day, news of Allied successes came fast and furious. Edie Rutherford complained that all the information was enough to give one 'mental indigestion'. On 20 July, an assassination attempt nearly took Hitler's life. 'What a pity that bomb didn't get Hitler,' Rutherford lamented in her diary. The bomb had been placed in the presence of Hitler and other high-ranking officers at their headquarters, Wolfsschanze (the Wolf's Lair), deep in the East Prussian woods at Rastenburg by the leader of the German opposition, known as the Schwarze Kapelle (Black Orchestra), Colonel Count von Stauffenberg.

The roots of the assassination attempt against Hitler went deep. As early as 1938, when Hitler announced his intention to go to war for territorial expansion, those in the army who did not agree with Hitler's policies were prepared to remove the Führer from power. As for young, thirty-three-year-old Count von Stauffenberg, his dislike of the Nazi leader reached even further back, to the Night of Long Knives in 1934, when Hitler orchestrated the deaths of the leadership of the SA (Stormtroopers), including Ernst Rohm. His hate deepened with Kristallnacht in 1938, when a concerted attack on Jews erupted across Germany. Stauffenberg expressed his assessment of Hitler on the eve of the Führer's triumphal entry into a prostrate Paris in June 1940, when he told fellow conspirators that Hitler was neither a great war leader nor a great law maker. Instead, the Count asserted, the man only desired destructive and all-consuming power. Hitler's lust for power could only destroy Germany, the conspirators reasoned.

After several failed plans to assassinate Hitler in the past, the recent success of the Allies in Normandy convinced the Schwarze Kapelle that the time had come to try once again. Operations in the east also signalled the right moment, too: Russians were quickly moving towards Berlin, and the conspirators wanted most of all to stave off utter defeat at the hands of the Soviets. So, Stauffenberg, summoned to headquarters to give a report to German High Command, armed the British-made bomb and placed it in the conference room. After the meeting started, the Count excused himself. Outside, Stauffenberg waited for the fireworks to start. Not long afterwards, a massive explosion ripped through the building. Convinced that Hitler had been killed, the Count quickly left the base to avoid detection and made his way to Berlin, where the Schwarze Kapelle were to complete their coup d'etat by blaming the murder on the SS and taking over the reins of government.

Although the explosion brought down the roof of the building, destroyed the hulking conference table and blew out windows, and though several high-ranking officers were killed, Stauffenberg's belief that he'd killed Hitler was incorrect. Fire from the blast singed Hitler's hair, his right arm was temporarily paralysed, a huge gash cut across his face and he suffered severe shrapnel wounds to his back, buttocks and legs; even the force from the explosion ripped off one of the Führer's trouser legs, but he escaped with his life.

Reading the news a few days later, Edie Rutherford thought it rather comical that Hitler had had his 'pants blown off him'. The Germans had no sense of humour, 'not as we understand it anyway', she told M-O. No self-respecting Briton would ever admit to having their pants blown off, Edie reasoned, 'as he would be ragged for the rest of his life'.

Hitler certainly did not take the attempt as a joke. He expected retribution. Despite their failure to kill the German leader, in the hours after the blast, the Schwarze Kapelle still had a good chance of success-fully completing their coup. By midnight, however, the game was up; the leaders of the movement, includ-ing Stauffenberg, had been apprehended, shot and dumped in an unmarked grave. Over the coming weeks, hundreds, if not thousands, fell under the veil of suspicion and were summarily dealt with.

Despite, or perhaps because of, Hitler's raving retribu-tion after the attempt, some people were convinced that the plot, successful or not, signalled the beginning of the end for Germany. At a RAF base in Normandy on 23 July, Churchill declared that recent events were 'grave signs of weakness in Germany. They are in a great turmoil inside. Opposite you is an enemy whose central power is crum-bling.'[6] Many perceived in the assassination attempt an end to Nazi domination over the German people and the end of the war. Irene Grant was one of the optimistic. Germany was in chaos, the Russians were advancing in the east and the troops in France were pushing on. 'War! Soon be over!' Irene exclaimed.

*   *   *

While the Allies forced their way from the beaches of Normandy into the interior of France that summer, Mitchell went on holiday with her husband in Devon, walking on the hills around Lynton and bathing by the sea. Her son's leave had been scheduled to correspond with their holiday, but he spent the summer in hospital due to a minor bicycle accident. After Peter had gone back to work, Mitchell moved back to Minehead, where the main topic of conversation and worry was not the invasion, but a new and menacing German weapon.

A week after the Allied landing in Normandy, residents of London and the south coast of England encountered a new form of airborne destruction. The Germans called it *Vergeltungswaffe Eins* or Revenge Weapon Number One; to the British, it was a flying bomb, doodlebug, or V-1. The V-1 made a high-pitched whining noise, similar to the humming of a 'model T Ford going up hill'.[7] But it wasn't the noise that people feared; it was the silence between the time the engine of the bomb cut out and the explosion. The explosion was devastating: since the bombs did not penetrate the ground, and therefore did not absorb at least some of the impact, the blast was worse than conventional bombs.

Four V-1s landed in and around London on the first day (one very close to Mitchell's home in Kent) – of these, only the bomb that fell on Bethnal Green produced casualties: six people killed and thirteen seriously wounded. Within days of the first V-1 attack, however, almost 500 people had been killed and more than 2,000 seriously injured. The bombs came over day and night – 100 to 150 a day were aimed at London during the summer and autumn of 1944. The indiscriminate pattern and constant menace of the V-1s disrupted people's routines, and morale plunged as quickly as the bombs themselves fell to the ground. Aside from taking shelter round the clock, there was little one could do against the bombs. Ack-ack guns, for instance, were of little use in populated areas, since shooting down a V-1 didn't stop the destruction.

After the attempt on Hitler's life in July, V-1 attacks were stepped up. Even though the bomb planted by the conspirators was British-made, MI-6 had little to do with the plot. The bomb was actually captured from Secret Operations Executive (SOE) stores in France; nonetheless, the discovery of the bomb convinced Hitler that the British had had a hand in the assassination attempt. In retaliation, he ordered a massive V-1 attack on the capital. Almost twice the usual number of bombs hurtled towards London that night, and the next night, 21/22 July, another 200 found their way to the capital.

Safely ensconced in Somerset, Helen Mitchell received letters from friends in Kent and London declaring that the doodlebugs were even more serious than before. As the V-1s pounded the south-east, more anxiety than usual crept into Helen's heart. Her husband, Peter, was in the centre of the storm and her son, William, was in hospital near London after a minor biking accident. She confided to M-O,

> Have often thought this is the worst part of the war, but just now with William in hospital among bombs, and Peter working among them, and not knowing whether one's possessions have gone, beats anything yet.

To Mitchell, the mere thought of the new weapon was unnerving. Her friends in London and in the south-east wrote and told her of the fear and devastation the bombs wrought, and she learned that her home in Kent was right in the middle of the fray. The house had been 'knocked about', ceilings were down and windows were broken in outbuildings round the house, but luckily, no one was hurt.

Characteristically, Mitchell felt the government did not handle the new threat well. She believed they should concentrate on boosting the morale of those in the path of the bombs, or at least move businesses and factories out of London. When she listened to Churchill's speech about the bombings, Helen scoffed, 'All very well, but no soldier is asked to be incessantly in the front line.' She knew all too well that she would soon be back in that front line herself.

In August, the Tanners spent three leisurely weeks in Scotland. Hugh's business afforded Natalie the opportunity to travel more than the average person in wartime. Throughout much of the war, the family took yearly holidays to Scotland or Wales. Hugh visited nearby factories while Natalie and James enjoyed the scenery; when Hugh was involved in meetings in Inverness, James and Natalie explored Loch Ness and the mountains from their hotel near Urquhart. They hiked the peaks or 'messed about' in a boat on the lake, soaking in the fine August weather. Some days, Hugh joined them or went off on longer hikes alone. On 6 August, Hugh headed off for a 20-mile hike while James and Natalie spent a quiet domestic day at the hotel, he making maps of the area and she washing shirts and darning socks. Without a radio and only the Scottish *Daily Express* – 'a foul paper', according to Natalie – to remind her of the war, the peace and idyll of the holiday made the conflict, she admitted, 'fairly remote'.

While the war seemed remote in the Highlands of Scotland in August of 1944, the Allies were clawing their way through France. Near Newcastle, Irene Grant spent the summer hanging on every scrap of news about Allied progress or setbacks on the Continent and lamented the 'slaughter' suffered on both sides. She found it particularly upsetting to hear about British and American troops 'wiping out pockets' of German resistance; it was too dehumanizing. On 25 August, after four years of Nazi rule, Paris was finally wrested from German hands. When Irene heard of London bells peeling in celebration, she wondered if it wasn't a little premature, 'Why could they not wait to be sure?' The battle for France had been too hard run for her to believe that the Allies actually had control over the capital. 'We cannot be sure of anything over the radio. Hear of town liberated, then next day still fighting,' Grant complained.

A day before the liberation of Paris, Helen Mitchell returned to Kent. On her journey through London and the south-east, she was 'horrified at all the new damage' the V-1s had inflicted on the region. Within days of Helen's return, British troops overtook V-1 launch sites on the French coast. While V-1s still dropped across Britain through Christmas, the threat from the doodle-bug had been largely contained. The official death toll from the summer of the V-1 numbered close to 5,500.

The end of the V-1 menace did not, however, spell the end to bombings in Britain. Indeed, just days after the liberation of Paris, Britons were greeted with a new form of attack, the V-2. This new 'revenge' weapon improved on the V-1 substantially. Now, civilians heard only the sonic boom of a rocket that flew faster than the speed of sound, followed by a bright blue flash of light across the sky and, finally, the massive destruction of a 1-ton warhead. The sound was so loud, people within ten miles of the rocket thought it was right over them. Once again, London and the south coast were in the crosshairs.

To this new hazard that confronted Helen when she returned was added the distant roaring of guns in France and Allied planes overhead, the singing of barrage balloon wires in the wind, as well as an entire house full of hungry tenants. In the housing crunch created by the combination of bombing and employment patterns, Helen's husband Peter felt compelled to offer his massive home to those in need. Her house now became a haven for workers and soldiers, and their families – all of whom expected to be fed and cleaned after.

To add to the insult and chaos of working-class (whom she called 'rough') lodgers invading Helen's home and middle-class sensibilities, the lodgers were 'carnivores' whose dinners required her to deal with animal carcasses that produced thick grease. For a vegetarian such as Helen it was a disgusting and degrading chore. 'One's life is a battle with grease, dust, food', she wrote at this time. On her fifty-first birthday, she began work at 7.30, 'collecting and cleaning vegetables, went to greengrocer. Mrs B. [a lodger] came about 12 and made pastry to last over weekend. Said she didn't have lunch, so I couldn't,' Helen complained. Afterwards, she 'finished cleaning up at 4, made the beds, dusted W's rooms, dug out sheets, pillows, etc. to air'. Exhausted, she then 'fell into a bath, read *Times* superficially, darned socks till time to get supper'.

'Will end of war liberate me from house-slavery?' Helen mused bitterly. Fearing the war would not end soon enough, she hoped her fifty-second year would be her last if her life did not change. Tortured by the continual rockets buzzing overhead, she did, however, confide to M-O that she 'preferred not [to be] done in by a bomb!'

CHAPTER THIRTEEN

ANYONE WANT TWO TIN HATS AND TWO GAS MASKS?

Nella Last looked out into her garden, surprised to find a cheeky little magpie staring back at her. It was 'so lovely a thing', and its playfulness was infectious. The gregarious little bird whistled and hopped, performing for a scrap or two from its new audience. Nella could scarcely disappoint.

Day after day, the little magpie returned to Nella's garden – always vigilantly watching for Murphy, the cat, but happy to perch just out of Murphy's reach and announce its presence. But never again did the cheeky magpie's antics raise a smile, for the day after its first appearance, Nella learned that her youngest son had been 'dangerously wounded' in Italy. From then on, the magpie would always remind her of 19 November 1944, when she received word of her son's condition. Cliff had safely fought his way through North Africa to El Alamein and up the Italian peninsula from Naples, but just outside Florence, he encountered a German machine-gun nest. As he advanced on the position, a grenade exploded nearby, shredding his thighs, ripping into his torso and tearing through his right hand.

Though Rome had fallen on 4 June 1944, the campaign to oust the Germans from Italy was nowhere near finished. Indeed, the capture of the Italian capital probably prolonged what was already a costly and nightmarish theatre of war. In the overall scheme of things, Rome was a diversion. Instead of doggedly pursuing the Germans up the peninsula or cutting them off just north of the city, American Lieutenant General Mark Clark sent the lion's share of his troops into the capital. Clark was known as a publicity hound, and Rome was certainly a perfect opportunity to capture the attention of the media. But while American troops were greeted with wine and flowers by thankful Romans, the Germans melted away to the north.

After Rome, the Germans retreated to the 'Gothic Line', just north of Florence, at the foot of the northern Apennines. Here, the Nazi troops built a formidable line of defence. Villages were razed to the ground and trees downed to give Germans clear lines of fire and to minimize the threat of surprise, while anti-tank ditches ran along the length of the German line. The approach to these ditches was littered with tree trunks and sprinkled liberally with barbed wire and landmines, as was the riverbed of the Foglia, which meandered through the region. The hilltops bristled ominously with machine-gun pillboxes. Martha Gellhorn, a *Collier's* magazine correspondent who witnessed the fighting in Italy, told her readers that the Germans had succeeded in 'turning the beautiful hills into a mountain trap four miles deep where every foot of our advance could be met with concentrated fire'.[1] These are the conditions Cliff Last encountered as his regiment slogged their way north of Florence.

The Allies would not punch through the Gothic Line until April 1945. The campaign that landed Cliff in hospital was the longest in Western Europe, fought under horrific conditions akin to the trenches, barbed wire, mud and death of the Great War thirty years earlier. More than 310,000 Allies and over 430,000 Germans were killed or injured in Italy.

Cliff recuperated from his grievous injuries in Italy for a time, allowing the future sculptor time to study Italian art and form. When he came home, he convalesced at Conishead Hospital close to home, just outside Barrow. Although Nella had much to be thankful for – a friend's son had been blinded in Italy and others had lost loved ones – it was a black time for her. 'Only my faith and a mother's anguish of mind kept me keeping on when Cliff was wounded,' Nella later remembered.

The mother who prided herself on a close relationship with her two sons – a closer bond than she had with their father, and, she liked to say, a stronger relationship than they had with him – found her sensitive younger son aloof, moody and difficult. The homecoming must have been disappointing for Nella, for Cliff seemed to harbour an '"agin everything" attitude'. For weeks afterwards, Nella found all her efforts to be close or helpful rebuffed. It seemed that Cliff found everything she did 'irritating', 'if not actually annoy[ing]'.

To make matters worse, the nature of Cliff's injuries further drove a wedge between the two. The grenade that had ripped through Cliff's body had imbedded shrapnel deep in his upper thighs and 'impaired' his penis and bladder. Nella desperately wanted to restore the deep connection she remembered having with her son as a boy and wished he would confide in her. But while she knew he was too 'shy' to talk to her about such injuries, she also worried that he had no one else to turn to: Will had never gained Cliff's confidence and his older brother, Arthur, lived in Northern Ireland. Still, it was the gulf that had opened up between mother and son that was heartbreaking for Nella.

Sometimes Nella blamed this distance on Cliff's injuries, while at other times she thought it an indication of the 'restlessness' of his generation – a characteristic she saw often in her beloved young neighbour, Margaret Atkinson. 'Margaret seems so unhappy and unsettled – she reminds me so much of Cliff,' Nella told M-O. 'I wonder if it's a kind of "modern way" for young things,' she mused. At times when Cliff pushed her away, Nella also recalled his waywardness as a child or chalked it up to a family trait found in roving ancestors who could never be content with their situation – an aimless angst buried deep in his make-up that made Cliff short with his parents and loathe the backwardness of Barrow.

Age or generational difference, personality or genetics, as with so many returning soldiers, Cliff's battlefield experience also contributed to the growing separation from his mother. Nella often called herself a 'soldier' and made parallels between herself and her soldier-son, considering her work in the community to be her patriotic contribution to the war. Nella knew the two were vastly different, however. Even at the beginning of the war, she feared the impact that an intimate knowledge of death and killing would wreak upon her sensitive son. She entered that dark world when, helplessly, she witnessed him 'thrash' about in nightmares, tormented by 'the fact he had killed people'.

He never talked about his battle experience; indeed, though he proudly showed his mother a letter stating he had been 'mentioned in despatches' for his action, he refused to reveal the circumstances that led to his being wounded. After a few months' convalescence, he did, however, begin to open up about his injuries. As his Medical Boards increasingly improved, in May 1945, Cliff proudly presented his mother with a report of his progress since Italy. Here, she learned the horrible extent of his injuries and quietly rejoiced that he had finally confided in her. Still, there was much left unsaid and slowly, agonizingly, the rift continued to grow.

As 1945 dawned and Nella tried to reconnect with her son after his injury, Helen Mitchell coped with the almost continual menace of the V-2 bomb. January 1945 was the worst time. Almost nightly, V-2s thundered overhead or struck nearby. Some nights, she switched on the radio to drown out the noise, but on other nights the rockets were so thick even this didn't mask their terrifying boom. On one such night, she ran round the house, looking for jobs to occupy her mind, until finally, she broke down and wept, 'the first time in ages', she admitted. Snow fell thickly and ice coated the streets in mid-month, but, 'Snow doesn't stop V2,' she thought bitterly.

While the V-2s harried residents of the south-east, Allied bombers headed eastwards to rain death and destruction over Germany. The last four months of the war represented the height of aerial bombings and destruction visited upon the enemy. From January 1945 to the end of the war, over 130,000 Germans were killed in Allied aerial assaults. On 13 and 14 February, the Allies bombed the historic town of Dresden and whipped up a firestorm of the order of the one that destroyed Hamburg in 1943. Hundreds of thousands of refugees fleeing the Soviet army in the east had poured into Dresden, only to face the terrible inferno fanned by the thousands of incendiaries dropped from above. At least 30,000 people perished in the bombing.

Edie Rutherford could feel little remorse over such destruction. The Germans, she reported with disbelief, seemed far from surrendering. 'We have battered them on all sides and from the air, and still they won't surrender,' she wrote to M-O. 'I do not understand how the Germans take all we do – such mesmerism has surely never occurred before in all history?' Edie wondered. Goebbels' defiant attitude towards the onslaught of Allied bombs convinced her that 'We'll have to cover every inch of Germany before we can truly say it's over.'

Although the horrific firestorm in Dresden and the destruction of hundreds of other German cities saddened Natalie Tanner greatly, it was the targeting of the beautiful Bavarian city of Würzburg which caused her the most grief. On 16 March, Allied bombers destroyed 90 per cent of the city in less than twenty minutes, killing at least 5,000 people. As a child, Natalie had spent 'four very happy years' in the ancient city on the Main river. Photographs of the rubble in *The Times* were difficult for Tanner to bear, and she made sure not to tell her mother, who lived up the road from Natalie, about the devastating fate of their beloved city. Natalie's mother, Audrey, did not keep up with the war news very often, but when she did, she became agitated and morose; the destruction of Würzburg would be particularly difficult. Unfortunately, one of her mother's friends – 'very kind, but exceedingly tactless' – presented Audrey with the very copy of *The Times* that Natalie was attempting to keep from her mother, leaving Natalie to pick up the pieces.

After over a month of constant battering from V-2s, the swelling in Helen's throat and an overexcited heart that had developed in the wake of the continual bombings sent Mitchell packing once more. This time, she rode out the danger at a convalescent home in Anglesey. Peter accompanied his wife on the exhausting trip westwards – the two left on the 6.07 train, four V-2s crashing nearby before they pulled away, and after a few bus rides and a final taxi run, arrived in Llanddona in midafternoon. 'Could not imagine more peaceful spot,' she wrote in her diary, 'beautiful country, no cars passing, no radio or children allowed.' Even better, there was only the rare plane heard overhead and no bombs. Peter spent the weekend walking the beaches and reading *Sense and Sensibility* to his wife before he went back to London, his work and more V-2s.

For Helen, March 1945 was a peaceful respite from the constant bombs and the usual lonely domestic grind. On her previous trips away during the war, Helen had often made arrangements with friends or acquaintances that required her to perform some domestic duties, whether cooking, cleaning or laundry. But this escape was different. There were no domestic obligations weighing her down, the town was largely quiet and the residents (what few there were) were as cultured as Helen believed herself to be. The owner of the convalescent home read Robert Browning to his guests, guests discussed poetry over tea and went for quiet strolls on the beach or into town. 'Wallow in absence of bombs, no sight of a kitchen, clean rooms and light,' she happily told M-O. Thinking of those she left behind, Helen added, 'Wish everyone else in Southern England could have a spell of such bliss.'

Despite Anglesey being by far the best escape of the war, the stay was not entirely free from wartime obligations and domestic concerns. One of the residents foisted balls of wool on Helen to knit socks for the army. 'Hoped to have holiday from male knitting but can't refuse,' she remarked to M-O. And, since Peter had returned to London, he had penned several letters informing her of a home in Beckenham that he wished to buy. Anxiety over this new turn of events crept into the 'bliss' of the Welsh island and, she confided in her diary, 'Cannot face future life of household drudgery in a town which is much grimmer than in [Kent].'

But knitting for the army was only a nuisance, which didn't seem to impinge too much on her routine in Anglesey, and the prospect of a new home in dingy surroundings was as yet only a dark cloud on the horizon. Helen continued to read, converse with the residents, go for restful walks and wallow in the peace of the countryside. However, 'such bliss' could hardly last. Three weeks after she'd arrived, with the Easter holiday looming and the expense of the home mounting, Helen made her way back to Kent.

The night of her return, she was greeted with a 'filthy night [of] frequent sirens and two V1s this way about 5 a.m.' The next three evenings would bring similar torment from the skies, and during the day, 'the little bastards' at the school behind her house did little else but 'singing or screaming in playground'. Adding to her grief, 'loathsome' children from the school knocked on her door admiring the daffodils in her front garden and asking permission to take some home; she gave a stern, but exasperated 'NO' to all. On 28 March, only days after she'd returned home, Helen noted with glee, 'Praise be to God! The school breaks up today!' That same night, it was quiet over Kent. During the day, there were no bombs to report either, which set Helen to wondering, 'Either a) It's all over or b) something dirtier is brewing.'

It was difficult for Helen to believe that the once seemingly invincible Germans didn't have something more dastardly waiting in the wings or that the fight was nearly finished in Europe, but the skies over Britain would soon be peaceful once again. The last V-2 fell on Easter Sunday, 1 April, about five miles from Mitchell's home in Kent, taking with it the last British civilian casualty of the war. In May, after the end of the war in Europe, Helen opened her newspaper and learned that the village next to hers had the distinction of being the heaviest-bombed area in Britain. Now, she understood the gravity of her experience. 'Feel less stupid about cracking up,' she told M-O, 'as I had to hear most of [the bombs] all by myself.'

As the war began to wind down, Edie Rutherford looked forward to a joyful and restful Easter break. It was a 'lovely morning' when she went to work on Good Friday to tie up loose ends before the holiday, but 'wind from a rainy quarter' did not bode well for good weather. Indeed, Sunday and Monday were both wash-outs. 'Horrid day,' she noted on Monday, 'cold wind, showery, dullish'. Although Edie and her husband had hoped to get out for a long walk, she didn't dare 'put my nose outdoors' the entire weekend. Sid went down to the cinema to book seats for an evening show, but it seems others had similar designs: the queue seemed a half-mile long, and he came home empty-handed.

A week later, the weather had hardly improved, but the couple finally managed to book seats for Noël

Coward's movie, *This Happy Breed*. Rutherford thought the tale of an ordinary British family living through the inter-war years 'splendid'. It was a welcome diversion from the recent health problems her husband had been experiencing since the beginning of the year. Sid's injuries from the First World War were catching up with him. Since January, Sid had suffered one illness after another. 'My husband isn't well,' Edie wrote to M-O in March, 'Feels life is a task too much for him. Drags wearily thru each day.' He spent several days at home that winter, forcing Edie to give up her diary for the day as the typewriter always bothered him. Edie attributed some of Sid's general lethargy to his recent commitment to quitting smoking – a decision she hoped would eventually aid his waning health – but she knew that his problems went much deeper. 'He never is well, being a last war wreck,' she confided. When Sid finally went to the doctor, he learned that his heart, liver, kidneys and right lung were in bad shape. Reporting his poor prognosis to Edie, he simply laughed it off, saying, 'Well, [at least] I have a good pair of boots!' She didn't find it amusing. For years, doctors had told her husband that his body was 'organically sound' and the true trouble was that he was 'just a nervous wreck'; to learn that his organs were beginning to shut down came as a heart-wrenching blow. That night, Edie's 'vivid imagination' filled her with a feeling of impending doom and haunted her with images of widowhood.

A week after the cold and dreary weather of the Easter holiday, Irene Grant toddled out to her garden to enjoy the warm sunshine and delight in the wallflowers that splashed cheerful colour across the small enclosure. Gathering strength from the warmth that surrounded her, for the first time in months Irene felt well enough to brave a walk outside. She made her way slowly up the avenue, noting with pride that of all the little gardens peeking out from behind the stubby brick walls, hers was by far the best.

Days later, on Friday 13 April, Irene and her family were 'profoundly shocked' to learn of President Roosevelt's death the day before. Irene felt his death deeply, as though she had lost a 'personal friend' and lamented that a champion of the people was now gone. Edie Rutherford noted his passing briefly in her diary, but seemed hardly moved, since, she argued, no one human being was 'indispensable'. Helen Mitchell thought otherwise. She worried that no one could possibly 'have his vision and give help so generously and amazingly as the Americans have done' under Roosevelt's leadership.

Although the pictures from the Yalta Conference in February had revealed a gaunt and sickly president, the news nonetheless also came as a shock to Natalie Tanner. She and her son, James, had been enjoying his Easter holiday together when word came through. Though the weather had been poor for most of the break, James and Natalie had nonetheless worked in the garden when the rain slackened, and made trips into Leeds for shopping, meals and movies. They had even found time, accompanying Hugh on a business trip to Newcastle one weekend, to enjoy James' favourite pastime: watching the engines pull into the station and keeping a log of their numbers. The day they learned of Roosevelt's death, mother and son went into Leeds for a movie and Natalie noted the pall of grief that hung over the city. She was convinced that Britons had far more respect for Roosevelt than did Americans and thus felt the loss more deeply. Certainly, all the women agreed, it was a shame that Roosevelt had not lived to see the peace that seemed likely any day that April.

Roosevelt's death was joyfully received by both the Japanese and Germans, who believed that the President's passing would mean an armistice. Some Germans hoped that the Americans would join forces with them against the Russians, with whom tensions presaging the Cold War had been brewing for some time. But the illusion was short-lived; despite the fault lines developing between them, the Allies remained focused on an unconditional German surrender. The death of the President could not thwart this objective, especially as Allied troops rapidly closed in on Berlin from both the east and the west. The Soviet army had been threatening Berlin from the east for several months, and in early March, British and American troops were finally across the Rhine.

As Allied troops marched into Germany, the horror of the Holocaust was increasingly revealed. In their campaigns through Poland, the Red Army had been the first to encounter concentration camps in late 1944, and western Allies finally witnessed the evil first-hand when they overran the Natzwiller camp in Alsace on the German–French border. The camp had been evacuated before the Allies found it: storerooms were bursting with prisoners' clothing and shoes, autopsy tables and gas chambers were still intact, but there was little power in these scenes. It seemed like a deserted lumber camp, a *New York Times* reporter noted in December 1944, 'There were no prisoners, no screams, no burly guards, no taint of death in the air.'[2]

Soon, however, Allied troops would encounter the full extent of human suffering in the camps. On 11

April, Americans liberated 21,000 emaciated survivors of Buchenwald and, four days later, British troops came face-to-face with the horror that was Belsen. Journalists found they had few words to explain the almost incomprehensible conditions of these camps, the living and the dead. Nonetheless, they were all gripped by a conviction that they must attempt to tell the story. News reports and photographs began to filter into Britain.

On 19 April, though the BBC initially refused to allow the shocking and gut-wrenching report, Richard Dimbleby recounted his harrowing experience of Belsen. 'I picked my way over corpse after corpse,' he solemnly intoned and described the sad scene as it unfolded before him. A young girl, 'a living skeleton', peered out of a face of 'yellow parchment' and called out for medicine. 'She was trying to cry but she hadn't enough strength,' he told his audience. Moving on, he encountered a pile of bodies that seemed so 'utterly unreal and inhuman that I could have imagined they had never lived at all'. It was, Dimbleby recalled, 'the most horrible day of my life'.[3]

Though Dimbleby's report was more descriptive and haunting, it would be CBS reporter, Edward Murrow's detail of his experience at Buchenwald on 16 April that received more press in Britain. Fighting down anger and physical revulsion at what he witnessed, he described, 'rows of bodies stacked up like cordwood. They were thin and very white. Some of the bodies were terribly bruised, though there seemed to be little flesh to bruise.'[4] Edie Rutherford was 'appalled' when she heard the broadcast, but she couldn't say she was surprised. For years, books had told the true story, she reminded M-O. Indeed, in December 1942, Murrow himself had warned that Hitler's regime was rounding up people for slaughter. 'But folk would not be told then,' Rutherford fumed. 'Now they HAVE GOT to be told and HAVE GOT to listen.'

Natalie Tanner echoed Edie's sentiments. Though most people in Leeds were exceedingly upset by the news, she noted with resentment and anger the apathy of most people towards the camps before the war. No one cared when Germans who opposed the Nazi regime before the war were thrown in concentration camps, she protested. Furthermore, 'no one seemed to mind' the reports coming out of the refugee camps of the gross maltreatment of Spanish Republicans during the civil war there in 1936–7. Still, Natalie reported with dismay, some simply could not believe the reports. As they had done for years, most sceptics argued that the 'atrocity stories' were simply trumped up, like the many reports of German abuses of women and children in Belgium during the First World War.

Alice Bridges heard first-hand about the conditions at Belsen from a soldier who had liberated the camp. The soldier reported images similar to those described in the media, but revealed a deeper, uncomfortable anger experienced by the liberators. 'He saw corpses lying on top of each other to the height and width of houses,' and reported cannibalism in the camp. Passing a chained SS guard, a fellow soldier said, 'What's he doing alive?' Bridges' friend pulled out his gun and shot him point blank.

Several months later, Edie Rutherford would confront the horror of the camps in person when a survivor walked into her office. He was a coal merchant from Prague and a friend of Edie's boss. The man had spent thirty-nine months in a camp, where he saw his

mother and brother sent to the gas chambers. He told
Edie of the numerous scars that criss-crossed his back
from being lashed by the guards, only now beginning
to heal. Once twelve stone, he walked into the office
a meagre six-and-a-half stone (approximately forty
kilos). Yet, she commented in amazement, he 'can still
smile and be courteous'. 'It shows the human spirit is
stronger than all,' Edie declared.

On the same day that Dimbleby went on air describ-
ing Belsen, pictures were released in *The Times* showing
the very same skeletons of living dead that Murrow and
Dimbleby depicted. Helen Mitchell opened the paper
that day and was 'much shocked by horror pictures'.
While reporters and soldiers on the ground were struggling with the question of the complicity of 'ordinary'
Germans in the atrocities of the camps, Helen nonetheless maintained that one could not blame them. 'It
is not the whole nation but *individuals* who do these
things,' she wrote in her diary. Irene Grant was clear
to distinguish between ordinary German and Nazis.
'The *SS*', she insisted, 'ought to be systematically shot.
Nothing could ever eradicate these cruel natures and
the world will be better without them.' On the ground,
although the Nazis were still the focus of the blame,
the problem seemed more complicated. Murrow told
a friend that he was certain that many Germans knew
of Buchenwald's purpose, but they stayed away out of
fear. 'The Nazis have succeeded in doing a much more
thorough job of brutalizing than I would have believed
possible,' he confessed.[5]

Soon after Buchenwald and Belsen, newsreels of the
camps were screened in cinemas across Britain. Some
felt compelled to watch, others simply couldn't bear
it, and many wept. To avoid the disturbing pictures,

and finding the photographs 'in the paper quite dread-ful enough', Nella Last refused to go to the cinema the last week of April. When she went to the movies the next week, however, someone requested the newsreels be played once again. Nella watched in horror. 'What kept them alive for so long', she sadly mused,

> . . . before they dropped as pitiful skeletons? Did their minds go first, I wonder, their reasoning, leaving noth-ing but the shell to perish slowly . . . Did their pitiful cries and prayers rise into the night to a God who seemed as deaf and pitiless as their cruel jailers?

Though a frequent movie-goer, Natalie Tanner also made a point not to watch the footage. She believed the films demonstrated the difficult reality of the camps once and for all to sceptics, but she was uncomfortable with those who watched and reported on the atrocities in social circles with perhaps more enthusiasm than was respectful of the dead. 'It's a hard thing to say,' she wrote in her diary, 'but it's quite obvious that certain sections of the German people enjoyed inflicting the torture.' At the same time, Natalie thought, 'Certain English people are getting a vicarious pleasure out of the pictures.'

Throughout late April, the Allies continued to dis-cover camp upon gruesome camp. Ten days after Richard Dimbleby broadcast his experience at Belsen, Americans came upon the Third Reich's original con-centration camp, Dachau. Less than ten miles from Munich, Dachau had opened in March 1933 – the first year of Hitler's reign – as a camp for political prison-ers. When Americans entered the camp on 29 April, the now familiar scenes of walking skeletons and piles of bodies played out once again. Few, however, could forget the railway cars lined up on the siding with thousands of decomposing bodies 'piled up like the twisted branches of cut-down trees'.[6] That day, 33,000 inmates were liberated, 2,500 of them Jews. Of those 2,500, fewer than 100 would be alive a month and a half later.

The day before Dachau's liberation, Edie Rutherford noted the 'fitting' end of 'Mussolini and Co.'. Italian partisans executed Mussolini, his mistress and several other supporters after they were caught attempting to escape to Germany. Their bodies were hung upside down from hooks at a petrol station in Milan. Anticipating messy legal battles after the war, Natalie Tanner was happy he was 'liquidated without all the fuss of a trial'. Days later, on 1 May, it was announced on German radio that Hitler, too, was dead. The original reports said he died valiantly in the defence of Berlin, but it was soon discovered that he had taken his own life as Soviet troops closed in on his bunker. Natalie Tanner suspected as much. 'If he is dead, I'm sure he didn't die a hero's death – he was probably bumped off or drowned himself,' she wrote. With no body recovered, there were always qualifications – always *if* he is dead. So many rumours of Hitler's demise had permeated throughout the war that people could hardly believe the news. On 2 May, Rutherford told M-O that she could 'not accept that Hitler is dead'. Four days later, Edie wrote that she could not believe the news until his dead body was recovered. Nella Last's son Cliff was convinced Hitler had slipped out of Germany and was on a submarine to Japan. Nor could any one in Nella's social circle believe he was actually dead.

With news of both Hitler's and Mussolini's demise, word came through that German forces in Italy had finally surrendered. By 4 May, German troops in north-west Europe had also given up the fight. All that was left was a formal surrender from German Supreme Command.

As the war in Europe rapidly drew to a close, wintry cold descended from north to south, and snow blanketed Britain. Rutherford complained that she had had enough of the cold, and Tanner's garden had a 'hang dog look'. In Newcastle, Irene Grant struggled with the anaemic coal supply to battle the 'freezingly cold' conditions in the north. Word was that next year, there would be less coal. 'We *cannot* do with less,' she protested. Taking occasional breaks from mending 'fairly hopeless dress and pyjamas', Helen Mitchell watched the snow fall outside and thought, 'How futile everything seems all over the world, despite how thankful one is to be able to sleep in peace.'

In the early days of May, everyone anxiously awaited news of the formal end of hostilities in Europe. Soldiers in the canteen in Barrow could not be dragged away from the wireless, for fear, Nella reported, that they might 'miss something'. Nella worked her way around the canteen as it buzzed with excitement, joking with the 'boys' and searching through the stocks to conjure up hot, satisfying meals. Other women at the canteen insisted the soldiers would be fine with cheese sandwiches, but Nella would have none of it. With Nella in charge, the grateful soldiers ate heartily: chips, carrots and casserole steak with gravy, topped off with pancakes, jam sauce and tea. 'Any minute now', was the consensus in the canteen as news from the wireless and papers was enthusiastically dissected.

Though the soldiers' revelry was infectious, and here and there gay red, white and blue dotted the streets in anticipation of VE (Victory in Europe) Day, there was a curious flatness to the wait. The end was too drawn out – 'normalcy' had slowly crept in, starting with the end of blackout restrictions months before. 'There would be no spectacular change to sweep things away on VE day,' no 'master-switch' turning on all the lights across Europe once again, Nella lamented. It was like watching a long drawn-out play where the actors left the stage one by one until someone slowly turned up the house lights and announced that the play was over, leaving the audience bemused and 'uncertain of the next move', until they too slowly dispersed.

Everyone waited on edge for the official declaration of VE holidays. Rumour buzzed and speculation raged as to when Churchill would declare the end and open victory festivities. Natalie Tanner's postman was sure that VE Day would be declared on 5 May. Tanner made sure to get in enough groceries before the celebrations – and the expected queues – developed. Aside from the potential crowds and queuing, Tanner was put out by the inconvenience of the wait. The 'whole affair has been badly managed', she declared. Hugh had appointments with clients that hung in the balance until VE was declared and she would have to plan to avoid the crowds of children who all had tickets to the cinema for VE Day. The government should simply set a date so that people could plan accordingly, Natalie argued.

On 6 May, Irene Grant wrote simply, 'War end watching hourly – When???' Helen Mitchell went into London to run errands on 7 May, in 'great state of fear that V Day would break'. 'Damn V Day,' she hissed.

While nerves were stretched and the holidays hung in the balance, Edie Rutherford and her friends had much cause to celebrate. Henry, the young RAF pilot whose wife Edie had comforted in 1943 when he had gone missing and was thought dead in a raid over Berlin, had safely returned home. He had baled out at 5,000 feet and was seriously wounded when he landed in a tree. For three days, he had stumbled through the French countryside, dazed and weakened from his injuries, until an old French couple finally took him in. The wife wanted to take him to the Resistance, but the husband was disgusted when the pilot could offer him no more than the £25 he had on him for his release. Henry was then dumped into a cart, wheeled to the nearest village and handed to the German authorities. As Russians closed in on Henry's prisoner-of-war camp, he and his fellow prisoners were forced to march 500 miles to the west in freezing conditions with little more than a loaf of bread for every four prisoners. In April, Henry's camp was finally liberated by American troops pushing eastwards.

Hoping to be free of chores on the big day, Alice Bridges spent the morning of 7 May cleaning her house in anticipation of the announcement. Edie Rutherford spent that day at work 'bewitched, buggered, and bewildered', waiting for word to come of VE Day. That night, she switched on the wireless for the 9 o'clock news and learned that the next two days were holidays. Nella Last felt let down by the announcement. A friend who was visiting simply said, 'What a FLOP,' over and over when he heard the news. Indeed, Nella thought the officials were holding back, not wishing people to get overexcited and forget that this was only one half of the war finished; Japan had not surrendered, there was more war to come. Excited by the news, Alice and her husband fashioned a flagpole and, after hours of rigging and admist a flurry of cursing, eventually managed to raise a large Union Jack to celebrate the occasion. When she went to bed that night, 'a most marvellous bonfire against a dark sky' glowed on the horizon, 'looking lovely and heralding tomorrow's peace'.

In Kent, VE Day dawned with 'flashes and uproar'. Helen Mitchell awoke with a start, thinking the noise was an air raid. Instead, it was a nasty thunderstorm passing overhead. After her husband woke up and left to check on the factory that morning, she tossed and turned, suffering from a 'foul headache' – the consequence of the night 'raid'. When she finally gathered the strength to drag herself out of bed, the gardener appeared and told her he was taking a holiday. When Cripps, her servant, showed up later, Helen offered her a holiday, but she turned it down and 'muscled in on the laundry', there being 'nothing amusing to do'.

With Cripps around, Helen braved a walk into the village. There was a 'rash of flags' about, one so large it nearly knocked her down when it fluttered in her face as she walked into a shop. When she came home, Cripps had finished all the housework and Helen went into the garden to collect spinach. She sat in the garden resting for some time, until the 'sultry enervating' weather drove her indoors. Later in the afternoon, her husband turned on the wireless to listen to Churchill's victory speech. Helen couldn't be bothered, 'as war is over and I don't want to hear any bilge and burp about it, nor false promises', and wrote up her diary entry instead.

Edie Rutherford went into town that morning to help a friend who was moving house. All along the bus route, people queued in the rain for fish and bread. She was home in time to hear Churchill's address at 3 p.m. Edie was proud of Churchill, his speech reminding her of the 'great gratitude' she felt 'for being born British'. At 5 p.m., she and Sid walked around town and saw thousands gathering around City Hall for a victory service. Many others simply wandered about, looking at decorations, which Edie thought so poorly done they were not worth mentioning. 'All the little mean streets had their decorations just as for Coronation and Jubilee,' she reported, 'I find them pathetic, tho' courageous.'

They returned home in the evening and walked around her shopping district for a time. A radio shop had fashioned large speakers outdoors, blaring festive music as people, many 'worse for drink', wandered about, 'looking sorry for themselves or just merry'. Outside her flats, a neon 'V' had been erected and people merrily danced to music emanating from a flat on a lower floor. Edie didn't dance, but she refused to grudge others their fun. By 2 a.m., however, others weren't so magnanimous: someone on a higher floor poured water on the revellers from above, at which the merrymakers soon melted away.

In Barrow, Nella Last met with throngs of schoolchildren milling about, harried housewives carrying heavy baskets and holding the tiny hands of their toddlers as they pointed out the festive decorations around town, and queues of women anxiously awaiting the arrival of the advertised 'fish later'. Feeling unsettled all morning, her 'wretched tummy . . . felt as if I'd swallowed butterflies', she went home and rested. Reciting comforting thoughts to settle her stomach, she decided it was VE Day and would not let it ruin the day. The family then hopped in the car and drove down to Lake Coniston. The trip tamed her uneasy stomach and eased her mind. 'Odd shafts of sunlight made long spans of sparkling silver on the rippled water, the scent of . . . damp earth', she wrote, 'lay over all like a blessing.' When they returned, they switched on the wireless to hear the King's speech, and 'drank a toast in beer and cider'. Despite the VE celebrations, Nella confided that she still felt a 'curious "flat" feeling'. By 10.30 p.m., she was in bed. Faint 'snatches of songs' wafted in through the open window. 'I've heard more "merriment" by a straggling crowd of soldiers as they went back to camp on a Saturday night,' Nella reported ruefully.

Dodging the raindrops, Hugh Tanner drove his wife and mother-in-law into Leeds for lunch, where they had champagne to celebrate the end of European hostilities. They stayed long enough to hear Churchill's speech, then drove back home to take care of gardening. Natalie 'decided that VE was just like any other wet Sunday. Everything', she sighed, 'seems flat and stale.'

With the direct threat to Britain finally over for certain, Edie Rutherford, so buffeted by the vicissitudes of British weather, was happy to note that weather forecasts were once again being reported. Feeling a little playful, she asked M-O, 'Anyone want two tin hats and two gas masks?'

WHO'D A THOUGHT IT?

Jimmy held out his hand to Alice. Taking hold, he gently lifted her into his delivery van and saw that she was settled in before he started the ignition and drove out of town. He had waited for her outside the Odeon theatre for their usual Tuesday date, but it was such a 'marvellous' June day that the two decided to skip the film and instead enjoy a jaunt into the countryside. Alice had spent the better part of the morning primping for the afternoon tryst. She put on a stunning green-and-brown silk dress she had made days before, a belt to match and lovely new suede shoes. It took her two hours to spiff up an old handbag, polishing it until it shone like new, and lovingly mending an old pair of gloves as she had failed to find new ones in the shops. Jimmy confessed he'd never seen her 'looking so nice'.

The two drove south out of Birmingham, passing sun-soaked verdant fields on their way to Sutton. Lounging along the reeded banks of Aqualate Mere, Alice thankfully breathed in the fresh air and enjoyed the warm sun as it played upon her face. While they relaxed, Jimmy and Alice reminisced about the past ten months they'd spent together. As she cast her mind to the past, Alice was slightly shocked to realize that, apart from her usual chats with men in the casino, she had been exclusively devoted to Jimmy.

Her husband, Les, still refused to take Alice out on the town and seemed relieved that Alice was perfectly happy going out on her own. He had no idea that she was seeing only one man and falling for him with each passing day.

She was forty-two and he was twenty-five. He was tall and thin, quiet and insecure. Unlike the other men she'd met in town, Jimmy was a perfect gentleman. It was rare and refreshing, she told M-O, to find a man who respected her wishes for platonic friendship and didn't press her for anything sexual. Her typical dates, on the other hand, showered her with 'friendship and adoration . . . till they find out it's a waste of time', and then bolted. That day at Aqualate Mere, Jimmy told her, 'He loves me more than ever,' but she didn't stonewall him as she did the others, who often professed love in hopes of a more physical relationship. Instead, she knew he truly meant it and was quietly pleased to hear the words.

He was handsome when he smiled, which, in the beginning of their relationship, was very rare. When she met him, Jimmy was overwhelmed by his job, and his home life was a mess. His mother drank both her wages and his, leaving him with 'no clothes, no shoes and no one to care for him'. In August 1944, Alice stepped in as the maternal figure he had never known. They met in town that August and instantly made a connection. For hours they sat in a churchyard, he talking about his problems, she listening intently. As they parted that day, he asked her earnestly for her friendship and she gladly assented. Though she was sceptical about a lasting friendship because of their age difference, she soon found age was easily overcome.

In the beginning, the age gap was bridged by Alice rationalizing that her role in the relationship was purely maternal. He worked part-time, and therefore, had his mornings free. They met at least once a week in the morning for a movie and lunch or for an exhilarating drive through the country. Slowly, Alice built up his confidence and became the bright spot in his week. She cleaned him up, gave him advice on his job and helped him with his mother. When they marked their first anniversary together, she noted proudly that he had gained weight, had more self-assurance and that his home life was on the mend. Alice told M-O that her mission was to help Jimmy find a young girl whom he could marry. But, on the night of their first anniversary, Jimmy confessed that he'd fallen hopelessly in love with her and no other woman could ever match her 'perfection'. 'Good gosh', she wrote with a rare tinge of humility, 'perfection?'

Alice was never abashed to tell M-O how ravishing she looked on her outings and rarely missed an opportunity to recount any man's compliment on her beauty. Indeed, when Jimmy dropped her off in town after the ride out to Aqualate Mere, she reported that a 'Yank' smiled and eyed her hopefully. Americans rarely took notice of her, Alice wrote, because she was never 'blatant enough'. That day, however, was different. 'In the sun my satin dress just hit the eye, so the Yanks were naturally attracted,' she smugly observed. A few days later, she told M-O she'd met an interesting man in the casino who asked to see her again. She set up a time to meet in a week, but sincerely hoped he wouldn't show – Alice didn't want to break his heart.

'The only trouble', she confessed, 'is if a friendship happens, he'll fall for me in a big way.' Her exploits and admirers certainly boosted her self-confidence, and Alice enjoyed telling M-O how fetching she was, both physically and intellectually (as she often told them, the men enjoyed her conversation as well as her looks). But Jimmy's compliments were deeper, more meaningful – professions that made her heart leap and her stomach plummet, professions that struck her as so sincere that she couldn't help but be modest.

Still, Alice protested strictly virtuous behaviour with Jimmy. Though she told M-O that there would never have been a relationship had Les kept up his marital end of the bargain, she always maintained her first love for her husband. 'Les was to fault', she wrote in her diary after seeing Jimmy, 'for never energizing himself to take me out. He is lucky to be able to neglect me and yet keep my love.' Despite all that, she was clearly smitten with Jimmy. When he told her he had finally landed full-time work after a year of seeing each other, she mourned the loss of their regular outings. 'I really felt like weeping, I have got so used to him and his fidelity and thoughtfulness that for a time I shall feel lost,' she confessed.

That summer, as the war in the Pacific raged on and Alice grew closer to Jimmy, the nation went to the polls. Two weeks after VE Day, party politics once again became a reality after five years of coalition under Churchill's command. Although the leader of the Labour Party, Clement Attlee, wanted to maintain the coalition government until the war with Japan was completed, Labour's National Executive Committee resoundingly rejected an offer made by Churchill to wait out the war. Labour formally left the coalition; the first general election in ten years was now scheduled for 5 July.

Incensed at Labour's defection, Churchill's opening salvo in the campaign was an ill-conceived mud-slinging and fear-mongering speech delivered on 4 June. Designed to strike fear into the nation of the dangers if Labour came to power, it instead smacked of a petulant politician playing politics as usual. Assuming the very word 'socialism' to be a dreadful bogey to the British people, the Prime Minister spiced his speech liberally with the term, very rarely referring explicitly to the Labour Party. 'I must tell you', Churchill schooled his audience, 'that a Socialist policy is abhorrent to the British ideas of freedom.' Indeed, he continued with an ominous tone, 'There can be no doubt that Socialism is inseparably interwoven with Totalitarianism and the abject worship of the State.' Furthermore, Churchill argued, a socialist government aimed at directing every aspect of society and industry could not suffer public discontent with its policies, and therefore, 'They would have to fall back on some form of *Gestapo*.' And if the spectre of a Nazi-like political police wasn't enough to warn the people off a disastrous vote for Labour, Churchill further warned the people that property and 'nest-egg[s], however small' were in dire jeopardy of 'shrivel[ling] before their eyes'.[1]

Most were shocked by Churchill's so-called 'Gestapo speech'. The revered and respected war horse had opted to appeal not to a higher sense of Britishness and optimism, but rather to continue the fear and uncertainty of wartime; it was as if he had forgotten (or, indeed, had never learned) all that the people had fought for in the People's War. Churchill and the Conservatives, dubbed the 'National Party' during this speech, seemed to have little agenda beyond rolling things back to the 1930s and running on the strength of the great man's popularity. Even those who held an 'admiration [for Churchill] . . . amounting to idolatry', as Vita Sackville-West confessed, were shaken by his speech.[2] Nella Last, who similarly harboured an unwavering love for Churchill, was also 'disappointed' with the speech. 'I felt it lacked dignity – was a bit too "puckish" for the time or place,' she wrote to M-O. 'It will', Nella was convinced, 'start a bit of mud slinging and ear slapping.' Those who were Labour supporters, like Edie Rutherford, listened with disgust. 'Same old thing, and he'll get in and all his pale,' she spitted, 'because most folk are still dead in ignorance in this country.'

When Clement Attlee took the microphone the next night, his voice calm and reassuring, he stressed that Churchill had made a gaffe, for the Prime Minister 'wanted the electors to understand how great the difference between Winston Churchill the great leader in war of a united nation, and Mr. Churchill the party leader of the Conservatives'.[3] Indeed, Attlee struck a deep chord here, for many – as noted by M-O – felt Churchill to be a great war leader, but as Irene Grant had stressed often in her correspondence with M-O, 'not for the people'. In fact, after Churchill's speech, Irene noted it was a 'grand marvellous Tory speech . . . we who wondered had he a *little* leftish feeling, now know he's pure Tory with not a thought for the people.'

From the beginning, when J.B. Priestley had gone on air in 1940 to push for a better future through the People's War, Churchill had always been reluctant to entertain such utopian sentiments. In 1942–3, as people excitedly discussed Beveridge's template for a new world order, he was obstinate. Churchill's Gestapo speech was not only in bad taste for connecting Labour with Nazism, but it also reminded the people that he refused to look to the future – a *better* future. Attlee's speech certainly threw a bit of mud, for instance, when he said, 'when [Churchill] talks of the danger of Labour mismanaging finance', he had conveniently forgotten 'his own disastrous record at the Exchequer' in the 1920s; but Attlee's speech was much more hopeful and focused on the future. 'The men and women of this country who have endured great hardships in the war are asking what kind of life awaits them in the peace,' he asserted. 'They seek the opportunity of leading reasonably secure and happy lives, and they deserve to have it.'[4] Attlee talked about the questions that mattered as Britain looked to the future.

The prime election issue, as Britons envisioned the future, was housing. Gallup polls in June found that 40 per cent of people considered housing to be the most important issue, far beyond even the next highest-rated, social security (14 per cent), and a majority polled believed Labour was the best party to handle it. The problem was massive: over three million properties, most of which were private dwellings, had been decimated in the Blitz. One answer to the problem was prefabricated houses. In Sheffield and its suburbs, new prefabs were erected and on view to the public in July. Edie Rutherford reported that the boxy non-descript houses looked 'awful' on the outside, but were 'well fitted up on the inside'. The cost was astonishing, she reported: £900, 'which seems terrible when one thinks of what one could get for that sum prewar'. Still, 'Anything is better than mother-in-law.' As one woman reported after visiting a post-war housing exhibition in London, 'I'm so desperate for a house I'd like anything. Four walls and a roof are the height of my ambition.'[5]

The extent to which the housing shortage was a major grievance that summer was illustrated in the actions taken by ex-servicemen in Brighton. Coming home from war and finding little or inadequate housing for their families, groups of ex-servicemen, dubbed 'vigilantes' by the press, began taking over empty houses. Many were frustrated at the bureaucracy involved in officially requisitioning unoccupied private property (some of which had stood empty for the entire war) during such a housing dearth and finally took the law into their hands.[6] Several times during July Edie cheered for the vigilantes. 'Hurrah for the Vigilantes. Maybe they are wrong, but why can't authority do what they are doing? Until it does, I hope vigilantism spreads,' she told M-O. Eventually, convinced by the movement, the Ministry of Health gave power to local authorities to speed up the process. Edie marked the news with a resounding, 'Hurrah!', happy to see 'democracy in action. Who says it doesn't pay to kick up a fuss agen all the laws?'

By the time the Ministry of Health acted in July, the election had taken place, and on 26 July the results of the 5 July election were finally trumpeted on the BBC. Although a great deal of cynicism and some apathy shot through the campaign, voter turnout was an impressive 73 per cent, helped, in part by the beautiful summer weather the nation enjoyed on election day. Edie Rutherford and her husband cast their votes for Labour, as did Alice Bridges, Irene Grant and Natalie Tanner. Tanner had spent most of June and early July stumping for the party, helping out with administrative matters and attending party meetings.

When she went into town on 5 July, Natalie ran into a friend who was a staunch Conservative, and, 'Despite my red rose [he] stood me a glass of beer and I stood him one despite his National colours.' After this friendly exchange, the man (a colliery owner) proceeded to tell Natalie that Labour simply could not nationalize coal mines. 'You must have discipline in mines,' he argued, 'and our mines are so peculiar anyway that you can't have up to date machinery in them, and anyway the miners don't want labour saving equipment.' Natalie felt as though she'd been transported back to the nineteenth century. Indeed, he even cited the machine-breaking Luddite movement of that century as evidence for his claims.

Nella Last spent the early days of July on holiday at an old guest house in Bardsea, just up the coast road from Barrow. On the 5th, she and her husband went to Barrow to vote – Conservative – and then off to the market town of Ulverston. Few in Ulverston or at the guest house in Bardsea seemed interested in discussing the election. 'I never saw so many people "caring less" about a thing,' she observed. Election day passed enjoyably in Ulverston, with little talk of electoral matters among the crowd from Bardsea, but change was in the air. Stopping in a pub for a chat and swift drink, Nella noticed most of the customers were young women. Although they looked like 'nice ones', they were seasoned pub-goers who clearly knew how to order a pint. As the women sat talking, Nella was alarmed to notice that upon crossing their legs, they showed 'well above bare knees'. With their cigarettes and relaxed attitude, 'They seemed so "independent".'

Election Day for Helen Mitchell was exhilarating and rewarding. The woman who could barely get through a day of domestic work without taking a nap spent fourteen hours that day helping out at the Labour committee rooms. It was, she told M-O, the 'most enjoyable day in years'. Unfortunately, the next day, she was 'the little woman again', doing laundry, sundry chores around the house and shopping in town. Later in the afternoon, she was amused to open the door to a gypsy, who told her fortune. 'Good luck coming,' Helen cheerfully announced, 'shall marry again and move, very lucky!'

Such promises were a welcome fantasy for Helen, who had been locked in a bitter struggle with Peter over living arrangements since April. It was an old tale – a story she'd relived over and over during thirty years of marriage. Peter had a predilection for what Helen called 'genuine olde-worlde houses' with history and charm, which she absolutely despised. For her, there was no charm, only dust, draughts and useless rooms that oozed centuries of filth that ensured her everlasting imprisonment in a domestic hell. He had moved her to Scotland after the First World War, quit his job in Scotland once she'd finally felt comfortable there and moved to another unmanageable home near London and finally settled in Kent, all without taking Helen's feelings into consideration or consulting her first. To make matters worse, Peter rarely lived in the houses to which he bound his wife. Instead, he treated his home as if it were a country hotel that he visited for the weekend, never considering that by doing so he made his wife no more than a 'servant in own house' – a phrase she used often to describe her situation.

Anticipating the war's end in April 1945, Mitchell began to look for a new home to replace the one she'd come to loathe. The media buzzed with excitement about rebuilding Britain with new efficient homes, and she hoped to find a small one that would enable her to keep up respectable appearances, and also allow time for her once again to teach elocution and become involved in theatre. Peter also seemed interested in finding a new home, but, as usual, the two had vastly different ideas. He wanted to move closer to work, and though he humoured her by looking at small houses, he soon became obsessed with yet another unwieldy home, in Beckenham. It was advertised in *The Times* as an 'attractive detached house' with nine bedrooms, three reception rooms, a billiards room, a three-car garage and garden – hardly the small modern home in the country Helen had envisaged.

As he had done throughout their thirty years together, Peter once again made the decision to buy the house without consulting his wife. Furthermore, he spent an additional £375 (the house cost £3,500) purchasing 'filthy old linoleum', curtains, billiard room fittings and electric fittings – again, without her approval. Helen was 'appalled' and 'shocked to the core' by his utter lack of economy and taste. When Peter showed her their new home, she told M-O it was,

Even more appalling than I thought . . . ragged linoleums . . . every room breaks out in the rich ornate vulgar style of the low wealthy business man. Kitchenry vast rambling and squalid. Whole place obscene. Light fittings give one stomach ache. I feel No! To live alone there and devote one's life to trying to do the daily cleaning ending with late evening meals, beyond my physical strength and an insult to my beliefs in design and taste.

She called it the 'horror mansion' or, in typically sarcastic fashion, 'Linoleum Lodge'. To make matters worse, her husband had bought the rambling house with his workers in mind. She, the middle-class aesthete, could now look forward to sharing the vulgar 'lodge' with 'toughs' from her husband's factory.

During the summer of 1945, as the election campaign raged on the national scene, Mitchell struggled to make her husband understand how she felt about the prospect of moving into Linoleum Lodge. The rambling old house, with multiple lodgers, would mean, she argued, the continuation of her slavish existence. Furthermore, it would exacerbate her condition, since the house was closer to Peter's work, and therefore, he would necessarily be home more often, wanting food and to be waited on. Neither Peter nor William would lend a sympathetic ear to Helen's concerns. They insisted she could call on servants to assist her, but she knew the reality of the situation. Even if she could procure help, she knew there were very few who could live up to her exacting standards. Night after night, she fought with her husband, tried to coax him to change his mind, cried and otherwise bemoaned her damnable existence.

In July and August, failing to dissuade her husband from his decision and confronting a vast mansion teeming with work and working-class lodgers, Helen toyed with ideas of escape. She could leave him; but Helen did not seem to entertain the idea of divorce so much as living apart. Though certainly fraught with problems, living separately had been a generally acceptable situation during the war – at least more successful than the prospects she faced that summer. Barring an 'act of God' or awaiting the second marriage that the travelling gypsy had assured Helen was her fate, it seemed the best option.

Yet reality soon crept in. Without the consent of her husband, and, more importantly, without his financial support, the plan could never work. Helen had no income of her own, and felt unable to support herself alone. In a particularly acrimonious fight in August, she learned that he would not condone or pay for separate accommodations. 'Consider my position slavish,' she fumed to M-O, 'work damned hard in a hellish house at jobs I hate and think marriage bloody awful.' The only available avenue of escape now was the one she took at the end of this harrowing evening, and would continue to do for months: 'to bed . . . doped heavily'.

Aside from polling day, the one bright spot in the summer was the election return on 26 July. Though she had spent the day working 'damned hard', packing and cleaning, and though a 'foul thunderstorm' wore down her nerves, the results were promising. 'Felt much less cynical and depressed as a result of the election,' she wrote in her diary.

Despite the auguries to the contrary (both a Gallup poll and Mass-Observation pointed to a Labour victory), most believed a Conservative victory to be a foregone conclusion. But Labour had won a landslide victory over Churchill's National Party. 'Well, well, well,' Edie Rutherford enthused on the 27th, 'who'd a thought it? Not I. Damn bad prophet me, but how GLAD I am.' Natalie Tanner danced about her room in glee, and local Labour canvassers came out to Alice Bridges' house to thank her for her support. 'Yippee', was all she had to say. Irene Grant was equally well chuffed.

Labour picked up 212 seats to win a solid majority

of 393 returned to Parliament, while the National Party could number only 213. Liberals were reduced to only twelve and, oddly enough, William Beveridge, the man who had whipped up such hope for building an equitable future in 1942, was among the casualties. Irene Grant's Common Wealth Party was decimated. The leader, Sir Richard Acland, renounced his seat and threw in his lot with Labour, but in fifteen of sixteen fights, Common Wealth did so poorly it lost its deposit. Irene was not disappointed, as she had followed Acland's lead and supported Labour, or more specifically, she stressed, 'Socialism'. Labour had won a resounding 47 per cent of the vote, while the Conservatives made a respectable showing with 39 per cent.

Nella Last and her entourage at the WVS were shocked at the loss. Mrs Lord, an organizer for the service, came in 'flushed and upset' at the news and 'feared riots and uprising'. Another woman was incensed that Nella seemed unfazed. 'You take things very calmly,' she admonished. 'Don't you realise we may be on the brink of revolution?' Although she felt the news was 'fate', Nella, the master of keeping up appearances, was inwardly stunned and 'would have given a lot to be able to reach . . . for a bottle of *sal volatile*'.

More than just the Conservative loss shook Nella's delicately built wartime façade of confidence and happiness that summer. The end of the death and destruction in Europe was certainly welcomed, but the victory was hollow. She felt 'no wild whoopee' on VE Day, a function of the drawn-out sequence of events leading to Germany's surrender, no doubt; but there was something deeper, for she looked at the end of the war as an end to her volunteer work.

The bitter prospects of returning to pre-war life and the confines of home chaffed her newfound independence.

With the war in Europe over, the existence of the WVS and other volunteer efforts was increasingly called into question. Nella began to have more free time, and capitalized on this freedom by frequenting the cinema and theatres more often – sometimes two to three times a week in June and July. She and Will spent a much-needed week-long holiday in Bardsea in the first days of July. But, while Nella enjoyed a welcome break after six years' hard work, she sadly watched the slow dismantling of those wartime institutions that had given her a little more gumption, and certainly a lot more confidence and recognition.

The realization that things were slowly grinding to a halt dawned on the women at the WVS and the shop in the waning days of May. The mood at the centre was sombre as women recalled the camaraderie and the good times they had together. There was a 'shadow' over them with the 'feeling we soon will be scattered . . . it's been grand to all work together,' Nella wrote. When times were tough, there was always someone who joked, smiled or comforted. One of the women said she'd miss Nella and her cheeky ways most of all. 'I'll have no one to tease and torment me,' she confessed to Nella. It suddenly struck Nella that everything was fading so quickly. Even the grouses and the office politics, the little arguments here and there, were passing. Their time together was now assuming a 'golden hue of "do you remember"', and the 'little troubles like the blitz and its effect on the old building, pipes bursting and heating, times when Mrs. Waite [a WVS organizer] was so cross and difficult' forgotten.

It was the closure of the Red Cross shop, which she had helped build into a thriving enterprise during the war, that underlined the ending of an era. Nella confessed feeling pride in every little parcel sent to a prisoner of war through her efforts at the shop. She had put so much sweat and toil into the shop: cleaning up the space, scavenging for goods to sell, lovingly repairing the odds and ends that weren't quite saleable, making dolls and clothes for sale, and – probably the most rewarding – chatting with customers and helping those in need. The young mothers and soldiers' wives who frequented the shop often found a helpful hand and a titbit of useful advice when Nella was there. Reflecting on the three years of its existence one day, she 'looked round the tatty shop . . . [and] thought of all the love and effort it had needed, like a sickly child, it had "taken a deal of mothering"'. She had poured so much into the shop, and 'Now it will just go like blackout etc., having served its purpose,' Nella wrote morosely.

What wasn't going away anytime soon was rationing and shortages. A week after VE Day, Edie complained that there was no cress, new potatoes or peas 'about just now'. Furthermore, the 'variety' of foods available was abysmal. The most worrying, however, was Sid's health. 'My husband is quite definitely suffering from poor nutrition,' she wrote. 'He NEEDS more milk, butter, cream.' This cry was not abnormal – many women complained throughout the war that there was not enough healthy and sustaining food available for husbands engaged in physical labour. But, already weakened by his multiple infirmities, Edie feared that austerity measures were further deepening his illness. 'I'm terribly worried about him,' she confessed. No ray of hope loomed on the horizon. Indeed, she reported, despite victory in Europe, 'There are suggestions that we are going to be worse off than ever for food.'

The devastation wrought by the war in Europe exacerbated food shortages. When the Nazi spectre began to recede, all that was left in its wake was utter ruin. Fertile farmland had been decimated, cities were reduced to rubble, homes destroyed, industry crippled and infrastructure systematically dismantled by Germans retreating from Allied troops at the end of the war. Millions of refugees and displaced people roamed the Continent, searching for loved ones, seeking shelter and desperate for food. Most Europeans subsisted on less than 1,000 calories a day – the Viennese got by on 800 calories, while those in Budapest lived on a paltry 550. The weekly ration for many in the Netherlands during the 'hunger winter' of 1944–5 was less than Allied soldiers were given per day; 16,000 Dutch perished as a result. To the chagrin of many, the Germans did remarkably well in comparison. The average German ate a little over 1,400 calories a day in 1945. As Allied governments tried to assuage the situation, the food crisis in Europe quickly became a problem for Britain. Less than three weeks after VE Day, cuts were made to fat, bacon and canned meat, even the Christmas sugar 'bonus' of half a pound extra was eliminated.

Edie Rutherford was incensed by the injustice of the situation. As many in Britain would ask over the next decade, she mused, 'I sometimes wonder who did win this war. When one thinks of the way the Germans looted . . . and then contrast it with a cut in rations which followed our victory.' On the other hand, she pointed out, the devastation of Germany would keep

Germans 'so busy for years, building, and keeping themselves fed etc that they should not have time to plan wars'.

The price of everyday items was also a worry. Shopping in town for household sponges, Edie complained that what had once cost her less than £1 was now going for £4, and shoetrees had jumped from 6d to £3. 'Rather than give in to such wicked profiteering ... I did NOT buy,' she said resolutely. The cost of clothing and fabric was so dear and of such poor quality that Irene Grant spent most of her days piecing together old bits of material and mending what she could. It all grated on her nerves and cut into her sense of respectability. 'Patch beside patch is neighbourly,' she quoted, 'but patch upon patch is beggarly.'

Even when Irene's husband, Tom, received a pay rise later in the month, things didn't get much better. Tom's wage was increased to £30 a month in May 1945, with four months' back-pay, and both Marjorie and Rita had also received raises. The family wanted to celebrate – Irene especially wanted to fit out their new home with new carpets and linoleum – but there was nothing to buy. They settled instead for 'a pinch of snuff' each.

Alice Bridges developed a lucrative side business capitalizing on the problems of shortages. An accomplished dressmaker, the days and nights she was not out on the town or with Jimmy, whom she called her 'strip of romance', Alice was hunting for fabric in town, fashioning and stitching together interesting designs. One customer was so tickled with Alice's avant-garde design of 'five knife pleats at right side front and three at left side back', that she paid her more than the agreed price. Alice also made dolls' clothes for girls in the neighbourhood. The extra money coming in was becoming a necessity, as Les' health took a turn for the worse that summer. Respiratory problems would increasingly plague Alice's husband and cause him to lose more and more days at work. When he could, Les pushed himself to work, since 12/- sick pay was nowhere near what the family needed to survive. But this determination to work in the face of what was becoming a serious illness only wore him down even further. Alice tried her best to bolster his health and keep him from sinking into depression, but there was little she could do beyond watch her once powerfully stout husband 'shrink' before her eyes.

The couple had a rare moment to celebrate and revel in each other's company, however, that summer. At midnight on 15 August, the new Prime Minister, Clement Attlee, announced Japan's surrender over the wireless. When they heard the news, Les cheerfully embraced Alice and broke out the bottle of port they'd been saving for months. Alice toasted, 'To us', and Les added, 'To peace – and you'. Alice sped up the stairs to wake Jacq, who was given a little glass, and then toasted, 'To the Children's Victory Party!'

Lights blinked on here and there down the road, and people began to fill the streets, women emerging from their homes, dazed and half-dressed, wondering if 'the News had come through'. Bonfires began to sputter to life across the neighbourhood to the sound of jubilant singing and shouting. Though she was fully enjoying the festivities, Alice still wondered, 'how it was the Japs had caved in so soon, it didn't seem like their fatalistics [sic]'.

When Germany crumbled in May, Japan had defiantly held on, pushed back across the Pacific until the island itself became the target of continual Allied bombing. The firestorms unleashed across Germany to devastating effect were also wrought upon Japanese cities. In the early hours of 9 March, over 300 American B-29 'Superfortresses' whipped up the superheated flames of destruction in just four hours. American incendiary bombs were developed to spew gelatinized petrol upon impact, making the fires that were started virtually impossible to quench. By the time the last B-29 made its way back to base, nearly 90,000 people had been killed.Over and over throughout the summer of 1945, the horrifying bombing of Tokyo was played out across Japan. Sixty-six cities were bombed, killing over 900,000 people.

Hiroshima and Nagasaki, two cities that had so far managed to escape the summer raids, would be forever etched as the tragic sites of the beginning of the nuclear age and the end of the war. Early on 6 August, the afternoon of the 5th in Britain, while many enjoyed a bank holiday weekend, close to 40,000 people were instantly killed when an atomic bomb was dropped on Hiroshima; in the coming days, 100,000 would perish as a result of the bomb. Nonetheless, believing the Americans could not possibly have enough radioactive material for another bomb, the Japanese leadership decided to hold on. On 10 August, they were convinced to seek an end to the war when Nagasaki experienced the same fate as Hiroshima, killing some 70,000 people in total.

Sleeping soundly in her Sheffield flat, Edie Rutherford and her husband awoke with a start when a man's voice cried out, 'Jap war's over! Hurrah!' After shaking herself awake and looking groggily at the clock, Edie realized that Clement Attlee's scheduled midnight announcement must have relayed the wonderful news. Fireworks, shouting and 'unharmonious' singing erupted minutes later.

Nella Last and Will were also shaken from their sleep at midnight. For them, it was ships' sirens and church bells, followed by a neighbour belting out the few verses she knew to 'God Save the King' over and over, as loud as she could. Some days before, she had informed Nella that when VJ (Victory in Japan) was announced, she would drink tumblers full of champagne and gin in celebration; it sounded as if she was keeping her promise. Will, who had slept in a separate room for several years now, peeked his head into Nella's room, saying, 'Sounds like it's all over'. From her window, Nella could see bonfires being lit, cars rushing up Abbey Road towards town, rockets and searchlights darting across the sky and neighbours rushing around looking to share the news with someone. After some time, ships' sirens still blasted through the air, dogs were barking ceaselessly at all the commotion and children outside the window made merry setting off their own tiny fireworks. The neighbour who had opened the festivities saving the King had now had a few more drinks and was, according to Nella, at the 'Yippieeeehk stage'. Will went to bed, muttering at all the noise. All the excitement worked Nella's stomach into knots, so she took two aspirins, curled up in bed again and read herself to sleep.

In the morning, Nella woke feeling worse for the unexpected disruption of sleep. The warm and glorious summer weather of the past few days had disappeared, grey skies crowded in and drizzle gently tapped at the windows. Despite the poor weather, Nella suggested they celebrate peace with a ride out to Ambleside. After a visit to Will's grumpy parents, with whom Nella had never got on and who dampened the spirit of VJ Day even more than the soggy weather, the two shed the gloom of the parents-in-law and enjoyed a picnic lunch, sheltering from the rain in their car. Returning home, they found neighbours had built a bonfire. In the drizzle, the fire sputtered and smoked while everyone stood around rather 'orderly and apathetic', as if queuing for fish, Nella thought. There was no 'festive air', and when the wind turned from the north, sending a cold chill through the crowd and bringing rain clouds, the older folk retired inside to tend their own modest hearth fires.

On holiday in Berwick-upon-Tweed, Natalie and her son James were so busy enjoying the sights of the border town that Natalie barely registered any of the coming peace in Japan in the early days of August. Like Nella and Edie, she was awoken by church bells and singing when the news came in at midnight on 15 August. That day was their scheduled departure, so, amid the merrymaking in Berwick, they boarded a train back home. The weather had been fine on the northern coast, but by the time they arrived in Leeds, it was steadily drizzling. Everything seemed rather desultory. A few 'bedraggled girls hung onto soldiers' arms with victory hats on, but it was a most depressing sight', Natalie recounted in her diary. Some hotels in town were dark: 'NO BEER', they advertised glumly. From their own hotel room in the centre of town, however, Natalie and James witnessed more excitement: people milled about in the square, setting off fireworks, dancing on top of air-raid shelters, climbing on the statue of the Black Prince, and 'yelling aimlessly'.

At Edie Rutherford's block of flats on VJ Day, one of the neighbours rigged up a set of speakers on the balcony and blasted dance tunes all night. Bonfires were lit and people danced into the small hours of the morning. Edie and Sid joined in until 1 a.m., and then left the celebrations to the younger crowd jitterbugging on the street.

VJ Days were 'hellish' in Kent. Firecrackers, off-key singing and carousing outside Helen Mitchell's door were hardly welcome. There was no joy in the end of the war, indeed, she felt 'rather shamefaced' that the way in which the surrender was secured was unsporting. 'Illogical, I know', she admitted, but nonetheless couldn't shake the guilt of the bomb. The 'shame' of the victory made it difficult to join in festivities, had she been so inclined, but the end of the war with Japan signalled no change to her domestic situation. Indeed, she was still entrenched in a major battle of her own over moving house. She had failed to persuade Peter to give up Linoleum Lodge, and so Helen spent the first weeks of August packing. The next skirmish came over Peter's insistence on keeping 'foul chairs, mirrors, tables, etc' left by previous owners. Helen protested, to no avail; Peter began 'throwing his weight about'. 'Go to hell,' she spat and stormed out of the room. While others were whooping it up over VJ, she 'spent most of evening weeping with rage and misery'.

Alice Bridges left her husband in the afternoon on VJ Day to set up speakers for the neighbourhood block party that night. Having anticipated VJ Day for a few days, Alice had already done her housework and was free to spend the day as she wished. As she had done on D-Day, Alice wanted to record Birmingham's reaction to the news; she also wanted to find Jimmy. On her odyssey through town, she noted the preparations for celebration teas buzzing about down every side street, 'heaps of Yanks about' and long queues at the casino. Jimmy caught up with her, and in the whirl of excitement, Alice gave him a kiss. He looked surprised, then, recovering his wits, said, 'Ah, a peace kiss I expect.' She said nothing, but made plans to meet him that night.

That evening, Alice searched desperately about for her 'young strip of romance', but the two never met up. Instead, she ran into a man she knew from the discussion group she attended regularly. He flirted shamelessly with her as she constantly looked over his shoulder for Jimmy. Finally, he asked her to take a drive with him. Alice turned him down flat, insisting she wasn't a 'basement bargain'. Putting on a swagger, he informed her that, 'I knew a charming person once who said she had always been true to her husband – she was very moral – but she didn't mind kissing me all over.' 'Did you enjoy it?' Alice enquired. 'Rather,' he replied, 'I like these unorthodox ways of making love.' 'Well, if that's an open invitation to me, I'm afraid you will be disappointed,' she retorted and stalked off to catch the bus home.

When she returned home at 9.30 p.m., the party had just begun. 'The scandal-making female from the bottom' looked at Bridges suspiciously on her late return and eyed another lady significantly. To annoy the gossip-makers, Alice put on her charm and 'got the men running round after me getting me a drink and a sandwich'. She then ignored the women and enjoyed the party. Les' speakers provided the music and the 'air was thick' with 'whoopee'. In the morning, Les brought up a pot of tea. Then they spent the 'next 3 hours very profitably, going all romantic'. 'I can't imagine', she confessed, 'anyone else being quite as nice as Les.' In the afternoon, she went out to see Jimmy.

*   *   *

Despite the joviality of VJ celebrations, there was an underlying unease. The war was over, but the peace seemed tenuous. Relations with the Soviet Union had soured significantly during the course of 1945 – highlighted recently by the USSR's declaration of war on Japan only *after* the first atomic bomb was dropped. Nella Last remembered three major conflicts in her lifetime, starting with the Boer War at the turn of the century, and a fourth one now loomed ominously on the horizon. Edie Rutherford noted the turn of affairs rather matter-of-factly and, perceiving the shape of the Cold War to come, pointed out the utility of harnessing Germany's aggressive tendencies on the side of Britain instead of against it.

The implications of the atomic bomb, however, lent a darker pall over the developing chill in international affairs. When word came through of the bombings of Hiroshima and Nagasaki, most people back home were shocked and fearful of the scale of death unleashed from a single bomb. Irene Grant could do little but stutter forth a halting, 'Atomic energy. What a frightening thing!!' When an Australian serviceman at the canteen in Barrow told Nella that only 'eight ounces of the "atomic" was used' in the bombs, she was sure he had misspoken. 'You surely mean eight pounds,' she suggested. But he replied, '8 lb. would blast England to Hell.' '*Pardon me*,' she replied, adopting a mock serious tone, 'don't judge England by Australia – *we* could go the other way.' The canteen roared with mirth at the joke, but the merriment masked the deep anxiety Nella felt about such weapons of slaughter.

Edie Rutherford's initial reaction to the news of Hiroshima was that 'Mankind will exterminate itself and this earth, if we don't soon exercise some restraint.'

In the same vein, but hardly optimistic that 'restraint' was possible, Helen Mitchell's reaction was, 'Well, if scientists are not drowned at birth . . .' On reflection, she wrote, 'Suppose the sooner we polish ourselves off the better.' Informally polling all as they walked by her front garden, Irene Grant was convinced that everyone understood the immense gravity of atomic potential.

Nella Last thought the bomb,

> . . . a crack in a hitherto unopened door. It opens up terrifying possibilities and makes the "end of the world" or rather of civilization a real possibility if another war ever comes – not a Wellsian dream or nightmare.

It was a nightmare that some felt they had only narrowly escaped. When the news came through of the huge explosion and mushroom cloud, Les Bridges told his wife that the description matched almost exactly the nightmares that had left him 'wringing wet with sweat' and terrified during the Blitz. Although Alice expressed her own concern over the potential of the bomb, her blitz experience left her bitter and vindictive. 'It is awe-inspiring and unbelievable', she told M-O, 'the only thing is in the case of Japan we didn't drop enough and it's a thousand pities that Germany caved in too soon.'

The shock and shame Helen Mitchell experienced over the bomb was soon somewhat attenuated when she reflected on its impact on the experience of air raids. Not yet informed of the long-term and widespread effects of radiation, Helen reasoned that war would be considerably shorter and more humane in the future. And, most importantly for Helen, psychologically scarred by the air war, there would be 'no long endurance of raids, terror, blackout' – 'One would be snuffed out quickly.'

Already perceiving the uncomfortable gravitational pull that set Britain between the two poles of the developing superpowers, however, 'The trouble is that one has a permanent background of uneasiness,' Helen noted. 'Who's going to use it next? Shall we be terrified of offending America or Russia or someone else?'

EPILOGUE

<hr>

Taking shelter from the dampened VJ festivities, and warmed by their little wood fire, Nella reminisced with her husband about the end of the last war. Will had been stationed in Southampton, Arthur was six and Cliff only a few months old. They were younger and much 'gayer' then, Will reflected, setting out at lunchtime with the kids, a pram brimming with tea and festive fare, and enjoying the excitement of the peace together until the small hours of the next morning.

Perhaps it was their youth, Nella agreed, that made them so light-hearted as they celebrated the Armistice and, looking fondly across the years, 1918 was certainly imbued with a warm glow of carefree happiness. Still, she reminded Will, there was little sense then 'that war could come home to us'. This time, war had 'come home' to Britain, and the People's War had demanded every ounce of dedication and sacrifice they had to give – and more – until all that was left was utter exhaustion. There was no excitement; only 'thankfulness' remained with which to celebrate victory. And in 1918, she argued, few could perceive 'war's backwash' of economic slumps and massive unemployment.

Knowledge of the past made the future look bleak. Will acquiesced, but added that he wished 'we had a Govt. that knew something of the ropes, it's dreadful to think of such drastic changes now'.

With change in the air and hopes for a more equitable People's Peace than what Nella and her contemporaries remembered after the First World War, Labour entered government on 1 August 1945. When her husband wrung his hands over the radical changes Labour proposed, Nella assured him that – despite anything he or she thought – their time had passed. In the post-war peace, a new generation was taking over, and social revolution was inevitable, perhaps preferable. Wholesale change was the order of the day, for, as Nella pointed out, 'It's no use putting new patches on old garments, we need new ones, even if the coarse sackcloth of them irks skins used to old comfortable garments.' For so long, she said, the world had been 'a whirl of battle and death'; now was the time for a rebirth and the attendant, often painful, spasms of creation.

For Alice Bridges and her family, Labour's post-war social initiatives were a godsend. Early in 1948, Les suffered a heart attack and collapsed. Scraping to feed her family and pay for Les' medication, she confessed that her family had 'nearly reached bottom' by the summer. Neighbours and family brought Alice what food they could to help them get by, but it never seemed to be enough. At the same time, Jacq, now fifteen and exhibiting a precocious talent for art, desperately wanted to go to college. But with the financial circumstances as they stood, they simply could not afford further education, and Alice wrestled with how to tell her daughter that she must leave school and get an office job.

The National Health Service saved the Bridges from reaching bottom. When the NHS opened its doors on 5 July 1948, Les' medical bills were now covered. Upon learning that her financial worries had been solved, Alice felt an incredible rush of relief. Now, she could focus on keeping her husband comfortable as his health slowly deteriorated. During Les' illness, Jimmy – now more confident and calling himself James – was still a constant companion in Alice's life, and often his presence helped her get through the day. But in late 1948, following the advice of his doctor – who felt it ill-advised for his patient to continue seeing a married woman – James found a new love.

In 1949, Alice wrote to M-O as a widow. Though grieving the loss of her husband, she was carrying on, she told M-O. Alice was now working part-time and making do with a life insurance pay out and National Assistance, and a new dance partner had recently come on the scene. Jacq had received education assistance and started her studies at the local college of art. The post-war changes that Will Last had so worried over had, at least for Alice and her daughter, provided some support in times of need. Despite the hardships she now endured, Alice wrote at the time, 'The country does not let me want.'

In the post-war years, Irene Grant continued to fight a losing battle with her rheumatism. Some days she was able to venture beyond her garden, but very rarely. After March 1950, a serious fall made it even more difficult to get out. The next year, Rita's epilepsy, which had been silent since late 1940, returned with a vengeance. She had 'ten fits (Major Mal) in a week'. Once again, angry confrontations ensued between Rita and her father, who, frustrated at the outbursts, often flew into a rage. Marjorie had married and moved out a few years before, so it was Irene alone who refereed the shouting matches. Irene would continue to write about her daughter's seizures until her last correspondence with M-O in the early 1950s.

Satisfied that her patriotic duty had been served, Edie Rutherford left her office job in June 1946, but she would continue to keep an eye on global and domestic events for M-O throughout the 1940s. In those years, she watched as the empire slowly unravelled. Though she believed in granting independence to India in 1947, she was nonetheless reluctant to see the imperial bonds break. The woman who had been so exercised over Gandhi's intransigence during the war that she fervently believed that, 'to be rid of Gandhi would be a good thing', reported with deep sadness Gandhi's assassination just months after India's independence. 'Oh, who could have done such a terrible deed as to kill Gandhi?' she lamented on 30 January 1948. 'He was the conscience of mankind, we all know in our better selves that what Gandhi stood for and lived for was the highest ideal.'

In the post-war years, Edie returned to being a full-time housewife, and Sid's health steadily improved. The long-term unemployment that had plagued the couple after the last war seemed a distant memory, as Sid's work in the timber trade was secure in the post-war building boom. By 1951, when Edie stopped writing for M-O, she jubilantly announced a return holiday to South Africa, after eighteen years away. 'Himself disgruntled,' she said of her husband, 'swears I'll never return.' She looked out of the window, gazing on the sunbeams as they danced upon the tiny, hopeful tree buds, awaiting the 'edge' of the cold April air to soften and allow the 'leaves to burst out'. 'Could be,' she jested, 'but I think I'll return alright.'

Helen Mitchell would have appreciated a holiday away – to America or Europe, or even just an extended cruise. After the war's end, Helen continued to search for ways to flee her domestic drudgery, her crumbling, loveless marriage and to escape the bonds of the country that 'enslaved' her in these conditions. Peter worked so much and controlled the finances so tightly that a holiday beyond British shores was out of the question. As in wartime, they did go out west for the occasional holiday, but it was never enough. Helen increasingly grew even more tired of Peter and only wished 'to get rid of him'.

By September 1947, she decided that her recounting the daily grind of peacetime was hardly worth M-O's time and left off writing in her diary. She did respond now and again to questionnaires sent over the next few years – one of her last was in 1951 when it was clear that she had not succeeded in escaping. 'I have now been 5 years in full-time domestic service,' she wrote:

In general it has wrecked my life. The non-stop responsibility hanging like a millstone round the neck. Chiefly the fact that I have been forced into it against my will makes the background of my mind one of sullen resentment. (I am a professional woman.)

As for Peter, 'I regard him as a stomach. We do nothing together, and to me he is now merely an employer.' This would be her last correspondence with M-O.

* * *

After the war, Natalie Tanner enjoyed more and more freedom. The rounds into Leeds and Bradford remained almost unchanged, but as travel restrictions lifted, her sphere of activity widened. The late 1940s would see her in London at least once a month, and in the 1950s, Tanner enjoyed trips to the Continent, thanks to the newly nationalized British European Airways (BEA). Natalie continued to write for M-O until 1968, sprinkling her diary liberally with film criticism, a rekindled love for the game of cricket, travel stories and commentary on international events, from the Suez scandal of 1956 to Britain's support of the US in Vietnam. Hugh and Natalie celebrated their fiftieth anniversary in the 1970s, quite fittingly, with a quick trip to the Middle East on the Concorde.

Only months after the war had ended, Nella Last lamented that all the volunteer work and the camaraderie that she had enjoyed over the war years had quickly ebbed away. The WVS still limped along, but her work there was hardly as empowering and energizing as it had once been. As the years receded away from the war, Nella also felt the emotional bond between herself and her sons strain, and eventually snap. After Cliff's injury, Nella never again felt as close as she had once been to her younger son. In 1946, he would make a new life for himself in Australia. Arthur married, had children and moved to London, but although she made clothes for the children and sometimes visited them, she increasingly felt that she was an unwelcome intrusion in her son's life. After Will retired in 1949, they spent most days at home, shut off from the friends Nella had made in the community during the war.

In 1945, Nella had solemnly vowed never to break down as she had done in the inter-war period. But in 1965, at the age of seventy-five, Nella submitted once again to the old 'nervous breakdowns' that war had temporarily cured. The once proud, confident, self-assured and spirited domestic soldier was reduced to a fear of going out of doors, of making decisions and of losing all control over her family and her own life. Within a year, she would stop writing for M-O and within two, she would be dead.

Mass-Observation continued to poll its participants well into the post-war period, sending out directives regarding politics, class and social change until mid-1951. In the 1950s, the group slowly turned from its initial mission to provide ordinary Britons a platform from which to 'speak for themselves' and became involved in consumer-oriented marketing and polling for corporations.[1] Despite this new direction, M-O continued to collect diaries from its correspondents, and for many the organization still played a significant role in their lives. M-O would be revived as an important social institution committed to its original endeavour of understanding British society in the 1980s and continues to this day. As in wartime, writing for M-O in the post-war peace was (and is) often a cathartic and empowering experience, and the organization remains an important social outlet – even a friend, as M-O certainly was for the increasingly isolated Nella Last.

Approaching the tenth anniversary of the beginning of war in 1949, Nella Last remarked with amazement that she had written a diary for nearly ten years – '3650 entries', she reckoned. 'I can never understand how the scribbles of such an ordinary person, leading a shut-in, dull life can possibly have value,' she humbly wrote. Looking back, she reflected upon the importance of the war and M-O in her own life, remembering the deep well of strength she tapped in wartime – a strength she had never known existed – and one, she lamented, that now seemed to have dried up. M-O gave Alice, Helen, Irene, Natalie, Edie, Nella and hundreds of others a voice to describe the war in their own words, from their own perspectives. Writing the war and peace for M-O provided an opportunity for them to reflect upon their experiences, to parade their talents and patriotism proudly to others or to grouse about restrictions and husbands. Without these diaries, their lives would have passed largely unnoticed by all but their families and their own social circle.

These women show us the personal, day-to-day battles of the People's War, and, through them, we can feel the profound effect the war had upon their lives both during the conflict and afterwards. Some women, like Natalie Tanner, felt their social lives were on hold while the war raged, waiting only for the peace to release them from their quiescence so they could 'get back to normal'. Others, like Nella Last and Alice Bridges, were energized by the war and found confidence and social experiences that were unlikely to have penetrated their cloistered domesticity otherwise. However, these largely positive experiences could ultimately have a negative effect, as some women found the depth of possibilities within themselves, only to be forced back into the home and unfulfilling relationships. For Last, the experience of war had particularly tragic consequences as, over the post-war years, she slowly descended into an abyss of loneliness and purposelessness.

For women like Helen Mitchell, the continual wartime call to the colours that so invigorated Nella and the constant air raids that battered Helen's nerves only deepened the profound depression of an unfulfilled life. Many, like Edie Rutherford, would find in the war a way to express patriotism through a commitment to work in meaningful employment. Others, like Irene Grant, did their best to steer their families heroically through the shortages and difficulties of wartime, despite their own personal challenges.

These women's experiences were unique and yet universal, bounded by the events and expectations of the time in which they lived, and yet also timeless. Their struggles and triumphs demonstrate the inherent human need to feel recognized and valued, to find purpose and meaning and to wrestle with the complexities of the global, national and local communities and our place within them. All of the women endeavoured to carve out their own sense of self, independent of those around them, while also yearning for deep and meaningful connections with others. Their experiences remind us that the military and political events of the day were important, but they were not the only battles waged in the People's War.

ENDNOTES

Introduction

1 Brian Braithwaite, Noelle Walsh and Glyn Davies, eds, *The Home Front: The Best of Good Housekeeping 1939–1945* (London: Ebury Press, 1987), p. 78.
2 With the exception of Nella Last, whose diaries have been published under her real name, the names in this book are pseudonyms to protect the identities of the women and their families.

Chapter One: The Last War

1 'Cheerfulness at the Front', *The Times* 5 November 1917, p. 5 col. c.
2 Paul Fussell, *The Great War and Modern Memory* (Oxford: Oxford University Press, 1975; reprinted 2000), p. 41.

Chapter Two: War, Again

1 Quoted in Juliet Gardiner, *Wartime Britain 1939–1945* (London: Review, 2005), p. 71.
2 J.B.S. Haldane, *A.R.P. Air-Raid Precautions* (London: Gollancz, 1938), p. 50.

Chapter Three: Very Well, Alone

1 J.B. Priestley, *Postscripts* (London: W. Heinemann, 1940), p. 2.
2 Quoted in Arthur Marwick, *A History of the Modern British Isles, 1914–1999: Circumstances, Events and Outcomes* (Oxford: Blackwell, 2000), p. 139.
3 Quoted in Winston S. Churchill, *The Second World War: Vol. 2, Their Finest Hour* (New York: Houghton Mifflin, 1949), p. 187.
4 Winston Churchill, *Never Give In! The Best of Winston Churchill's Speeches*, ed. Winston S. Churchill (New York: Hyperion, 2003), p. 218.
5 Ibid., p. 229.
6 David Low, *Europe at War: A History in Sixty Cartoons with Narrative Text* (Harmondsworth: Penguin, 1941), p. 81.

Chapter Four: Oh God, What a Night

1 Quoted in William L. Shirer, *The Rise and Fall of the Third Reich: A History of Nazi Germany* (New York: Simon & Schuster, 1990), p. 749.
2 Quoted in Gardiner, *Wartime Britain*, p. 332.
3 Angus Calder, *The People's War: Britain, 1939–1945* (London: Jonathan Cape, 1969), p. 141.
4 Ibid., p. 144.
5 Quoted Gardiner, *Wartime Britain*, p. 307.
6 Quoted in William Shirer, *The Berlin Diary: The Journal of a Foreign Correspondent, 1939–1941* (Baltimore, MD: Johns Hopkins University Press, 2002), p. 496.
7 Quoted in Martin Gilbert, *The Second World War: A Complete History* (New York: Macmillan, 2004), p. 122.
8 T.C.G. James, *The Battle of Britain*, ed. and with an introduction by Sebastian Cox, (London: Frank Cass, 2000), p. 294.
9 Gardiner, *Wartime Britain*, p. 350.
10 Mass-Observation diarist 5318, 13 October 1941.
11 Quoted in Calder, *The People's War*, p. 204.
12 Ibid., p. 179
13 Quoted in ibid., p. 171.
14 Carlton Jackson, *Who Will Take Our Children?: The British Evacuation Program of World War II* (Jefferson, North Carolina: McFarland and Co., 2008), p. 14.

15 Clyde Binfield, *The History of the City of Sheffield, 1843–1993* (Sheffield: Sheffield Academic Press, 1993), vol. 2, p. 243.

16 Mary Walton and Joseph Lamb, *Raiders Over Sheffield: The Story of the Air Raids of 12th and 15th December 1940* (Sheffield: Sheffield City Libraries, 1980), p. 7.

17 Ibid., pp. 12–17.

Chapter Five: Domestic Soldiers

1 Quoted in James Hinton, 'Voluntarism and the Welfare/Warfare State: Women's Voluntary Services in the 1940s', *Twentieth Century British History* vol. 9, no. 2 (1998), p. 280.

2 Gary Cooper, 'I Like Women', *Good Housekeeping*, June 1944, p. 1.

3 Quoted in Calder, *The People's War*, p. 277.

4 'What Women Are Doing and Saying,' *Woman's Own*, 9 January 1942, p. 16.

5 'Letters from the Home Front', *Woman's Own*, 20 November 1942, p. 18.

6 Priestley, *Postscripts*, p. 68.

7 Lord Woolton, BBC broadcast, 8 April 1940. Joanna Bourke and Tim Piggott-Smith, *BBC Eyewitness 1940–1949* (London: BBC Audiobooks, 2004).

8 Ministry of Fuel advertisement, *Good Housekeeping*, September 1943, p. 25.

9 Ministry of Food advertisement, *Woman's Own*, 5 March 1943, p. 2.

10 Abram Games, Imperial War Museum, IWM PST 2865 in online collections, http://www.iwmcollections.org.uk.

11 Braithwaite, Walsh and Davies, eds, *The Home Front*, p. 72.

12 The National Archives maintains a website exploring Second World War propaganda and art, illustrating many propaganda messages listed here. See National Archives, *The Art of War* http://www.nationalarchives.gov.uk/theartofwar/prop/home_front/

13 Braithwaite, Walsh and Davies, eds, *The Home Front*, p. 78.

Chapter Six: A Few Hours of Happiness

1 Quoted in Claire Langhamer, 'Adultery in Post-War England', *History Workshop Journal*, vol. 62 (2006), p. 103.

2 Ibid., p. 100.
3 Rosita Forbes, 'Be a Success', *Woman's Own*, 22 June 1940, p. 28.
4 Quoted in Phil Goodman, '"Patriotic Femininity": Women's Morals and Men's Morale During the Second World War', *Gender and History*, vol. 10, no. 2 (August 1998), p. 282.

Chapter Seven: The Sun Never Sets

1 Quoted in Arthur Herman, *Gandhi and Churchill: The Epic Rivalry that Destroyed an Empire and Forged our Age* (New York: Random House, 2008), p. 500.
2 Clementine Churchill, quoted in Mary Soames, *Winston and Clementine: The Personal Letters of the Churchills* (New York: Houghton-Mifflin Harcourt, 2001), p. 460.
3 Winston Churchill, *The Second World War: Vol. 3, The Grand Alliance* (New York: Houghton-Mifflin Harcourt, 1986), p. 551.
4 Quoted in Christopher Alan Bayly and Timothy Norman Harper, *Forgotten Armies: the Fall of British Asia, 1941–1945* (Cambridge, MA: Belknap Press, 2005), p. 120.
5 Churchill, *Vol. 3, The Grand Alliance*, p. 539.
6 Anne O'Hare McCormick, 'Churchill Rises to "Grand Proportions" of History', *New York Times*, 27 December 1941, c18.
7 'Churchill Speech Hailed in Congress', *New York Times*, 27 December 1941, p. 3.
8 Quoted in Herman, *Gandhi and Churchill*, p. 478.
9 Churchill, *Never Give In!*, p. 330.
10 Quoted in Calder, *The People's War*, p. 274.
11 Quoted in Herman, *Gandhi and Churchill*, p. 481.
12 Calder, *The People's War*, p. 272.
13 Quoted in Herman, *Gandhi and Churchill*, p. 489.
14 Quoted in ibid., p. 489.
15 Quoted in ibid., p. 493.
16 Herbert Morrison, in Hansard Parliamentary Papers, Written Answers, 23 September 1943.
17 Edith Summerskill, in Hansard Parliamentary Papers, Written Answers, 7 August 1941.
18 Winston Churchill, *The Second World War: Vol. 4, Hinge of Fate* (New York: Houghton-Mifflin Harcourt, 1986), p. 344.
19 Quoted in Calder, *The People's War*, p. 305.

Chapter Eight: Fight Like Hell Until All Are Equal

1 Priestley, *Postscripts*, p. 42.
2 Ibid., p. 21.
3 Ibid., p. 7.
4 Ibid., p. 33.
5 Ibid., p. 45.
6 George Orwell, *Homage to Catalonia* (New York: Houghton-Mifflin Harcourt, 1980), p. 104.
7 'Beveridge Plan Criticized', *The Times*, 8 May 1942 p. 4E; 'Parliament and the Beveridge Plan', *The Times*, 6 October 1942, p. 5E.
8 Jose Harris, *William Beveridge: A Biography* (Oxford: Clarendon Press, 1997; 2nd edn), p. 376.
9 Calder, *The People's War*, p. 527.
10 Quoted in Harris, *William Beveridge*, p. 413.
11 Quoted in ibid., p. 413.
12 *ITMA* transcript, 4 December 1942, BBC Written Archives Centre, Caversham Park.
13 Quoted in Michael Bromley, 'Was it the *Mirror* Wot Won it? The Development of the Tabloid Press During the Second World War', in. Nick Hayes and Jeff Hill, eds, *'Millions Like Us'? British Culture in the Second World War* (Liverpool: Liverpool University Press, 1999), p. 114.
14 Harris, *William Beveridge*, p. 366.
15 Ibid., p. 420.
16 Quoted in Calder, *The People's War*, p. 530.
17 Harris, *William Beveridge*, p. 429.
18 William Beveridge, 'Social Insurance and Allied Services Report – Executive Summary', Cmd 6404, November 1942, at http://www.fordham.edu/halsall/mod/1942beveridge.html
19 *Woman's Own*, 5 March 1943, p. 7.
20 *Good Housekeeping*, March 1943, p. 1.
21 Calder, *The People's War*, pp. 547–9.
22 Winston S. Churchill, *His Complete Speeches, 1897–1963: Vol. 7, 1943–1949*, ed. Robert Rhodes James (New York and London: Chelsea House Publishers, 1974), 21 March 1943, pp. 6755–65.

Chapter Nine: Don't Let's Be Beastly to the Hun

1 Quoted in Thomas R. Brooks, *The War North of Rome: June 1944–May 1945* (Cambridge, MA: Da Capo Press, 2003), p. 2.

2 Winston S. Churchill, *The Second World War: Vol. 5, Closing the Ring* (New York: Houghton-Mifflin Harcourt, 1986), p. 380.

3 Quoted in Nicola Lambourne, *War Damage in Western Europe: The Destruction of Historic Monuments During the Second World War* (Edinburgh: Edinburgh University Press, 2001), p. 140.

4 Quoted in Martin Gilbert, *The Second World War: A Complete History* (New York: Macmillan, 2004), p. 500.

5 Keith Lowe, *Inferno: The Fiery Destruction of Hamburg, 1943* (New York: Scribner, 2007), p. 64.

6 'Hamburg Smoke Four Miles Up', *The Times*, 31 July 1943, p. 4 col. F.

7 'Evacuation of Hamburg', *The Times*, 2 August 1943, p. 4 col. G.

8 Lyrics in Noel Coward, *The Complete Lyrics*, ed. Barry Day (Woodstock, NY: Overlook Press, 1998), p. 207.

9 William Gallacher, Hansard Oral Answers to Questions, 4 November 1943.

10 Quoted in Francis L. Loewenheim, Harold D. Langley and Manfred Jonas, eds, *Roosevelt and Churchill: Their Secret Wartime Correspondence* (New York: E.P. Dutton, 1975), p. 10.

11 Winston Churchill, Hansard Oral Answers to Questions, 4 November 1943.

12 'Housekeeping Savings', *The Times*, 9 November 1943, p. 2, col. D.

13 Stephen Michael Cretney, *Family Law in the Twentieth Century: A History* (Oxford: Oxford University Press, 2003), p. 117.

14 George Woods, Hansard Commons Sittings, 1 December 1943.

15 Kevin Jefferys, *The Churchill Coalition and Wartime Politics, 1940–1945* (Manchester: Manchester University Press, 1995), p. 122.

16 *Brains Trust* transcript, 13 September 1943, BBC Written Archives Centre, Caversham Park.

Chapter Ten: Can You Beat That?

1 'Lady Bountiful Fraud Charge', *Daily Mirror*, 5 February 1944.

2 'Jekyll–Hyde Mind of Lady Bountiful', *Daily Mirror*, 17 March 1944.

3 Herbert Morrison, Hansard Oral Answers to Questions, 16 December 1943.

4 Calder, *The People's War*, p. 407.

5 Edward Smithies, *Crime in Wartime: A Social History of Crime in World War Two* (London: George Allen and Unwin, 1982), p. 62.

6 Ibid., p. 74.
7 'Rescue Squad Men Guilty of Looting', *The Times*, 13 February 1941, p. 2 col. D.
8 Quoted in Calder, *The People's War*, pp. 178–9.
9 'Bombs in Cargo of Oranges', *The Times*, 15 January 1944, p. 2 col. D.

Chapter Eleven: Worst Raid Ever Last Night

1 Quoted in Lambourne, *War Damage in Western Europe*, p. 150.
2 Quoted in Fred Taylor, *Dresden, Tuesday February 13, 1945* (New York: HarperCollins, 2004), p. 128.
3 Quoted in Gilbert, *The Second World War*, p. 319.
4 Jörg Friedrich, *The Fire: The Bombing of Germany, 1940–1945* (New York: Columbia University Press, 2008), p. 169.
5 Gardiner, *Wartime Britain*, p. 547.
6 Quoted in Ibid., p. 610.
7 Churchill, *His Complete Speeches, 1897–1963: Vol. 7, 1943–1949*, 26 March 1944, p. 6907.

Chapter Twelve: Oh! What a Leisurely War

1 Gardiner, *Wartime Britain*, p. 620.
2 Stephen Ambrose, *D-Day, June 6, 1944: The Climactic Battle of World War II* (New York: Simon & Schuster, 1994), p. 54.
3 Gardiner, *Wartime Britain*, p. 620.
4 Ambrose, *D-Day*, p. 44.
5 Quoted in Gardiner, *Wartime Britain*, p. 146.
6 Quoted in Anthony Cave Brown, *Bodyguard of Lies: The Extraordinary True Story Behind D-Day* (New York: Harper and Row, 1975; reprinted New York: HarperCollins, 2002), p. 769.
7 Gardiner, *Wartime Britain*, p. 638.

Chapter Thirteen: Anyone Want Two Tin Hats and Two Gas Masks?

1 Quoted in Donald L. Miller and Henry Steele Commager, *The Story of World War Two* (New York: Simon & Schuster, 2006), p. 242.
2 Milton Bracken, 'Alsace Nazi Prison Neat and Efficient', *New*

York Times, 5 December 1944, p. 7.

3 Quoted in Ben Flanagan and Donald Bloxham, *Remembering Belsen: Eyewitnesses Record the Liberation* (London: Vallentine Mitchell, 2005), p. xii.

4 Quoted in Ann M. Sperber, *Murrow, His Life and Times* (New York: Fordham University Press, 1996), p. 251.

5 Ibid., p. 253.

6 Quoted in Gilbert, *The Second World War*, p. 678.

Conclusion: Who'd a Thought It?

1 Churchill, *His Complete Speeches, 1897–1963: Vol. 7, 1943–1949*, 4 June 1945, pp. 7169–74.

2 Quoted in Gardiner, *Wartime Britain*, p. 677.

3 'Labour Case to Socialism: Mr. Attlee's reply to Mr. Churchill', *The Times* 6 June 1945, p. 2, col. A.

4 Ibid.

5 Quoted in David Kynaston, *Austerity Britain, 1945–1951* (London: Bloomsbury, 2007), p. 72.

6 For example, 'Vigilante Fined: "Complete Defiance of Law and Order"', *The Times*, 17 August 1945, p. 2, col. D.

Epilogue

1 Quoted in Ben Highmore, *Everyday Life and Cultural Theory: An Introduction* (London: Routledge, 2002), p. 87.

BIBLIOGRAPHY

For nearly thirty-five years, Angus Calder's *The People's War* (1969) has stood as the definitive social history of Britain in wartime. Only Juliet Gardiner's *Wartime Britain* (2005) comes close to providing a recent work that can stand with it. Both were indispensable in my writing of the historical background in this book.

M-O Diarists

D 5296
D 5353
D 5372
D 5420
D 5447
D 5445

Journals, Newspapers and Other Primary Sources

Beveridge, William. 'Social Insurance and Allied Services Report – Executive Summary', Cmd 6404, November 1942. http://www.fordham.edu/halsall/mod/1942beveridge.html
Brains Trust transcripts, BBC Written Archive Centre, Caversham Park
Good Housekeeping

Hansard Parliamentary Papers
Housewife
ITMA transcripts, BBC Written Archive Centre, Caversham Park
New York Times
The Times
Woman's Own

Books and Articles

Ambrose, Stephen. *D-Day, June 6, 1944: The Climactic Battle of World War II* (New York: Simon & Schuster, 1994)

Baggott, Rob. *Health and Health Care in Britain* (Houndmills Macmillan Press, 1994)

Bayly, Christopher Alan and Timothy Norman Harper. *Forgotten Armies: The Fall of British Asia, 1941–1945* (Cambridge, MA: Belknap Press, 2005)

Binfield, Clyde. *The History of the City of Sheffield, 1843–1993* (Sheffield: Sheffield Academic Press, 1993), vol. 2

Bourke, Joanna and Tim Piggott-Smith, *Eyewitness 1940–1949* (London: BBC Audiobooks, 2004)

Braithwaite, Brian, Noelle Walsh and Glyn Davies, eds, *The Home Front: The Best of* Good Housekeeping *1939–1945* (London: Ebury Press, 1987)

Bromley, Michael. 'Was it the *Mirror* Wot Won it? The Development of the Tabloid Press During the Second World War', in Nick Hayes and Jeff Hill, eds, *'Millions Like Us'? British Culture in the Second World War* (Liverpool: Liverpool University Press, 1999)

Brooks, Thomas R. *The War North of Rome: June 1944–May 1945* (Cambridge, MA: Da Capo Press, 2003)

Brown, Anthony Cave. *Bodyguard of Lies: The Extraordinary True Story Behind D-Day* (New York: Harper and Row, 1975; reprinted New York: HarperCollins, 2002)

Calder, Angus. *The People's War: Britain, 1939–1945* (London: Jonathan Cape, 1969)

Churchill, Winston S. *The Second World War: Vol. 2, Their Finest Hour* (New York: Houghton Mifflin, 1949)

Churchill, Winston S. *His Complete Speeches, 1897–1963: Vol. 7, 1943–1949*, ed. Robert Rhodes James (New York and London: Chelsea House Publishers, 1974)

Churchill, Winston S. *The Second World War: Vol. 3, The Grand Alliance* (New York: Houghton-Mifflin Harcourt, 1986)

Churchill, Winston S. *The Second World War: Vol. 4, Hinge of Fate* (New York: Houghton-Mifflin Harcourt, 1986)

Churchill, Winston S. *The Second World War: Vol. 5, Closing the Ring* (New York: Houghton-Mifflin Harcourt, 1986)

Churchill, Winston S. *Never Give In! The Best of Winston Churchill's Speeches*, ed. Winston S. Churchill (New York: Hyperion, 2003)

Coward, Noël. *The Complete Lyrics*, ed. Barry Day (Woodstock, NY: Overlook Press, 1998)

Cretney, Stephen Michael. *Family Law in the Twentieth Century: A History* (Oxford: Oxford University Press, 2003)

Dimaak, Max. *Clifford Last* (Melbourne: Hawthorne Press, 1972)

Fenwick, I.G.K. *The Comprehensive School, 1944–1970* (London: Methuen, 1976)

Flanagan, Ben and Donald Bloxham. *Remembering Belsen: Eyewitnesses Record the Liberation* (London: Vallentine Mitchell, 2005)

Freedman, Jean Rose. *Whistling in the Dark: Memory and Culture in Wartime Britain* (Lexington: University Press of Kentucky, 1999)

Friedrich, Jörg. *The Fire: The Bombing of Germany, 1940–1945* (New York: Columbia University Press, 2008)

Fussell, Paul. *The Great War and Modern Memory* (Oxford: Oxford University Press, 1975; reprinted 2000)

Gardiner, Juliet. *Wartime Britain 1939–1945* (London: Review, 2005)

Gilbert, Martin. *The Second World War: A Complete History* (New York: Macmillan, 2004)

Goodman, Phil. '"Patriotic Femininity": Women's Morals and Men's Morale During the Second World War', *Gender and History*, vol. 10, no. 2 (August 1998)

Haldane, J.B.S. *A.R.P. Air-Raid Precautions* (London: Gollancz, 1938)

Harris, Jose. *William Beveridge: A Biography* (Oxford: Clarendon Press, 1997, 2nd edn)

Hart, B.H. Liddell. *History of the Second World War* (New York: Da Capo Press, 1999)

Hennessy, Peter. *Never Again: Britain 1945–1951* (London: Jonathan Cape, 1992)

Herman, Arthur. *Gandhi and Churchill: The Epic Rivalry that Destroyed an Empire and Forged our Age* (New York: Random House, 2008)

Highmore, Ben. *Everyday Life and Cultural Theory: An Introduction* (London: Routledge, 2002)

Hinton, James. 'Voluntarism and the Welfare/Warfare State:

Women's Voluntary Services in the 1940s', *Twentieth Century British History*, vol. 9, no. 2 (1998)

Holland, James. *Italy's Sorrow: A Year of War, 1944–1945* (New York: HarperCollins, 2008)

Hough, Richard and Denis Richardson. *The Battle of Britain: The Greatest Air Battle of World War II* (New York: W.W. Norton, 2005)

Howkins, Alun. 'A Country at War: Mass-Observation and Rural England, 1939–1945', *Rural History: Economy, Society, Culture*, vol. 9, no. 1 (1998), pp. 75–97

Hubble, Nick. *Mass-Observation and Everyday Life: Culture, History, Theory* (Basingstoke: Palgrave MacMillan, 2006)

Jackson, Carlton. *Who Will Take Our Children?: The British Evacuation Program of World War II* (Jefferson, NC: McFarland and Co., 2008)

James, T.C.G. *The Battle of Britain*, ed. and with an introduction by Sebastian Cox, (London: Frank Cass, 2000)

Jefferys, Kevin. *The Churchill Coalition and Wartime Politics, 1940–1945* (Manchester: Manchester University Press, 1995)

Judt, Tony. *Postwar: A History of Europe Since 1945* (London: Penguin, 2005)

Kavanagh, Tom. *ITMA*. (London: The Woburn Press, 1974)

Kynaston, David. *Austerity Britain, 1945-1951* (London: Bloomsbury, 2007)

Lambourne, Nicola. *War Damage in Western Europe: The Destruction of Historic Monuments During the Second World War* (Edinburgh: Edinburgh University Press, 2001)

Langhamer, Claire. 'Adultery in Post-War England', *History Workshop Journal*, vol. 62 (2006)

Last, Nella. *Nella Last's War: A Mother's Diary 1939–1945*, ed. Richard Broad and Suzie Fleming (Bristol: Falling Wall Press, 1981)

Loewenheim, Francis L., Harold D. Langley and Manfred Jonas, eds. *Roosevelt and Churchill: Their Secret Wartime Correspondence* (New York: E.P. Dutton, 1975)

Low, David. *Europe at War: A History in Sixty Cartoons with Narrative Text* (Harmondsworth: Penguin, 1941)

Lowe, Keith. *Inferno: The Fiery Destruction of Hamburg, 1943* (New York: Scribner, 2007)

McKay, Robert. *Half the Battle: Civilian Morale in Britain During World War II* (Manchester: Manchester University Press, 2002)

McKibbin, Ross. *Classes and Cultures: England 1918–1951* (Oxford: Oxford University Press, 1998)

Marwick, Arthur. *A History of the Modern British Isles, 1914–1999: Circumstances, Events and Outcomes* (Oxford: Blackwell, 2000)

Miller Donald L. and Henry Steele Commager, *The Story of World War Two* (New York, Simon & Schuster, 2006)

Morgan, David and Mary Evans. *The Battle for Britain: Citizenship and Ideology in Second World War Britain* (London: Routledge, 1993)

Morgan, Kenneth O. *The People's Peace: British History Since 1945*, 2nd edn (Oxford: Oxford University Press, 1999)

Nicholas, Sian. '"Sly Demagogues" and Wartime Radio: J.B. Priestley and the BBC', *Twentieth Century British History*, vol. 6, no. 3 (1995), pp. 247–66

Nicholas, Sian. *The Echo of War: Home Front Propaganda and the Wartime BBC, 1939–1945* (Manchester: Manchester University Press, 1996)

Nicholas, Sian. 'The People's Radio: The BBC and its Audience, 1939–1945', in Nick Hayes and Jeff Hill, eds., *'Millions Like Us'? British Culture in the Second World War* (Liverpool: Liverpool University Press, 1999)

Orwell, George. *Homage to Catalonia* (New York: Houghton-Mifflin Harcourt, 1980)

Priestley, J.B. *Postscripts* (London: W. Heinemann, 1940)

Rubinstein, David. *The Labour Party and British Society, 1880–2005* (Brighton: Sussex Academic Press, 2006)

Sheridan, Dorothy, Brian Street and David Bloome. *Writing Ourselves: Mass-Observation and Literacy Practices* (Cresskill, NJ: Hampton Press, 2000)

Shirer, William L. *The Rise and Fall of the Third Reich: A History of Nazi Germany* (New York: Simon & Schuster, 1990)

Shirer, William L. *The Berlin Diary: The Journal of a Foreign Correspondent, 1939–1941* (Baltimore, MD: Johns Hopkins University Press, 2002)

Smith, Harold L. 'The Effect of the War on the Status of Women', in Harold L. Smith, ed. *War and Social Change: British Society in the Second World War* (Manchester: Manchester University Press, 1986)

Smithies, Edward. *Crime in Wartime: A Social History of Crime in World War Two* (London: George Allen and Unwin, 1982)

Soames, Mary. *Winston and Clementine: The Personal Letters of the Churchills* (New York: Houghton-Mifflin Harcourt, 2001)

Sperber, Ann M. *Murrow, His Life and Times* (New York: Fordham University Press, 1996)

Summerfield, Penny. 'Mass-Observation: Social Research or Social Movement?' *Journal of Contemporary History*, vol. 20, no. 3 (July 1985), pp. 439–52

Summerfield, Penny. *Reconstructing Women's Wartime Lives: Discourse and Subjectivity in Oral Histories of the Second World War* (Manchester: Manchester University Press, 1998)

Summerfield, Penny and Corinna Peniston-Bird. *Contesting Home Defence: Men, Women and the Home Guard in the Second World War* (Manchester: Manchester University Press, 2007)

Taylor, Fred. *Dresden, Tuesday February 13, 1945* (New York: HarperCollins, 2004)

Waller, Maureen. *London: 1945, Life in the Debris of War* (New York: St Martin's Press, 2004)

Walton, Mary and Joseph Lamb, *Raiders Over Sheffield: The Story of the Air Raids of 12th and 15th December 1940* (Sheffield: Sheffield City Libraries, 1980)

Zweiniger-Bargielowska, Ina. *Austerity in Britain: Rationing, Controls, and Consumption, 1939–1955.* (Oxford: Oxford University Press, 2000)

INDEX

INDEX

Mitchell, William 11, 19, 20, 146, 188, 262, 263, 281
Mitchison, Naomi 253
Mitford, Tom 211
Mitford, Unity 211
Montgomery, Field Marshal Bernard 162
moral dilemmas 203–54
moral panics 126–7, 160–1
morale 4, 45, 59–60, 92, 94, 177, 221, 248, 271, 283
Morocco 162
Morrison, Herbert 159, 161, 211–12, 221, 231–2
Morrison shelters 81, 238
Mosley, Lady Diana 211–12
Mosley, Sir Oswald 211–13
Mulberry harbours 260
Munich Crisis (1938) 25–6
Murrow, Edward R. 226–7, 299–300, 301
Muslim League 152, 153
Mussolini, Benito 197, 265
  execution of 303

Nagasaki 330, 335
national anthem 17
National Health Insurance scheme 185
National Health Service 180, 186, 190, 341
National Loaf 95–6
National Trust 189
nationalization 319
Natzwiller camp 298
Nazi-Soviet non-aggression pact 22, 251
Nehru, Jawaharlal 152, 153
Netherlands 38, 43, 327
New British Broadcasting Station 56
new world order, visions of 167–8, 169–72, 181, 189, 190–1, 317, 340
Newcastle 6, 18
News Chronicle 177
Night of the Long Knives (1934) 278
Noel-Baker, Philip 231
Normandy landings 267–8, 277–8
North African campaign 162, 166, 197, 251–2, 253
Norway, Nazi invasion of 37–8, 43
Norwich 55, 249
Norwood Report 255

Operation Fortitude 262–4
Operation Gomorrah 199–201
Operation Overlord 262
  see also Normandy landings
Operation Sea Lion 53–4, 61, 79
Operation Steinbock 238, 247
orange shipments, destruction of 229–30
Orwell, George 55, 172
Ouistreham 267

pacifism 17
parachute mines 67
Paris
  German entry into 47
  government evacuation of 38–9, 47
  recapture of 284
Pas-de-Calais 263, 264
Passchendaele 10
patriotism 104
Patton, General 264
Pearl Harbor 138, 142
Penang 139–40
People's Peace 168, 181, 340
People's War 2–3, 44
  exhortations 105, 106, 107, 108, 112
phrase coined 2
peripatetic lives 245
Personal Injuries Act 161
Pétain, Marshal 48
Phoney War 35, 37, 41, 72
phospherine tonic 59
Plymouth 82–3
Poland
  British-Polish pact 22, 23
  government-in-exile 229
  Nazi invasion 23–4
  Soviet invasion 33, 35
Poor Law Guardians 17
postal service 4
Postscript 44, 104, 152, 168, 170
Pound, Sir Dudley 139
prefabs 317
Price, George 158
Priestley, J.B. 44, 104, 168–71, 316
  and the 1941 Committee 189
  and a new world order 168–71
Prince of Wales, sinking of 139, 140
prisoners of war 200
profiteering 328
proportional representation 189